The *Annals* of Quintus Ennius and the Italic Tradition

The *Annals* of Quintus Ennius and the Italic Tradition

JAY FISHER

Johns Hopkins University Press
Baltimore

Printed in the United States of America on acid-free paper
2 4 6 8 9 7 5 3 1

Johns Hopkins University Press
2715 North Charles Street
Baltimore, Maryland 21218-4363
www.press.jhu.edu

Library of Congress Cataloging-in-Publication Data

Fisher, Jay, 1969–
The *Annals* of Quintus Ennius and the Italic tradition / Jay Fisher.
pages. cm.
Includes bibliographical references and index.
ISBN-13: 978-1-4214-1129-3 (hardcover : alk. paper)
ISBN-13: 978-1-4214-1130-9 (electronic)
ISBN-10: 1-4214-1129-6 (hardcover : alk. paper)
ISBN-10: 1-4214-1130-X (electronic)
1. Ennius, Quintus. Annales. 2. Latin poetry — History and criticism. I. Title.
PA6382.F57 2014
873'.01—dc23 2013010980

A catalog record for this book is available from the British Library.

Special discounts are available for bulk purchases of this book. For more information, please contact Special Sales at 410-516-6936 or specialsales@press.jhu.edu.

Johns Hopkins University Press uses environmentally friendly book materials, including recycled text paper that is composed of at least 30 percent post-consumer waste, whenever possible.

To Robin McCombe Fisher

UXORI CARISSIMAE

CONTENTS

ACKNOWLEDGMENTS

The idea for this book (and many other books, I imagine) first came to me while I was writing a paper for a graduate seminar taught by Joshua Katz, who also supervised the dissertation that further developed my ideas about Ennius and the Italic tradition. Before that paper became a dissertation, Corey Brennan supervised a master's thesis on the same topic at Bryn Mawr College. There could have been no better committee for my dissertation at Princeton than Joshua Katz, Denis Feeney, and Andrew Ford. I also offer my heartfelt thanks to all of my teachers at Richard Stockton College, Bryn Mawr College, and Princeton University, as well as to those who directly guided me from that seminar paper to my dissertation.

The Department of Classics at Yale, my current place of employment, put me in a position to refine a collection of different impressions into a coherent argument about Ennius and the Italic tradition. I could not have asked for better, smarter, and more helpful students on the graduate and undergraduate level than I have at Yale. I owe a special debt to Christopher Simon, Sean Northrup, Tom Biggs, Josh Fincher, Tom Beasley, Matt Newman, and Caroline Mann for reading different versions of different chapters. I have had some very stimulating conversations with my colleagues at Yale, and Kirk Freudenburg in particular read several drafts of my introduction. I am also grateful to Yale University for a Morse junior faculty fellowship in the academic year 2009–10. During my time at Yale I was very fortunate that Lowell Edmunds agreed to help me cast my ideas into something resembling readable prose. I hope that I have at least sometimes been able to present my ideas in an engaging way, as he kept telling me to do.

I am in the debt of Matt McAdam at the Johns Hopkins University Press for his encouragement and for shepherding this book through the various steps of publication. I am even more in the debt of the anonymous reader who made not only helpful global comments about my manuscript but also concrete suggestions that have improved my prose in general. To paraphrase Charlotte Bronte, "Reader, I did my best!"

Although I have not given in to the temptation of listing all those who intervened in the process of writing this book, I hope that anyone who helped will read this book with the satisfaction of knowing that it is much better because of their help. Because I have benefited from the advice and help of so many, I must emphasize that I am to blame for all errors of fact, analysis, and style.

In addition to the help I have received on a professional level, I would like to thank my family for their love and support. My parents and my in-laws chipped in with emergency childcare at a late stage of this project, and my brother Jamie gave me an affordable place to live when I was writing my dissertation. Because this book is as much about multiculturalism as it is about Latin poetry, it is fitting that I credit my grandparents, three of whom gave me first-hand examples of multiculturalism as the children of immigrants from Eastern Europe and Ireland. My maternal grandmother in particular taught me to question my assumptions about assimilation and identity in two ways. It was only when I was in my mid-twenties that I learned that my grandmother's first language was Polish, not English. When I was in my thirties I also came to understand that my grandmother's father, a native of Vienna who spoke Yiddish fluently, was not raised Catholic.

The *Annals* of Quintus Ennius and the Italic Tradition

Ennius and the Italic Tradition

If a classic is "a book which people praise and don't read,"[1] then for all practical purposes the *Annals* of Quintus Ennius was a classic by the time of the emperor Domitian. The epic poet Silius Italicus, one of Domitian's contemporaries, caps his description of the deeds of Ennius at a battle fought during the Second Punic War with an intervention by the god Apollo, who saves Ennius from a spear hurled by an enemy named Hostus and then chides the would-be slayer of the poet of the *Annals* with a prophecy of his future fame:

> Resonare docebit
> Hic latiis Helicona modis nec cedet Homero honore
> Ascraeo famave seni. (SIL. 12.411–13)

> He will teach Mount Helicon to resound with Latin meters and he shall not yield to Homer in honor or the old Ascraean in fame.[2]

Apollo predicts that the reputation of Ennius is destined to be as good as those of Homer and Hesiod (the Ascraean), but Silius demonstrates little direct acquaintance with the *Annals.* Although Silius occasionally turns a phrase reminiscent of Ennius,[3] few, if any, of these verbal echoes are not actually allusions to Vergil, who often alludes to the *Annals* in his poetry, especially in the *Aeneid.*[4] There is also "no clear evidence" that the rhetorician Quintilian, another author who wrote under Domitian, had firsthand knowledge of the poem, since he cites only parts of the *Annals* that are known from other sources (with one exception).[5] The *Annals* apparently was praised but read only cursorily or not at all under Domitian. In sum, the *Annals* was a classic by one definition.

Nevertheless, there were times when the *Annals,* an epic poem that once told the story of Rome from its mythical foundations to the lifetime of Ennius in eighteen books, was read and praised. It seems that it was the first Latin poem to be a serious object of scholarly criticism in the second century BCE, roughly the generation after it was written.[6] Cicero not only praises Ennius on several occasions; he also quotes from the *Annals* liberally.[7] There was also a revival of interest in Ennius and other earlier poets during the reign of Hadrian, who preferred Ennius to Vergil, if the writer of his biography is to be trusted (*SHA*

Hadrianus 16.6). The miscellanist Gellius, who wrote in the time of Hadrian, mentions public recitations of the works of Ennius (*NA* 18.5.2), a poet who also wrote tragedy, satire, and several other poems besides the *Annals.*

Although the *Annals* has survived antiquity only in fragments quoted by later authors, it is enjoying more popularity as an object of scholarly attention than it has since the reign of Hadrian. Two editions of the fragments with commentary have been published within the last thirty years. Two volumes of papers dedicated to Ennius have also been produced within only the last six years.[8] Even the traditional focuses of Ennian scholarship—the collection of the fragments, the reconstruction of the epic from these fragments, and textual criticism—have made unexpected progress between the editions of Skutsch and Flores, since a series of papyrus fragments from Herculaneum is now known to belong to book 6 of the *Annals.*[9] Among other things, this flurry of research has revealed the unconscious assumptions of the later authors who preserve the remains of the *Annals,* since the fragmentary state of the poem makes modern interpretations susceptible to the biases of Cicero and the other ancient authors who quote the *Annals,* as James Zetzel and Jacqueline Elliott have observed.[10]

Because later Latin authors preserve what we know of the *Annals,* they also pass on their unconscious biases, such as the notion that the poem is an archaic and clumsy attempt at epic poetry in the Homeric mode. Such a view of Ennius may have originated, as Zetzel suggests, in Cicero's use of Ennius as the antithesis of "neoteric" poetry written by Latin poets, such as Catullus, who were deeply influenced by postclassical Greek poets, like Callimachus and Apollonius of Rhodes, who for the most part worked in Alexandria in Egypt in the third and second centuries BCE. Because the neoteric poets themselves do not seem to have accepted this simplification, the idea of Ennius as something that neoteric poetry is not (i.e., archaic and clumsy) may have originated with a single, influential Latin author rather than as a shared assumption among Latin authors of the late Republic.[11] Even if there was such a shared assumption, the literary tastes of an influential group do not constitute an objective fact about the poetry of Ennius.

In fact, Ennius was able to grasp the intricacies of intertextuality in a manner that recalls the same neoteric poets whose work Cicero saw as the antithesis of the *Annals.*[12] If the diction of the *Annals* is compared with the language of the types of texts that were available to him, Ennius is revealed to be a deft and sophisticated poet who can control and manipulate other texts in order to endow his own text with layers of meaning, and a poet who is able to challenge the reader to reconsider the narrative in light of these other texts. The crucial difference between Ennius and these other poets lies in the kinds of Latin texts that Ennius appropriates. Vergil, for example, had more than two centuries of Latin poetry to draw from, whereas Ennius had only about two generations. As a result, there was little Latin literature available for Ennius, but there did exist a variety of other texts in Latin that were available as raw material for the poetic register of the *Annals.*

These texts are not literary compositions like the *Iliad* or the tragedies of Euripides, or even texts at all in the sense of a written, narrative composition, but rather the formulaic language of significant cultural practices in the Roman Republic such as warfare and ritual. The textual parallels that I will adduce in the course of my argument, then, are evidence that the language of these linguistic registers was specific enough to convey meaning when taken out of context and imported into the diction of the *Annals,* and yet these texts were still not literary compositions or coherent narratives. The largest and most diverse body of "texts" falls within the sphere of ritual; there are prayers, ritual instructions, and technical discussions of specific rituals. Furthermore, the various cult titles of gods and goddesses can communicate something about the meanings that these cult titles had for the audience of the *Annals.*

Because of the nature of these texts, the essential unit of my analysis is not the literary allusion but rather what I will term the "traditional collocation." There are two key elements that differentiate a collocation, a "habitual meaningful co-occurrence of two or more words,"[13] from a nonce phrase: frequency and "semantic relevance," or the irreducibility of a phrase "to a combination of any of the dictionary senses" of its individual words.[14] Due to the paucity of archaic ritual Latin texts, I will, out of necessity, emphasize "semantic relevance" over frequency. Moreover, the difference between the literal meaning of the individual elements of the collocation and the collocation itself can be very subtle in some cases, since it can generate connotative as denotative meaning. In addition to its irreducibility on the level of meaning regardless of context, or denotation, a difference of meaning between a combination of the meanings of its individual words and the irreducible meaning of a collocation may arise from its original context or connotation. In other words, a traditional collocation can recall its original context in a new context even when the basic meaning of the phrase is transparent.

Although a traditional collocation is similar to a "formula" as defined by Milman Parry (i.e., "a group of words which is regularly employed, under the same metrical conditions, to express a given essential idea"),[15] it is more flexible than a Homeric formula, because it is not a "fixed" or "frozen" formula bound by meter. The presence of the two (or more) elements of a collocation in proximity to one another is usually enough to trigger "a meaning of [its] own."[16] The constituents of a collocation also do not need to occur in a specific order or even consecutively to generate an irreducible meaning and invite a comparison between its present poetic and its already established cultural context, much as a literary allusion invites a similar comparison between the present and previous literary contexts of a given phrase. As I hope to demonstrate, it is also possible to allude to a collocation as well by altering one of its constituent roots to a phonetically or semantically similar root, a type of transformation that is common in allusions to previous poetic texts in later Latin poetry.

What is more, many of the traditional collocations of Latin ritual bear a striking resemblance to expressions that occur in the ritual texts of other languages of the central Italian *koinê*. Many of these parallels are likely to be the verbal traces of a ritual tradition common to the speakers of Oscan, Umbrian, Etruscan, and even Greek that developed in the period of the seventh through the fourth centuries BCE, a time of intense mutual influence among the cultures of ancient Italy.[17] In addition to a common ritual tradition, the members of the *koinê* shared similar onomastic practices and employed a similar style of architecture in an increasing number of urban centers.[18] Angelo Mercado and Joseph Eska have gone as far as to claim that an underlying seven-syllable line structures inscriptions in archaic Latin, Paelignian, and Vestinian (the latter two languages are either closely related to or are dialects of Oscan).[19]

Even some of the most recognizably Greek elements of the *Annals* were so nativized that Ennius and his audience would have perceived them as Roman, because many elements of Greek culture were absorbed by Roman culture during the central Italian *koinê* period along with elements from the other cultures of the *koinê*. Hercules and Apollo, for example, are Greek deities, but the cults of both gods were as much a part of Italic culture as Greek. Even when poet and audience could trace some of these nativized elements back to their Greek origins, they still had culturally specific meanings to the audience of the *Annals*. Other Greek elements of the *Annals*, however, such as the Homeric dactylic hexameter, the meter of the *Annals*, did not have such a meaning for Ennius' original audience. Outside of these obviously direct borrowings, Ennius and his audience may have perceived many of the "Greek" elements in the diction of the *Annals* as "Roman."

Traditional collocations, besides being fascinating on their own terms, play a crucial role in the confirmation of hypotheses put forth by a number of scholars. The identification and interpretation of traditional augural collocations, for example, may help to solve problems of interpretation in the augural contest between Romulus and his brother (*Ann.* 72–91), thereby justifying the efforts of generations of scholars who have valiantly attempted to tease out the relationship of the fragment to augural practice.[20] Ilia's dream contains traditional kinship collocations that bring the issue of gender into focus (*Ann.* 34–50), an issue that has been discussed by several critics in the last generation or so. (It will become clear how much I owe to these scholars in my discussion of the dream of Ilia in chapter 5.) Nor are these the only fragments where the traditional phraseology of specific Roman cultural practices generates layers of meaning that were previously suspected but not apparent on the surface of the narrative. In sum, the identification and interpretation of these collocations in the *Annals* provides another means of testing the findings of previous readings—and of enriching them.

The identification and study of the relationship of these "systems of non-poetic discourse," or what Lowell Edmunds calls "system reference,"[21] to the *Annals* not only refines our understanding of the poem, it also opens a window into the crucial period when Latin authors began wholeheartedly to embrace Greek models. This turning point in Latin literature is one of the most important events in all of Western literature—it led to Vergil's *Aeneid* but also, eventually, to Dante's *Divine Comedy* and Milton's *Paradise Lost.* It is not hyperbolic to say that there are few moments in Western literary history of greater significance than the reinvention of the dactylic hexameter in Latin. The Italic contribution to the *Annals* should serve as a powerful reminder that Latin, and later Western literature, is not simply Greek literature translated into another language but rather a hybrid of cultural elements that underpins our very understanding of what it means to be "literature" and what it means to be "poetry."

Jupiter Stator and the Italic Tradition in the *Annals*

Without a close analysis, however, it is not always obvious that Ennius has appropriated, or is alluding to, a traditional collocation. Because of this difficulty, I will begin with a specific example, so as to illuminate something of the "nuts and bolts" of my thesis. The following fragment, perhaps from a hortatory speech delivered by Hannibal to his army before his historic march across the Alps, is a good place to start, since it illustrates precisely the linguistic calculus that is necessary to reveal the deeper traditional strata that underlie what is, on the surface, deceptively straightforward language:[22]

> Non semper vostra evortit nunc Iuppiter hac stat (*Ann.* 232)

> Not always does Jupiter upset your plans; now he stands on our side. (trans. Warmington)[23]

The phrase *Iuppiter . . . stat* comprises the same roots as the Latin cult title *Jupiter Stator.* The phrase *Iuppiter hac stat* is not a quotation of the cult title *Iuppiter Stator,* but the presence of *Iuppiter* and a form of the verb *stare,* the two underlying roots of the collocation *Iuppiter Stator,* nevertheless invites a comparison between the context of the Ennian line, whatever it may have been, and the discourse of the cult of Jupiter Stator.

The collocation of *Iuppiter* and *stare* is meaningful because the same roots co-occur in the collocation Jupiter Stator and because the cult title is "semantically relevant." In other words, the meaning of *Iuppiter hac stat* is more than the sum of its parts, by virtue of the existence of the traditional ritual collocation Jupiter Stator. Although collocations are often implicit and unremarked upon by speakers, Cicero explicitly discusses the significance of this collocation in his first oration against Catiline. In the first Catilinarian Cicero thanks Jupiter Stator (whom he calls *antiquissimo custodi huius urbis,* "the most ancient guardian of this city") that the Republic had already escaped unscathed from various plots of Catiline to overthrow it (*Catil.* 1.11). Because Cicero not only calls Jupiter Stator "the most ancient guardian of the city" but also claims that the cult of Jupiter Stator was founded by Romulus at the same time as the city (*isdem quibus haec urbs auspiciis a Romulo es constitutus* [*Catil.* 1.33]), the collocation has connotations of venerability in addition to a specific denotation as the god who upholds and protects the interests of the city of Rome. The cult title Jupiter Stator therefore has a specific semantic valence both as a guardian of the city of Rome in the late Republic and as the god who evokes the context of the foundational narrative of the city.

Because Cicero refers to Catiline as *hostis,* "foreign enemy," he hints that the collocation Jupiter Stator has military connotations that fit the proposed context of the quotation from Ennius and reflect the history of the cult title. According to tradition, Romulus vowed the first temple during a battle with the Sabines (LIV. 1.12.3–6), even though the temple was never built. Marcus Atilius Regulus vowed and actually built a temple of Jupiter Stator while fighting the Samnites at the edge of the territory of Luceria (LIV. 10.36.11) in the early third century BCE. After the first battle with the Samnites left the Roman army exhausted and dispirited, Regulus forced his rank and file to engage the Samnites the next day by sheer force of will (LIV. 10.35). When the Romans began to give way to the Samnites and retreat to their camp, Regulus refused to grant them entry. He instead vowed to build the temple for Jupiter Stator if the Roman battle line would cease from flight and defeat the Samnites. Jupiter Stator must have heard Regulus' prayer, since the Roman army turned back the Samnites and won a significant victory (LIV. 10.36). Because the temple of Jupiter that Regulus built in fulfillment of a vow made during the Third Samnite War was still standing in the age of Ennius, the cult title Jupiter Stator likely had military as well as ritual connotations for the poet and his audience.

The primary function of Jupiter Stator is, in fact, the protection of Roman interests against hostile powers throughout the tradition. He protects the Roman army in the story of Regulus and the Samnites, and the city of Rome in the story of Romulus and the Sabines. Moreover, Cicero delivered the first oration against Catiline to the senate when it was convened at the temple of Jupiter Stator, a symbolic gesture implying that Catiline is no different from the Sabines who threatened the nascent foundation of Rome, or from Samnites who endangered the lives of Roman soldiers, since Jupiter Stator evoked an image of conflict against foreign enemies.

In light of the opposition of *evortit* and *stat* in Ennius, Cicero's use of the gerundive *evertenda,* "to be overturned," in close proximity to *exstitit,* "has come into existence," to describe the actions of Catiline in the first oration may indicate that roots of *evortit*—another form of *evertenda*—and *stat* in Ennius are a collocation that forms part of the traditional discourse of Jupiter Stator:

> Nullum iam aliquot annis facinus exstitit nisi per te, nullum flagitium sine te; tibi uni multorum civium neces, tibi vexatio direptioque sociorum inpunita fuit ac libera; tu non solum ad neglegendas leges et quaestiones, verum etiam ad evertendas perfringendasque valuisti. (*Catil.* 1.18)
>
> No crime has come into existence except through you, no outrage without you; you alone have killed many citizens, harried and despoiled the allies unpunished and free; you have been able not only to neglect the laws and courts, but even to thwart and destroy them.[24]

Although *evertere* may have suggested itself independently to Cicero and Ennius as an appropriate antonym to the root of *stator,* the fact remains that both roots are opposed in both authors. It is also possible that Cicero is alluding to the fragment from the *Annals,* even though such a possibility is not likely, since there are no obvious and specific contextual connections between the Hannibalic War and the conspiracy of Catiline. Whether or not Cicero is alluding to Ennius, there is evidence suggesting that the proximity of *evertere* to *stare* in both authors is not empty wordplay.

Because Regulus built the temple as a consequence of his vow during a battle against Oscan-speaking Samnites, the proximity of *evortit* to *Iuppiter* in the Ennian fragment may be an allusion to an Oscan cult title of Jupiter. The root of the verb *evortit* is etymologically equivalent to the root of the Oscan epithet Fερσορει in ΔιουFει Fερσορει, *Iovi Vertori* (the cult title is written in the Greek alphabet after the orthography of the original inscription), a cult title of Jupiter in an inscription from Lucania (Rix Lu 25). Regulus may therefore have deliberately vowed a temple to Jupiter Stator because Jupiter Versor was worshipped by all Oscans, even though the cult is only attested for Lucania, or because he assumed that all Oscans worshipped Jupiter Versor. If so, the vow would have a deep symbolic value that could have been preserved in the historical record or in the oral tradition about the temple. The collective memory of Atilius' challenge to Jupiter Versor would explain why Ennius transformed the cult title of an Oscan deity and how a Roman audience would be able to make a connection between *non semper vostra evortit* (*Iuppiter*) and ΔιουFει Fερσορει (*Iovi Versori*).

If the building of the temple of Jupiter Stator was a commemoration of a response to Jupiter Versor in the Third Samnite War, as I have suggested, then the opposition of the Oscan and Roman Jupiter is not only an example of the intense cultural interaction in the central Italian *koinê* period but also serves as evidence for why it ended. The Third Samnite War was fought at the very beginning of the third century, the tail end of three centuries of mutual influence. If Regulus did not simply appropriate Jupiter Versor but rather opposed this form of Oscan Jupiter with an antonymic Latin form, then it suggests that the Romans were beginning to differentiate themselves more distinctly from the other cultures in the *koinê*. This emphasis on difference over sameness would eventually conceal much of the influence of the central Italian *koinê* on Roman culture behind a teleological narrative of imperial expansion that would end in the triumph of Greco-Roman culture and the eclipse of the Etruscans, Umbrians, and Oscan-speaking Samnites and their cultures.

The beginning of the second century was a time when separate "plural" identities were the norm, but it is unlikely that Ennius is expressing his "local" identity along with his Roman identity by alluding to Jupiter Versor.[25] Because the collocation of the name *Iuppiter* and the verb *evortit,* as well as others that I will adduce in the course of my argument, consists solely of Latin words bound by Latin syntax, the parallel between Oscan ΔιουFει Fερσορει (*Iovi Vertori*) and *evortit* (*Iuppiter*) in Ennius suggests that Jupiter Versor was a traditional collocation *in Latin.* In other words, if the collocation was borrowed from Oscan into Latin, it was nativized generations before Ennius wrote the *Annals.* As I hope to demonstrate, the diction of the *Annals* in general is characterized by the cultural hybridity that deeply influenced Roman culture during the central Italian *koinê* period of the seventh through the fourth century BCE rather than the independent "coexistence of elements of Roman and native culture" of the second century BCE, as Andrew Wallace-Hadrill understands the relationship between Latin and Oscan at that time.[26]

Jupiter Versor may also have been a hybrid of Oscan and Greek cult titles. Because the Oscan title ΔιουFει Fερσορει is so similar to Ζεὺς Τροπαῖος, "Zeus the giver of victory," the possibility that the Oscan collocation is a borrowing from Greek cannot be eliminated.[27] If the collocation is Greek in origin, however, then it is an example of a Greek cultural phenomenon that attained a life of its own in the Italic tradition. Whatever the Greek phrase originally might have meant for those who borrowed it, that meaning would have been lost with the passage of time, since the collocation was very likely a traditional, inherited cult title to the Oscan worshippers of Jupiter Versor, no matter what its ultimate origin may have been, just as it would have been for Latin worshippers of Jupiter Stator by the time of Ennius. Moreover, Jupiter Versor would have originally been an Oscan cult title to the Romans, who likely encountered the deity for the first time in the Samnite Wars.

If this single line from the *Annals* alludes to the Roman cult of Jupiter Stator and its origin as a response to Oscan Jupiter Versor, then the fragment alludes to local cult in a manner that recalls the Alexandrian poets who so profoundly influenced later Latin poets. The Alexandrian poet Callimachus had an avid interest in local cults, like those represented in his hymns to Delian Apollo and Argive Athena. Ennius, too, alludes to a local cult: in this case, the Roman cult of Jupiter Stator and possibly the Oscan cult of Jupiter Versor, "Jupiter the Overturner." Because Callimachus similarly alludes to Egyptian cult in his poetry,[28] a simultaneous and oblique reference to Roman and to Oscan cult is directly parallel to Callimachean practice. The line *non semper vostra evortit nunc Iuppiter hac stat* may also refer indirectly to a myth of origin of the cult of Jupiter Stator, or an aetiology, a reference that may be indicative of the influence of Callimachus, who was so interested in aetiologies that he wrote an epic-length poem on the subject, the *Aetia*.

There is, nevertheless, a crucial difference between Ennius and Callimachus with respect to their source material. Although Callimachus may have had firsthand knowledge of some of the local cults that he describes and explains, much of what he knew must have come from literary or at least written texts, such as the historian Xenomedes, an authority whom the Greek poet explicitly cites in the *Aetia* (fr.75.54). In contrast, Ennius would have had direct knowledge of the cult of Jupiter Stator. As a resident of Rome, he could have heard the story of the vow of Regulus and the building of the temple from a number of people without consulting a text. Unlike Callimachus, Ennius seems to be alluding not to a learned treatise or poem but to a ritual discourse.

Whether or not the allusion to Jupiter Stator was inspired by the work of the Alexandrian poets, it is subtle and sophisticated. Ennius does not baldly name Jupiter Stator but rather plays with the basic meaning of the two elements of the collocation. Nor does he place his allusion to Jupiter Stator during his narrative of the Third Samnite War, the obvious place for it. Because Macrobius assigns the fragment to book 7 of the *Annals,* where Ennius begins his treatment of the Punic Wars, which began at least a generation after the Third Samnite War, the location of the line in his narrative creates a sort of temporal displacement. If Hannibal is the speaker of this line, Ennius may also be forecasting the eventual outcome of the Second Punic War. After all, in the experience of the audience, Jupiter Stator stabilized and assisted the Romans against the Samnites. As history had already demonstrated by the time of the *Annals,* he came to their aid against Hannibal too.

What's in a Name? The Olympian Gods and the Common Italic Tradition in the *Annals*

However ΔιουFει Fερσορει became a cult title in Oscan, it could have been seen as a Greek cult title by a later generation accustomed to drawing a sharper distinction between Greek and Oscan than was operative in the central Italian *koinê* period and its aftermath. If there was, in fact, a cult title Jupiter Versor at Rome, later Romans too could come to understand a reference to Jupiter Versor as an allusion to Greek cult once the Romans became conscious of Greek Ζεὺς Τροπαῖος, "Zeus the giver of victory," even though neither Ennius nor his audience would likely have understood it thus. In other words, the act of privileging the Greek origins of some of the features of the *Annals* over the horizon of expectation of the poet and his audience can obscure the interplay between the foreign and the familiar that the original audience of the epic would have been able to perceive and appreciate.

The following fragment is a case where, in addition to the meter, the content could be seen as entirely Greek:

> Iuno Vesta Minerva Ceres Diana Venus Mars
> Mercurius Iovis Neptunus Volcanus Apollo (*Ann.* 240–41)

Ennius names twelve gods in the distich, the canonical number of Olympian gods in Greek culture. Although most of the names are Latin, every god named has a Greek counterpart who precisely matches in a scholion to the *Argonautica* of Apollonius Rhodius, provided Carl Wendel has reconstructed it correctly.[29] Ennius also casts his list in two lines of the Greek dactylic hexameter.

The Ennian *duodekatheon* is independent of its Greek models because of its form, but the changes are wrought by means of a combination of Greek meter and a canonical list of twelve gods, a Greek concept. The naming of gods is also paralleled by the practice of naming deities in Greek vase painting, even though Pindar and the other Greek poets who came before Ennius refer to the twelve gods without naming them.[30] In light of the evidence as it stands, a list of the twelve Olympians within the dactylic hexameter is an innovation that must be attributed to Ennius. Because the couplet is a recombination of Greek elements, however, its originality becomes manifest only when the Ennian list is compared to similar lists compiled by Greek writers and the use of those lists by Greek poets.

There are, again, indications of the influence of the Alexandrian poets in the *duodekatheon*. In what appears to be a poetic dream in the *Aetia* (fr. 2), Callimachus directly names Hesiod and refers to his *Theogony,* a poem that catalogues immortal beings by name in a manner recalled by the Ennian couplet, including the Muses, while narrating the creation of the cosmos and eventual triumph of Zeus. If the Ennian *duodekatheon* is derived from the prose writer Herodorus, then the use of this prose source is also roughly parallel to Callimachus' explicit citation of the historian Xenomedes. The postclassical Greek poet Aratus not only used a prose source but also cast that source, the *Phaenomena* of Eudoxus, a prose treatise on astronomy, into verse. The casting of the *duodekatheon* in verse by Ennius is an example of the same process in miniature. Moreover, there may be a hint of an *ekphrasis,* a poetic description of a work of art that is characteristic of Alexandrian poetry, if the gods named are actually statues in a *lectisternium,* as Otto Skutsch suggests.[31]

Although the idea of twelve supreme gods originated in Greek culture, Ennius had to decide whom to include and whom to exclude, or at least whose version of the *duodekatheon* he would adopt. Nor are his decisions disinterested in a Roman context. The most significant inclusion in Roman terms is Vesta, the Roman analogue of Hestia, perhaps the most Roman of Roman goddesses, who had an extensive role in Roman public cult. Ennius can also exclude certain figures. Although Dionysus appears in two sixth-century vase paintings of twelve gods that may be examples of a *duodekatheon,*[32] his Latin counterpart Liber is not named by Ennius. The exclusion of Liber may have been motivated by the disfavor the cult of the god had fallen into after the conspiracy of 186 BCE.[33] Ennius therefore made a selection that reflected the realities of Roman cult (and perhaps Roman politics), even though his *duodekatheon* is modeled on Greek precedents.

If the context of the distich is the *lectisternium* from the year 217 BCE as described by Livy (22.10.9), then the context is Roman although the content appears to be Greek. Even if the context is not particularly Roman, all the gods were worshipped at Rome under the names listed by Ennius. What is more, the names of these gods are all of Latin origin, with the exception of Apollo. In spite of his Greek name, even Apollo cannot be said to be wholly Greek, because the cult of the god was well established at Rome and throughout Italy in the age of Ennius. Even the Greek name Ἀπόλλων has been nativized in Latin to Apollo, as can be seen most clearly in the genitive form *Apollinis* in Latin when it is compared with the Greek genitive Ἀπόλλωνος. The same form could underlie both the Greek and the Latin genitive, but the last two vowels in *Apollinis* appear to have undergone vowel weakening, a change that affected unstressed syllables in Latin. Because the Romans were already celebrating the *Ludi Apollinares* in the Second Punic War, Apollo was a figure of Roman cult regardless of whether his name was nativized. It is therefore impossible to separate the Roman cult figures from the Greek gods, because the couplet comprises Latin names.

It is especially difficult to separate Jupiter from his Greek counterpart Zeus or from his Oscan counterpart in order to characterize him as "Latin," "Greek," or even "Oscan." As Denis Feeney has already noted, in the *Annals,* Jupiter is "the son of a euhemeristic Saturn, a cosmic force of cohesion, something on a couch at a Roman *lectisternium,* a dedicatee for a Greek king, a Zeus-figure chairing a meeting of factious kin, a clap of thunder."[34] If the form *Iovi Diano* (*CIL* V 783) is not a nonce formation, then Diana could also evoke another cult title of Jupiter.[35] Even the form of the name Jupiter is not culturally unambiguous, since the Umbrians worshipped **Iupater** (Rix Um 1 IIb 24) and an Oscan inscription refers to *Ioves patres* (Rix MV 1). Moreover, Latin, Umbrian, and Oscan all had a form of Jupiter without the *pater* element (e.g., Latin *Iovem,* Umbrian **Iuve,** and the aforementioned Oscan ΔιουϜει).[36]

Jupiter is not the only god whom Oscan or Umbrian speakers could claim as their own. Minerva is also named in Oscan inscriptions. Although the name Ϝενζηι in an Oscan inscription from Lucania appears to be a borrowing of Latin Venus (Rix Lu 31) (as is the case for ΔιουϜει Ϝερσορει, quotations from Oscan inscriptions written in the Greek alphabet are quoted in the Greek alphabet),[37] the mere occurrence of the name suggests that some speakers of Oscan in southern Italy worshipped Venus. If so, it may no longer have been obvious that the name was a borrowing. Ceres was an especially important Italic goddess, as evidenced by her importance in the Agnone Tablet (Rix Sa 1) and in other Oscan inscriptions.[38] Nor is Apollo a distinctly Roman cult figure. Three separate Oscan inscriptions from Pompeii and Messina deploy the title **Appelluneís,** a name that appears to be derived from *Apello,* the Doric form of Apollo.[39] What is more, the Umbrians also conceived of Mars as part of a triad with Jupiter, just as the Romans dedicated temples to divine triads, such as the Capitoline triad, which included Jupiter, Juno, and Minerva. The Ennian distich is therefore a hybrid not only of Greek and Latin but also of Oscan and Umbrian divinities that cannot be separated into elements belonging only to one culture or another.

In addition to the actual names of the gods, the form of the list may have native precedents. A striking parallel to the form of the Ennian couplet may be seen on a Praenestine bronze *cista* that lists a similar series of gods, albeit in a haphazard fashion, in a depiction of Minerva holding up baby Mars:

> Iuno, Iouos, Mercuris, Apolo, Leiber, Hercle
> Victoria, Menerva, Diana, Mars, Fortuna (*CIL* I^2 563)[40]

In spite of the fact that the Praenestine inscription is a jumble of names rather than the two, well-delineated lines implied in the text, the Ennian list and the Praenestine *cista* share seven of the same names. Although the abstractions Victoria and Fortuna are found alongside Leiber, the Italic equivalent of Dionysus, and Hercules rather than names of Olympians on the *cista,* the existence of a parallel list of deities in this context raises the possibility that such lists reflect a nativized Latin practice as well as a learned Greek *duodekatheon.*

Because the Praenestine *cista* is not a ritual text, however, more evidence is necessary in order to determine whether the Ennian distich had any ritual connotations. If Gellius is quoting verbatim from his sources, there is at least one ritual text that is roughly parallel to the *duodekatheon* in the *Annals:*

> Conprecationes deum inmortalium, quae ritu Romano fiunt, expositae sunt in libris sacerdotum populi Romani et in plerisque antiquis orationibus. In his scriptum est: "Luam Saturni, Salaciam Neptuni, Horam Quirini, Virites Quirini, Maiam Volcani, Heriem Iunonis, Moles Martis Nerienemque Martis." (GEL. 13.23.2–3)

> The invocations of the immortal gods, which are made in the Roman rite, are put forth in the books of the priest of the Roman people and in many ancient treatises, in which it is written [names of goddesses follow].

Ennius may have had a similar list of gods and goddesses in mind when he composed the Olympian couplet. Gellius also provides a poetic enumeration of deities from the *Satires* of Varro in his discussion of the *conprecationes:*

> Te Anna ac Peranna, Panda Cela, te Pales
> Nerienes <et> Minerva, Fortuna ac Ceres. (GEL. 13.23.4)

It may be significant that two lists of female divinities have survived antiquity and that Ennius divides his own list by gender. Because long lists of deities were invoked in Roman prayer (*conprecationes*) according to Gellius, the *duodekatheon* of Ennius may evoke these sorts of prayers. Moreover, the first six names in the couplet may evoke a particular type of native prayer addressed to goddesses.

Long lists of deities are apparently not exclusive to Latin ritual texts, either, to judge from the names of a variety of deities in the Agnone Tablet:

> 1. **aasas. ekask. eestínt.** 2. **húrtúí.** 3. **vezkeí.** 4. **evklúí.** 5. **fuutreí** 6. **anter** {.} **stataí** 7. **cerrí.** 8. **ammaí** 9. **diumpaís** 10. **líganakdíkeí. entraí.** 11. **kerríiaí** 12. **anafríss** 13. **maatúís** 14. **diúveí. verehasiú.** 15. **diúveí. piíhiúí regatureí** 16. **hereklúí. kerríiúí** 17. **patanaí. piístíaí** 18. **deívaí. genetaí** (Rix Sa 1)

> These altars stand in the enclosure for Venisci, for Euklos, for the Daughter, for Interstitia, for Ceres, for Amma, for the Nymphs, for Liganacdica Interna of Ceres, for the Rains, the Matis, for Jupiter the Overturner (?), for Jupiter the pious ruler, for Heracles of Ceres, for Patina Pistia, for Divine Genita.

The syntagm **kerríiúí hereklúí,** "Cerean Hercules" or "Hercules of Ceres," is parallel to the list of feminine divinities qualified by a genitive of a deity in Gellius. I emphasize again that a similar phenomenon in Oscan is not indicative of direct influence but rather evidence that even a simple list of theonyms could have ritual connotations among the member cultures of the central Italian *koinê,* connotations that may have existed in Latin and that could color the meaning of twelve names in the *Annals.*

Plautus once refers to Jupiter and the eleven gods besides him (*undecim deos praeter sese* [*Epid.* 610]). The *Bacchides* of Plautus, however, yields another extended invocation of multiple gods that has a distinctive Italic coloring:

> CHRYSALUS: ita me Juppiter, Iuno, Ceres
> Minerva, Lato, Spes, Opis, Virtus, Venus
> Castor, Polluces, Mars, Mercurius, Hercules
> Summanus, Sol, Saturnus dique omnes ament,

Ut ille cum illa neque cubat neque ambulat
Neque osculatur neque illud quod dici solet. (*Bac.* 892–97)

As truly as Jupiter [etc.] may love me he is not lying with her, not walking with her, not kissing her, not doing the thing that is usually said.

If Ceres were removed from the sequence *Jupiter, Iuno, Ceres / Minerva*, then all three members of the so-called Capitoline triad would be named together. Ceres may have been inserted for metrical reasons, since Minerva cannot end an iambic senarius, the meter of the Plautine prayer. The order of *Jupiter, Iuno, (Ceres) / Minerva* also matches an inscription set up by a *collegium* of Faliscan cooks:

Iovei Iunonei Minervai Falesce quei in Sardinia sunt donum dederunt . . . (*CIL* I^2 364)

The Faliscans who are in Sardinia gave this gift to Jupiter, Juno and Minerva . . .

The inscription verifies that some Latin speakers associated Jupiter, Juno, and Minerva in a triad, and it also implies that there was a relatively fixed expression of the triad. A comparison with the Plautine list suggests that this triad did not vary in the order of the names. However traditional the rest of the Plautine invocation may be, it seems that the close proximity of Jupiter, Juno, and Minerva is a nod toward a traditional triad of Roman cult. Whether or not Plautus is alluding to a traditional collocation of the names of the members of the Capitoline triad, the enumeration of divine names in prayer parallels the *conprecationes* quoted by Gellius above. These multiple invocations are therefore not only structurally parallel to the *duodekatheon* of Ennius but also suggest that the fragment from the *Annals* has native ritual overtones.

Because the Plautine list is an invocation of multiple Roman deities with Umbrian and Oscan equivalents, it has a marked Italic flavor. The presence of Hercules and the Dioscuri add to that Italic flavor, since they had been worshipped so long in Italy and in Rome that, to the Romans of the second century BCE, they were as traditional as Jupiter. A fragment of an altar from nearby Lanuvium dates the cult of the Dioscuri in Latium to the fifth century BCE:

Castorei Podlouqueique qurois (*CIL* I^2 2833)

For Castor and Pollux the κοῦροι.

Although *qurois* appears to be a transliteration of the dative plural of the Greek word κοῦροι, the second element of Διόσκουροι, "the sons of Zeus," a Greek epithet of Castor and Pollux, the form *Podlouquei* is not a transliteration of the dative of Πολυδεύκης the Greek name for Pollux. The inscription is therefore a hybrid of Greek and Latin elements. There are also a number of Latin dedications to Hercules dated before the end of the Second Punic War (*CIL* I^2 30, 61, 62, 394, 607, and *CIL* I^2 2887b) that testify to the popularity of the cult of this god. Because these inscriptions demonstrate that speakers of Latin had been worshipping them for generations before Plautus wrote the *Bacchides*, invocations of gods such as Castor, Pollux, and Hercules would likely have been considered a native practice by the audience of the play. Although Ennius does not name Castor or Pollux in his list of Olympian deities, the mixture of Greek and Latin elements in the dedication to the Dioscuri demonstrates that cultural and linguistic hybridity was a feature of Latin cult centuries before Plautus and Ennius created their own hybrid lists of gods.

Some of the names in the *duodekatheon* from the *Annals* also have close Etruscan parallels. The Etruscans made dedications to a goddess called ***Menerva,*** a name likely borrowed from one of the other languages of the central Italian *koinê*.[41] Helmut Rix has suggested that the Etruscan god *Neθuns* may be a borrowing from the unattested Umbrian counterpart of Latin *Neptunus*,[42] a hypothesis that is supported by the existence of other verbal parallels in Etruscan and Umbrian ritual texts.[43] It is also possible that the name Uni, the Etruscan analogue of Hera, has been influenced by the name Juno.[44] A borrowing from an Italic language into Etruscan differs from a borrowing from Oscan, or even Greek, into Latin, since Etruscan is not an Indo-European language. In other words, it does not have the similar inventory of sounds and basic words that all the other attested member languages of the *koinê* have by virtue of being genetically related. In order for Etruscan to exercise an influence on the language of ritual in central Italy and to be influenced by other languages, a prolonged period of cultural contact would have been necessary, contact so intense that even the names of gods were subject to mutual influence.

Even the idea of twelve gods divided into an equal number of male and female deities may owe something to the influence of the Etruscans. Seneca the Younger says that the Etruscans believed that Jupiter (or Tin, his Etruscan counterpart) had a council of twelve gods (*Nat.* 2.41.1). Arnobius tells us that Varro knew of the same group and that he claimed they were equally divided into male and female halves, just as in the Ennian distich (*Adv nat.* 3.40). Moreover, one of the earliest images of twelve gods anywhere is on an Attic black figure *kyathos* that was found in a tomb in Etruria.[45] Whether or not the idea of a *duodekatheon* divided into six gods and six goddesses spread to Rome and Latium from Etruria some time before Ennius wrote the *Annals,* it is likely another instance of a Greek idea that was adapted by a member culture of the *koinê* that was in turn borrowed by other member cultures, including the Romans, so early that it had become native for at least some of these other cultures.

If the source of Festus' explanation of the name *Mamertini* is accurate, the *duodekatheon* was meaningful to at least one group of Oscan speakers before the First Punic War:[46]

> Nomen acceperunt unum ut dicerentur Mamertini, quod coniectis in sortem duodecim deorum nominibus, Mamers forte exierat; qui lingua Oscorum Mars significatur. (FEST. 158M)

> They took one name so that they were called the Mamertines because when the names of the Twelve Gods were shaken together for drawing lots, Mamers by chance fell out, which means Mars in the language of the Oscans.[47]

The names of the twelve gods included at least one specifically Oscan deity, *Mamers,* a form of Mars particular to Oscan, the language of the Mamertines. Because the Mamertines appear in the historical record when they occupy Messana before the First Punic War, the significance of the number twelve for the gods for speakers of Oscan may be dated to at least a generation before Ennius was born.

Although I have discussed the traditional ritual character of the Ennian distich, I have not established whether this bare list can be a traditional collocation. It is possible that Ennius constructed his list around a "core" collocation of Mars and Mercurius. Plautus also places Mars and Mercurius together to form an alliterative doubling figure in the passage from the *Bacchides* quoted above:

> CHRYSALUS: ita me Juppiter, Iuno, Ceres
> Minerva, Lato, Spes, Opis, Virtus, Venus
> Castor, Polluces, Mars, Mercurius, Hercules
> Summanus, Sol, Saturnus

The names *Mars* and *Mercurius* not only form an alliterative doubling figure but also straddle the break between the first and second lines in the couplet from the *Annals:*

> Iuno Vesta Minerva Ceres Diana Venus Mars
> Mercurius Iovis Neptunus Volcanus Apollo.

The phonetic shape of the names could independently suggest such an arrangement, but *Minerva* is not placed alongside *Mercurius* or *Mars* in Ennius or Plautus, even though her name also alliterates with *Mercurius* and *Mars*. Even if *Minerva* traditionally needed to be near *Iuno* and *Iuppiter* in the *Bacchides, Mars* or *Mercurius* could have followed *Minerva*. It is therefore possible that both Plautus and Ennius built their lists around a traditional collocation of *Mars* and *Mercurius*.

The twelve names of gods in Ennius could themselves be a traditional collocation. The fact that Livy and Ennius list the same exact twelve gods in a different order suggests that the Roman *duodekatheon* had become canonical after 217 BCE. Livy could be alluding to Ennius, but his list is organized very differently:

> Iovi et Iunoni unum, alterum Neptuno ac Minervae, tertium Marti ac Veneri, quartum Apollini ac Dianae, quintum Volcano ac Vestae, sextum Mercurio et Cereri. (LIV. 22.10.9)
>
> One (couch) for Jupiter and Juno, another for Neptune and Minerva, a third for Mars and Venus, a fourth for Apollo and Diana, a fifth for Vulcan and Vesta, a sixth for Mercury and Ceres.

There is little in Livy beyond the names themselves that suggests that he is alluding to Ennius. The order of the couches in Livy also places Minerva next to Jupiter and Juno, an order that may be traditional but is not found in the arrangement of Ennius. The difference in the presentation of the same twelve names between the poet and the historian points to a common source that Ennius seems to have altered in order to render it into hexameters, since it is not chronologically possible that the poet is alluding to the historian. The list seems to have remained consistent for approximately two centuries, likely because it appears to be part of a commemoration of a specific historical event that was memorable both because it followed the defeat of the Roman army at Lake Trasimene by Hannibal and also because it may have been the first time twelve gods were supplicated instead of six.[48] Whatever explanation there may be for the stability of the canonical list, it may have become a traditional collocation with twelve rather than two constituents early enough that the audience would have recognized the *duodekatheon* in Ennius as a traditional collocation.

If Ennius is not alluding to a traditional collocation of names, the Ennian couplet itself seems to have become a traditional way to name the twelve gods in later Latin. Both Apuleius and Martianus Capella quote the distich. Although Apuleius, who was active in the Antonine age, could have read the *Annals*,[49] Capella, a fifth-century CE author who could not have read the *Annals*, also quotes the distich in his encyclopedic treatise *De Nuptiis Philologiae et Mercurii* (1.42). Whether Martianus took the quotation from Apuleius or from another source, he explicitly attributes it to Ennius. The use of the quotation and the implicit appeal to the authority of Ennius in two different authors suggests that his list had become an authoritative list of the chief gods of the Roman pantheon by the Antonine age, if not before.

If equal attention is paid to the Roman, Greek, and general Italic elements of this very short fragment in Ennius, a sense of cultural hybridity emerges. The fragment is not a Hellenizing revelation so much as a presentation of a nativized concept recharacterized by novel Greek elements. Most of the gods in the Greek *duodekatheon* had equivalents not only in Roman but also in Umbrian, Oscan, and even Etruscan cult. The Etruscans borrowed much of the content and style of their mythic tableaux from the Greeks, but they had been producing images of groups of explicitly named gods on objects like mirrors and gems for centuries before the arrival of Ennius at Rome. The naming of the images of gods on the Praenestine *cista* also suggests that the practice was well established in Latium. If the *duodekatheon* is, in fact, a naming of the gods whose statues were included in the *lectisternium,* then Ennius, too, is naming images of gods. Whether or not Etruscan or Praenestine works of art inspired the Ennian distich, the twelve gods in Ennius owe something to common Italic ritual as well as to Greek literature.

Prayer in the *Annals*

By now I hope to have demonstrated that there is a relationship between ritual and text in the two fragments of the *Annals,* but it is often difficult to decide where the ritual ends and the literary text begins, or vice versa. As Denis Feeney has argued, ritual is an open-ended system of signification, and it is therefore subject to the influence of literature.[50] It is always possible that a given "traditional" collocation was once, in fact, a literary creation that was co-opted into Roman ritual.[51] Nor was every utterance in Roman ritual archaic or traditional. The consuls ordered Livius Andronicus, for example, to compose a hymn for Juno Regina in response to portents in 207 BCE (LIV. 27.37.7). The text of the *Carmen Saeculare* of Horace has not only survived, but there is also direct, contemporary evidence that it was performed at the close of the Secular Games of 17 BCE (*CIL* VI 32323.147–49). It is also possible that a literary representation of ritual or a prayer could combine traditional ritual collocations in new ways that allowed the new prayer to be traditional in every sense of the word in spite of its novelty.

Yet another single line from the *Annals* can demonstrate just how complicated the relationship between literary text and ritual utterance can be. Skutsch suggests that Livy may "quite possibly [be] reflecting what Ennius said" in a prayer of Horatius Cocles to the river god Tiberinus:[52]

> Tum Cocles "Tiberine pater," inquit, "te sancte precor, haec arma et hunc militem propitio flumine accipias." (LIV. 2.10.11)

> Then Cocles cried, "O Father Tiberinus, I solemnly invoke thee; receive these arms and this soldier with propitious stream!"[53]

Although the prayer in Livy has a "dactylic rhythm," as Skutsch observes,[54] it is the verbal echoes of Ennius that suggest the influence of the poet on the historian:

> Teque pater Tiberine tuo cum flumine sancto (*Ann.* 26)

> And thee, Father of the Tiber, with thy hallowed stream. (trans. Warmington)

Whether or not Livy is alluding to Ennius, Vergil apparently does allude to the fragment from the *Annals* in the *Aeneid:*

> Tuque o Thybri tuo genitor cum flumine sancto (*A.* 8.72)

> And you Tiber o begettor with thy hallowed stream.

However the relationship between Livy, Ennius, and Vergil is understood, all three prayers appear to be related to one another in some way.

The wording of Ennius' prayer possibly influenced Livy and certainly Vergil, but there is evidence that Ennius is alluding to the traditional wording of a prayer that existed outside of the literary tradition. Servius quotes a traditional invocation of Tiberinus that appears to be the basis of the line in the *Annals:*

> Adesto Tiberine cum tuis undis (*ad Aen.* 8.72–73)

> Be present Tiberinus with your waters!

The similarity of context and word choice indicate that *cum tuis undis* likely underlies the expression *cum flumine sancto.* The use of the vocative *Tiberine* in the context of a prayer may also have alerted the audience to the possibility that Ennius is alluding to the prayer that Servius is quoting, or at least that Ennius is using language appropriate and traditional for Roman prayers.

The words *pater* and *sanctus* are not only present in Ennius and Livy, they are also constituents of the traditional ritual collocation *sancte pater.* The collocation appears in Livy, Propertius (4.9.71), and Ovid (*F.* 2.127), among others. If the manuscript reading *sancto* does not in fact conceal an original *sancte,*

Ennius refrains from an outright quotation of the collocation. Although there are no examples of *pater sancte* before the Augustan age, the use of *sancte* in an address to a god is demonstrably older than Ennius. Phanostrata the matron invokes *Spes . . . sancta,* "holy Hope," in the *Cistellaria* of Plautus (*Cist.* 670), and Sceparnio the slave invokes *Palaemo[n] sancte Neptuni comes,* "Palaemon, holy companion of Neptune," in the *Rudens* (*Rud.* 160). The vocative phrase *sancte . . . Victor,* "holy (Hercules) Victor," in an inscription of Republican date (*CIL* I^2 632), suggests that the use of *sancte* in prayer was not limited to literature.

By altering *cum tuis undis* to *cum flumine sancto,* Ennius is able to allude not only to the traditional address of the river god Tiberinus but also to the ritual collocation *sancte pater* without having recourse to direct quotation. Although there are no exact matches between the prayer in Servius and in Ennius besides the vocative Tiberine and the preposition *cum,* the similarity is enough to prompt the audience of the *Annals* to recall the prayer and compare the version preserved by Servius with the Ennian. The prayer in the *Annals* is playfully allusive, and it also adds some semantic weight by evoking the traditional collocation *sancte pater,* an expression that is not found in the Servian prayer. On the assumption that the prayer in Servius is traditional, Ennius has taken a traditional address of the river god and turned it into a literary allusion that is even more traditional because it includes a ritual collocation that was not part of the original prayer.

The combination of the same traditional elements in the prayer of Cocles in Livy could be the result of the influence of Ennius, but there are alternate explanations. With the exception of the pronoun *te,* the only exact verbal parallel between Ennius and Livy is *Tiberine,* an element that appears to be a traditional part of any address to Tiberinus. Because the combination of *pater* and *sanctus* seems to be a traditional collocation in its own right, it is also possible that both authors independently included the expression to add to the solemnity of the prayers in their narratives. It is even possible that Livy, consciously or unconsciously, recalled the prayer from the *Annals* because Ennius was the first author to combine these traditional elements in one prayer. To whatever extent that Ennius influenced the prayer of Cocles, the relationship between the prayers from the *Annals* and Livy is only part of a much larger series of prayers to the river god Tiberinus within, and perhaps without, the literary texts that depict prayers to this divinity.

Another fragmentary prayer, presumably from the end of book 1 of the *Annals,* presents a similar situation. Someone, perhaps Romulus on the occasion of the agreement to share the kingship with the Sabine king Titus Tatius, pronounces a blessing:

> Quod mihi reique fidei regno vobisque, Quirites,
> se fortunatim feliciter ac bene vortat (*Ann.* 102–3)

> And may this, I pray, turn out in fortune prosperous and fair for me, our task, our plighted troth, our kingdom, and for you, my citizens. (trans. Warmington)

Skutsch has noted a number of parallels for the passage, most significantly a report from Cicero that earlier generations began prayers with the following invocation:[55]

> Quod bonum faustum felix fortunatumque esset (*Div.* 1.102)

> May this be good, auspicious, happy, fortunate.

Skutsch also notes several Plautine parallels. The most striking of them is from the *Aulularia:*

> (LYCONIDES:) Nunc quae res tibi et gnatae tuae
> Bene feliciter vortat—"ita di faxint" inquito (*Aul.* 787–88)

> May this matter now turn out well and happy for you and your daughter—
> Say "may they grant this."[56]

Because *bonus* and *felix* are the common denominators between all three authors, it is likely that Ennius, Cicero, and Plautus are alluding to a traditional collocation that had the roots *bonus* and *felix.* Moreover, the use of *fortunatim* in Ennius and *fortunatum* in Cicero likewise suggests that a form of *fortunatus* was also a constituent of this fairly extensive traditional ritual collocation. Varro quotes a prayer from the ritual of lustration in what he calls the "Tables of the Censors" (*Censoriis Tabulis*), which supports the thesis that the collocation consisted of three roots, *bonus, felix,* and *fortunatum:*

> quod bonum fortunatum felix salutareque siet populo romano Quiritium reique publicae populi romani Quiritiumque mihique collegaeque meo fidei magistratuique nostro (*L.* 6.86)

> May this be good, fortunate, lucky and healthy for the Roman people of the Quirites and the Republic of the Roman people of the Quirites, and for me and for my colleague and for my faith and our magistracy.

On the basis of this prayer, it appears that *fortunatim feliciter ac bene* in Ennius, *bonum faustum felix fortunatum* in Cicero, and *bene feliciter* in Plautus transform the underlying traditional collocation *bonum fortunatum felix* that is found in the censorial prayer.

In addition, the expression *mihi reique fidei regno vobisque, Quirites* in Ennius appears to allude to *populo romano Quiritium reique publicae . . . mihique . . . meo fidei magistratuique nostro* in the censorial prayer. Whereas the datives of beneficiaries in Varro's prayer are roughly parallel to *tibi et gnatae tuae* in the *Aulularia,* the detail *fidei regno* in Ennius is an especially striking correspondence to *meo fidei magistratuique nostro* in Varro. Neither *fides* nor *magistratus* is an obvious choice for a beneficiary. *Regno* appears to have been changed in order to make it relevant to the regal period, when there were no elected magistracies. Ennius has therefore added a touch of realism while foreshadowing the coming of such institutions after the expulsion of Tarquinius Superbus.

The enumeration of beneficiaries in Ennius, Varro, and Plautus is not only a verbal template for Roman prayer but for Umbrian prayer, too. The Umbrian phrase *mehe. tote. iioveine. esmei. stahmei. stahmeitei.* (Rix Um 1 VIa 5), "for myself, the Iguvinian people, for this established ordinance," bears a general resemblance to all the lists of beneficiaries so far discussed.[57] *Stahmei stahmeitei,* "the established ordinance," is not an obvious choice of beneficiary any more than one's faith or "plighted troth" (*fides*). It is also a political institution roughly analogous to *magistratus* in Varro and *regnum* in Ennius. The evidence suggests a common Italic template that consists of individuals as well as political concepts as beneficiaries in public prayer, a template that surfaces in Latin and Umbrian.

Although there is an apparent relationship between the Ennian fragment and the censorial prayer, the phrase *bene vortat* in Ennius may be a literary conceit rather than a traditional collocation. Frances Hickson has suggested that the multiple occurrences of the phrase *bene vortat* in Livy have been influenced by Ennius.[58] If so, then the ultimate source of influence is likely Plautus, who also uses the verb *vertere* with the traditional collocation of *bonus* and *felix*. The fact that Hickson can suggest a relationship, however, is an indication that there is no single direction of influence between ritual and literature. Even if Plautus is the inventor of the expression *bene vertere,* the phrase was already part of the Latin literary tradition when Ennius appropriated it for the *Annals*. In other words, the collocation *bene vertere* was already traditional for Ennius no matter what its original context may have been.

Three Hearts Beat as One: New Models for Understanding the *Annals*

In his *Noctes Atticae* Gellius recounts that Ennius claimed to possess three hearts—one Latin, one Greek, and one Oscan:

> Quintus Ennius tria corda habere sese dicebat, quod loqui Graece et Osce et Latine sciret (GEL. 17.17.1)
>
> Quintus Ennius used to say that he had three hearts on the ground that he knew how to speak in Greek, Oscan and Latin.

Because the verb *sciret* is in the subjunctive mood in a relative clause, an indication of indirect discourse in Latin, Gellius is most likely reporting what Ennius wrote, not his own interpretation.[59] On the most obvious level, three hearts signify the three languages spoken by Ennius: Greek, Latin, and Oscan. Because Gellius also discusses the ability of Mithradates to speak twenty-five different languages in the same context, the claim of Ennius is almost certainly of a linguistic nature.

Because Ennius hails from the territory of Messapic speakers rather than Oscan speakers, a number of solutions have been proposed for what exactly Ennius may have meant by *Osce.* Werner Suerbaum allows for the possibility that Ennius' third *cor* is Messapic. Such a suggestion, however, would mean that Ennius, a man of obvious linguistic talent, elided the difference between Oscan and Messapic, languages that differ so much that they are not even considered to be within the same branch of the Indo-European family.[60] Andrew Wallace-Hadrill suggests that "Oscan stands for the local language neither Greek nor Roman."[61] Emily Gowers suggests that the three hearts could be cultural "memory-banks" or "literary identities" as much as languages.[62] Thomas Habinek also interprets Ennius' three hearts in terms of culture rather than language.[63] Given how little is known of Ennius' biography, it may be a more productive approach to interpret the three hearts of Ennius as cultures, as Gowers and Habinek suggest.

As a native of Rudiae in ancient Calabria, Ennius, who was born in the second generation after the Pyrrhic War, would have needed three, if not four, languages to negotiate the mix of cultures in southern Italy. Rudiae was located in the territory of the Messapii, who spoke a different language from Latin, Oscan, and Greek. The *nomen* Ennius, however, is apparently Oscan.[64] Ennius' native town was also less than a hundred miles from the Greek colony of Tarentum, perhaps the city that gave birth to Livius Andronicus.[65] Rudiae may have had a

Greek-style amphitheater.[66] Moreover, the Roman colony of Brundisium was even closer than Tarentum. Both cities were also connected by the Appian Way, the road that connected the settlements physically and symbolically to Latin-speaking Rome.

Ennius began his life, and may have ended it, as a member of a multicultural community. Cicero reports that Ennius was granted Roman citizenship when he received land at a colony founded by Marcus Fulvius Nobilior (*Brut.* 79), who founded two colonies, Potentia and Pisaurum (LIV. 39.44.10). If Ennius was enrolled at Pisaurum, as Skutsch assumes,[67] then he was at least nominally part of a community that produced a series of inscriptions dedicated to gods who are "important to the folk of central Italy, not just of Rome and its vicinity" and populated by a "Latin/Italic and Roman constituency."[68] It is possible that his experience with the multicultural population of Pisaurum, however limited it may have been (Ennius presumably remained in Rome after he was granted citizenship), affected Ennius' poetry on some level.

Whatever Ennius meant when he wrote *Graece, Latine,* and *Osce,*[69] I would like to propose a new understanding of the fragment. Because the ability to speak Greek, Latin, and Oscan assumes both a linguistic and a cultural competence, as Gowers implies, it may be better to understand the contrast in Ennius as one between Greek, Roman, and common Italic culture. By Greek, I mean the elements of the *Annals* that were foreign to Rome, such as an epic composed in dactylic hexameter that contains allusions to Greek poetry. By Roman, I mean the elements of Roman culture that had served to differentiate the Romans from the other cultures in ancient Italy, like the cult of Jupiter Stator, as opposed to the undifferentiated Italic god Jupiter. By common Italic, I mean the elements of Roman culture that had been borrowed from or shared with the participants of the central Italian *koinê,* including elements of Greek culture that were familiar to Ennius and his audience because they had already been nativized centuries before. The most obvious of these borrowings is perhaps the alphabet that Ennius used to write down the poem.

Although this tripartite model of cultural influence on the *Annals* is useful for understanding the multicultural underpinnings of the form and content of the poem, the audience would likely have categorized the various elements of the poem as familiar and foreign. If Jupiter Versor was, in fact, part of the discourse of the cult of Jupiter Stator at Rome, the former would have been a familiar cultural element in spite of the Oscan origins of the cult title. The *duodekatheon* had its roots in Greek and Etruscan culture, but it would likely have evoked the *lectisternium* of 217 BCE for a Roman audience rather than the scholarly lists of the twelve Olympians put forth by Greek intellectuals or the Etruscan concept of an advisory board for the god Tin. The wish for a good result of one's *fides* and magistracy would likely be familiar to an audience that had heard the latter during the ceremony of lustration. Although there are parallels in the other cultures of the central Italian *koinê* and in Greek literary texts for some of these phenomena, the audience was very likely familiar with them because they had been or become part of Roman culture by the time Ennius wrote the *Annals.*

Whether the audience perceived these ritual practices as familiar or foreign, I hope to have demonstrated that the poem is a testament to the hybridity of Roman culture not only in the second century BCE but also in the earlier central Italian *koinê* period. If the Romans have influenced our view of poetry because they adopted the same Greek models that would later be adopted (and adapted) by other cultures throughout Western Europe, the impact of the central Italian *koinê* on the Western conception of poetry should be explored, even though much of the evidence of its influence has been lost. The Oscans, Umbrians, and Etruscans have influenced our conception of classical literature, if only by subtly altering some of the Greek cultural elements that Ennius incorporated into the *Annals.*

The fact that Ennius sometimes failed to follow his Greek models closely could be seen as a failure on his part, either due to a lack of ability or because it required several centuries of painstaking work by generations of poets to reach the Heliconian heights of Greek perfection. I prefer to think that Ennius was creating a hybrid form that mirrored the success of Rome in incorporating elements of different cultures into a new paradigm. Because the Italic elements in the *Annals* continued to influence epic poetry that came after Ennius, if only indirectly, the Italic tradition is a part of our own tradition, and understanding its role in the *Annals* can help us understand the role of multiculturalism, past and present, in modern ideas about poetry in a world where the multicultural is now the norm.

The Annals *and the Greek Tradition*

If later generations emphasized the Greek features of the *Annals,* they had good reasons to do so. Ennius, after all, seems to have claimed that the soul of Homer lived on in his body.[1] Moreover, the dactylic hexameter would have been foreign to the audience of the *Annals,* since it was unique to the Greek tradition before Ennius. Although Greek meter was familiar to those who attended the performances of Roman comedy and tragedy, the iambic meters of the theater were characterized by a tolerance for substitution in a manner unknown to Greek iambs.[2] In contrast, Ennius conformed, with some exceptions, to the rules of prosody and substitution of the Greek hexameter. What is more, the occurrence of other borrowings of Greek words and imitations of Homer throughout the fragments leaves little doubt that the *Annals* owes a great deal to the Greek epic tradition.

Once it is established that the *Annals* is profoundly influenced by Greek poetry, however, it is easy to identify other elements of the poem as Grecisms that were Greek in origin but that had been fully nativized and were familiar to the original audience of the poem. If one emphasizes the Greek origin of the twelve gods named in *Annals* 240–41 over the synchronic Roman practice of the *lectisternium,* for example, such an emphasis can disguise the rich, multicultural texture of the passage. Even the concept of a canonical list of twelve gods in Roman culture may have owed more to Etruscan than to Greek thought. Nor is the *duodekatheon* the only passage from the *Annals* where Greek origins threaten to obscure Italic horizons of expectation. I now hope to demonstrate that even the most Homeric passages in the *Annals* are as deeply engaged with the native, Roman tradition as the poem is with the Greek.

Although the *Annals* consistently engages the Greek language and its poetic tradition, Ennius employs multiple strategies for this single purpose in his poem. On the level of language, Ennius borrows many Greek words, such as *Musa* and *melos* (from Greek μέλος, "song"), and it is possible that Ennius changes the gender of a Latin noun in order to make it conform to the gender of its Greek equivalent. The Latin masculine noun *pulvis,* "dust," for example, is feminine in the *Annals,* as is its Greek equivalent κόνις.[3] Even if the change in gender is due to the vagaries of Latin grammar in the second century BCE, the phrase *vicit Olympia* (*Ann.* 523) is a "clear Grecism," to be more specific, an adoption of a Greek grammatical construction analogous to a change in gender under Greek influence, according to Skutsch.[4] In addition to single words, Ennius also translates and adapts formulae and sometimes entire passages from Homer, such as the one from the *Iliad* describing Ajax as he is beaten back by the Trojans (*Il.* 16.102–11). Ennius borrows and adapts this passage in order to describe a Roman tribune in battle against the Histrians (*Ann.* 391–98).

Many, if not all, of these Grecisms are not simply borrowings, however, but rather single elements of a multicultural hybrid form that would continue to characterize Latin poetry. Any use of the Greek language in a Latin text must inevitably generate a linguistic hybrid. Words such as *Musae* (*Ann.* 1) and *melos* (*Ann.* 293) occur alongside more familiar Latin words such as *pedibus, quae* (*Ann.* 1), and *pangit* (*Ann.* 293). Even the "clear Grecism" *vicit Olympia* (*Ann.* 523) consists of a native Latin word and a Greek toponym in spite of its bold use of a place name with specifically Greek connotations as the object of the verb *vinco.* The imitation of a Homeric passage to describe the actions of a Roman tribune is so obviously a cultural hybrid that it requires no detailed explanation. In sum, it is simply not possible for a poem that draws its inspiration from one language but is composed in another to be anything but a hybrid.

It remains difficult to fully appreciate the hybrid and multicultural nature of the *Annals,* however, since many of the Roman cultural elements that are mixed in with the Greek elements are not easily recovered. The implicitly invited comparison between Homer and Ennius is doubly pernicious in this respect. On the one hand, the Latin elements of the diction of the *Annals* are especially difficult to perceive because they are obscured by the Homeric influence on the poem, a phenomenon easily perceived by anyone familiar with Greek literature. On the other hand, the Italic contributions come not from a famous poem but rather from more elusive forms of language that require a deeper, and considerably more complicated, investigation before such parallels can be identified in the fragments of the *Annals.* The familiarity of many Greek cultural elements at Rome in the second century BCE further obscures the hybrid nature of the poem if any of these features has been nativized to the point where it could be understood as a feature of Roman culture, even though there may be some lingering awareness of their foreign origin. In more positive terms, the hybrid of

Greek and Latin in the *Annals* is so successful that it is often extremely difficult to separate the individual contributions of Greek poetry and Roman culture from one another.

Because Ennius is not the first poet to combine the Greek and Roman, moreover, multiculturalism had, in fact, already become a common feature of all Roman literature. The first epic ever composed in the Latin language had retold the story of Homer's *Odyssey* in Latin. Plautus and Terence were forced to remove elements in the Greek originals of their Roman comedies that had no relevance to their Roman audiences and to find Roman equivalents for other Greek cultural practices. This tradition of literary hybridity may be traced back early in the Italic tradition, as can be seen in inscriptions that could not have been written in languages like South Picene or Faliscan if some form of the Greek alphabet had not been adopted by speakers of these languages in the first place. Moreover, Calvert Watkins suggests that the epigrams in the aforementioned languages are representative of Greek poetic genre.[5] In sum, cultural hybridity itself is a native feature of the *Annals*.

All of these issues may already be observed in what is almost certainly the first line of the *Annals*:[6]

> Musae quae pedibus magnum pulsatis Olympum (*Ann.* 1)
>
> Muses who with your feet beat mighty Olympus. (trans. Warmington)

On the linguistic level, Greek borrowings occur along with native Latin words that communicate how deeply the rest of the epic will engage with the Greek language. *Musae* and *Olympum* are not only borrowings from the Greek language, but the form of *Musae* is ambiguous enough to raise the possibility that it is an example of "code switching," a technical term for importing a word or phrase from one language into another with the grammar of the original language intact. Ennius does not just borrow freely from Greek in this line, he also appears to allude to Greek epic poetry. In addition to his use of the dactylic hexameter, the meter of the Homeric epics, there is more than one phrase from Greek epic that could be the model for *Annals* 1. Given the obvious importance of the Greek language and poetic tradition in the first line, it is no wonder that few have felt compelled to seek out still more sources for the *incipit* of the *Annals* and by extension for what remains of the epic.

Nor is Homer the sole epic influence at work on this line. By invoking the Greek Muses, Ennius invites comparison between the first line of the *Annals* and of Livius Andronicus' translation of the *Odyssey*, since Andronicus translates Homer's Muse with the native Roman analogue *Camena:*

Virum mihi Camena insece versutum (*Od.* 1)

Tell me O Camena of that wily man.

This implicit invitation is made explicit later in the *Annals* in a fragment that invokes the Muse with a form of the extremely rare Latin verb *insece,* also used by Livius (*Ann.* 322). An invocation of the Muses in the first line of the *Annals* may have also recalled the beginning of the *Bellum Poenicum* of Gnaeus Naevius:

Novem Iovis concordes filiae sorores

Nine daughters of Jupiter, harmonious sisters.

The allusion to dancing in the *Annals* may, in fact, have been influenced by the musical meaning of *concordes,* and the unnamed nine daughters of Jupiter in Naevius could either be Muses or *Camenae.* Because the genre of Latin epic had already been founded by Livius and taken up by Naevius, moreover, the idea of epic was not new to the audience of the *Annals,* even though the use of dactylic hexameter in Latin was.

In addition to these literary precedents, Maurizio Bettini has noted verbal parallels in a description of the dance that accompanied a hymn composed by Livius that Livy describes in his narrative of 207 BCE, as well as in the poetry of Horace.[7] These parallels, I suggest, indicate that the expression *pedibus . . . pulsatis* is a traditional ritual collocation that may be quite venerable if it is related to a similar expression found in Umbrian ritual. Whether or not the collocation can be traced back to the central Italian *koinê* period, Plautus appears to allude to a collocation of *pes* and *pulsare,* yet another connection between the *Annals* and the Latin literary tradition.

Such a hybrid of the Greek and Latin language, Greek and Latin poetry of various genres, and Roman ritual language sets the tone for the rest of the epic and prepares the audience for an encounter with different forms of meaningful language from more than one culture. The line begins with a Greek word that triggers the recall of previous Latin epics. The meter of the line further establishes the *Annals* as an epic text, a genre that already existed in Latin in spite of the use of a different meter in the previous Latin epic poems. Some members of the audience may have been struck by the use of the phrase *pedibus . . . pulsatis,* which I suggest is a Roman ritual collocation that bridges the dance of the Homeric Muses with the ritual dances performed in Rome and in different parts of

Roman Italy. Although it is not as easy to see the use of ritual system reference through the network of literary references, I hope to demonstrate that the hybrid nature of the line can be truly appreciated only when all its cultural facets are identified and the multicultural dialogue that underlies the first line of the *Annals* as well as the epic in its entirety is restored.

Once I have established that the language of Roman ritual is present, even in imitations of Homeric formulae, I will submit the radical thesis that a single Ennian imitation of a passage from the *Iliad* alludes to the language of Italic curse tablets. When Ennius imitates Homer's claim that he could not speak without the help of the Muses even if he had ten tongues and a heart of bronze (*Ann.* 469–70), his mention of his tongue and the inability to speak may have been sufficient in itself to recall similar wishes that a victim of a curse lose his or her ability to speak. Various indications that the gods of the underworld are particularly active in book 6, which begins with Ennius' nod to Homer, may have also prompted the audience of the *Annals* to perceive the similarities between such curses and the language of the Ennian fragment retroactively. Moreover, the difficult syntax of the fragment is a virtual enactment of the desired result of so many curse tablets: the loss of the ability to speak. If my suggestion is correct, then the audience will have been prepared for a narrative with darker, chthonic overtones that will allow Ennius to imply that the forces of chaos nearly overcame the forces of order in the war against Pyrrhus and his Greek allies.

Ennius and Roman Epic

There are passages from the *Annals* that encouraged later readers to view Ennius' epic as a break with the nascent Roman epic tradition. A close reading of these passages, however, suggests that there is continuity as much as rupture between Ennius and his two epic predecessors. Most significantly, Ennius' disparagement of the verses sung by *Faunei vatesque,* "Fauns and Seers," need not imply an attack upon Saturnian poetry as a whole (*Ann.* 206–7) but rather focuses on the Saturnian meter. Even if it is an attack, Naevius and Livius are at least a little above Fauns and Seers, who sang (*canebant*) sometime in the past rather than wrote (*scripsere*), as Ennius does in the present and as Livius and Naevius did in the recent past.[8] When Cicero, who quotes the fragment, claims that Ennius did not treat the First Punic War (*Brut.* 76), the subject matter of Naevius' *Bellum Poenicum,* he contradicts what is known about the *Annals* from other sources. However undesirable the title *vates,* "Seer," appears to be to Ennius neither the

Greek title *poeta* that he gave to Homer, and to himself in his *Satires,* nor the Greek term *poema* was new to Latin literature.

Ennius' famous disparagement of his Saturnian forbears is worded in such a way, though, that it could leave the impression that his epic has little to do with the poems of his Latin epic predecessors Andronicus and Naevius:[9]

> Scripsere alii rem
> vorsibus quos olim Faunei vatesque canebant (*Ann.* 206–7)
>
> Others have written of the matter in verses, which once upon a time the Fauns and Seers used to sing. (trans. Warmington)

Given that the *Annals* employs the Homeric dactylic hexameter, these written (*scripsere*) verses (*vorsibus*) almost certainly refer to the Saturnian meter of Livius and Naevius, an intuition confirmed by Cicero's identification of Naevius as the target of the attack (*Brut.* 75).[10] This emphasis on verses sung by Fauns and Seers implies that the use of Homeric meter in the poetry of Ennius is markedly different, and presumably better than the earlier Latin epic poets.

The disavowal of the title *vates,* a native Latin word with the primary meaning of "prophet" or "oracle," also gives the impression of a rupture with native Roman culture and a close continuity with the Homeric poems. Although there is no explicit contrast between the terms *poeta* and *vates* in the extant fragments, Ennius associates the Saturnian meter with the *vates,*[11] whereas Homer, a poet who uses the dactylic hexameter is a *poeta:*

> Visus Homerus adesse poeta (*Ann.* 3)
>
> Homer the poet appeared at my side. (trans. Warmington)

Moreover, Ennius explicitly names himself a *poeta* in a fragment from the *Satires:*

> Enni poeta, salve, qui mortalibus
> versus propinas flammeos medullitus (*Saturae* fr. 11)[12]
>
> Your health, poet Ennius, who pass to mortal men a cup of flaming verses drawn from your very marrow! (trans. Warmington)

If Ennius and Homer are *poetae* who write in a meter other than one used by *vates* and *Faunei,* it is a reasonable inference that, in the eyes of Ennius, the *vates,* who employ the Saturnian meter, are inferior to *poetae,* who compose in hexameters.

The contrast is implicit, but *carmen,* the nominal counterpart of *canebunt,* also appears to be inferior to Ennius' *poemata:*

> Quomque caput caderet carmen tuba sola peregit
> et pereunte viro raucum sonus aere cucurrit (*Ann.* 485–86)
>
> And when his head was falling, the trumpet finished alone its tune; and even as the warrior did perish, a hoarse blare sped from the brass. (trans. Warmington)

There may be a touch of irony in this description, but the *raucum sonus* of the *carmen* of the *tuba* does not imply a favorable attitude toward *carmen.* In contrast, the *poemata* of Ennius will be heard among widely spread peoples:

> Latos <per> populos res atque poemata nostra
> <clara> cluebunt (*Ann.* 12–13)
>
> My subject and my <famous> poem shall have renown among [widespread] peoples.[13]

Finally, the pipe of the Muses produces neither *carmen* nor *poemata* but *melos:*

> Tibia Musarum pangit melos (*Ann.* 293)
>
> The flute composed a song of music. (trans. Warmington)

Because the substitution of other Greek terms for native (or nativized) Latin word seems to imply that the *poemata* of Ennius is superior to any texts that may be categorized as *carmina,* the Greek word *melos* may also indicate that the "song of music" is superior to the songs of the *vates,* an intuition that the genitive *Musarum,* the Greek version of the *Camenae,* supports.

Cicero also creates the impression of a rupture between the *Bellum Poenicum* and the *Annals* on the level of content in his discussion of the relationship between the two authors:

> tamen illius, quem in vatibus et Faunis adnumerat Ennius, bellum Punicum quasi Myronis opus delectat. Sit Ennius sane, ut est certe, perfectior: qui si illum, ut simulat, contemneret, non omnia bella persequens primum illud Punicum acerrimum bellum reliquisset. (*Brut.* 75–76)
>
> For all that Ennius counts Naevius among primitive bards and Fauns, his *Bellum Punicum,* like a work of Myron, still yields pleasure. Grant that Ennius is more finished, as undoubtedly he is; yet if Ennius had really scorned him,

> as he professes, he would not in undertaking to describe all our wars have passed over that stubbornly contested first Punic War.[14]

If Cicero's statement is taken at face value, then Ennius did not treat the First Punic War, the subject of the *Bellum Poenicum* of Naevius.

Although such an interpretation of Ennian polemic seems plausible at first, a close examination of the evidence does not support the hypothesis of a total rupture with the Saturnian tradition. Ennius does seem to have told the story of the First Punic War in the *Annals* in some form, even though Cicero claims that Ennius did not treat the subject matter of the *Bellum Poenicum* of Naevius.[15] Even if the testimony of Cicero and the evidence could be reconciled, Cicero claims that Ennius borrowed *multa* from Naevius. Nor does Ennius explicitly say that he will not treat the unspecified subject matter of the "others," only that the "others" treated it. If the unnamed *alii* are in fact the Saturnian poets, they wrote (*scripsere*) their verses just as Ennius must have, as I have already observed, thereby generating a hierarchy that places Naevius closer to Ennius than the unnamed Fauns and prophets, not a simple binary opposition between two poets, as Cicero implies in his discussion.

Even the use of the word *poeta* in Ennius is not an unambiguous assertion of the superiority of his poetry over the work of Naevius and Livius. Ennius is not the first Latin author to use the word *poeta*. It occurs in Plautus no fewer than six times (*As.* 748, *Cas.* 861, *Mil.* 211, *Ps.* 401 and 404, *Cur.* 591, and *Capt.* 1033),[16] in addition to a single occurrence of the word *poema* (*As.* 174). Because later generations would identify the unnamed *poeta barbarus* mentioned by Plautus in the *Miles Gloriosus* as Gnaeus Naevius, it was possible for the readers of a later age, if not in the lifetime of Plautus, to refer to a Saturnian author as a *poeta* rather than a *vates:*[17]

> (PERIPLECTOMENUS:) Nam os columnatum poetae esse inaudivi barbaro
> quoi bini custodes semper totis horis occubant (*Mil.* 211–12)

> I've heard that a barbarian poet has a pillared face, a man on whom two guards each always lie and keep watch at all hours.[18]

Paulus ex Festo seems to refer to this line when he writes *unde Plautus Naevium poetam Latinum barbarum dixit* (PAUL. Fest. 36M). Although it may have been composed after the lifetime of Ennius, the retort, *malum dabunt Metelli Naevio poetae* (Caesius Bassus (*G.L.* 6 p. 266), is another possible example of the use of the title *poeta* for a Saturnian author.[19] Plautus goes one step further than Ennius by directly importing the Greek verb ποιέω in the *Pseudolus* (*Ps.* 712), though not in the sense of poetic composition. What is more, Ennius' model Homer never called himself, or anyone else, a ποιητής.[20] This independence from Homeric usage and the possible dependence on Plautus in his use of *poeta* are symptomatic of the difficulty of disentangling the Latin from the Greek tradition in Ennius and of the dangers of overinterpreting fragmentary evidence.

Even if a complete break with the Saturnian tradition could have been accomplished (it was not), Ennius' dismissal of the verses of *Faunei* and *vates* is still colored by the language of native Latin ritual. The mere presence of terms such as *vates* and *cano* in Ennius' polemic evokes native Latin cultural practices. Varro identifies a form of *cano* in a fragment of the *Carmen Saliare,* one of the most venerable of all Latin prayers (*L.* 7.27). If no evidence existed for the ritual character of *cano* in traditional Latin sources, the imperative **kanetu** (Rix Um1 IV 29), the Umbrian congener of *cano,* suggests that the verb had ritual connotations in common Italic by virtue of its presence in a series of ritual instructions. Furthermore, Peter Wiseman suggests that the word *Faunus* had a marked association with cult and prophecy for the audience of the *Annals.*[21] At the risk of stating the obvious, the use of the Latin language simply forbids a complete break with the native Latin tradition.

Code Switching in the *Annals*

Because *Musae,* the very first word of the *Annals,* can be transliterated Greek, it may also be an example of code switching, an important indicator that an individual Grecism is truly foreign rather than a familiar nativization, as appears to be the case for the word *poeta.* The fact that Ennius himself may have explicitly glossed *Musae* at some point in the *Annals* may also signify that *Musae* is, in fact, a transliteration of Μοῦσαι:[22]

> Musas quas memorant nosce nos esse Camenas (*Ann.* 487)
>
> You shall know that we whom men call the Muses are *Camenae.* (trans. Warmington)

Because there is no perceptible phonetic difference between the first declension Latin accusative plural ending and the Greek, *Musas* may also be a Greek form (Μούσας) embedded in the Latin. As the first word, *Musae* leaves the language of the entire poem in doubt in the split second it takes to reach *quae,* a word that indicates that the language of the *Annals* will be Latin not only because the Greek nominative plural feminine relative pronoun was αἵ but also because the initial sound of *quae* did not exist in Greek.

It is unlikely that *Musae* is an instance of code switching, but an obvious example may be seen in a Latin inscription from Paelignian territory:

> Sa(lvios). Seio(s). L(ouci). f(ilios). Herclei. donom ded(it) brat( ) datas; [L(oucios)] Seio(s). Sa(lvi) f(ilios) Herclei victurei.[23]

> Salvius Seius the son of Lucius made this dedication to Hercules because of a favor having been given.
> Lucius Seius the son of Salvius (made this dedication) to Hercules Victor.

Although the inscription is largely in idiomatic Latin,[24] *brat datas*, "because of a favor having been given," is an Oscan formula. *Brat* is an abbreviation of *brateis,* the Oscan cognate of Latin *gratis.* The formula is therefore a "tag," a formulaic expression and an example of code switching since it retains the grammatical form of the source language (L_1) in the target language (L_2). Because Musae is not unequivocally a Greek form, it is not necessarily an instance of code switching. Since Ennius could have emphasized the foreign quality of the Greek word by using a Greek ending in a manner analogous to Vergil's use of the form *Aenean* instead of *Aeneam,* the lack of a definitive Greek form of *Musae* suggests that it is a borrowing rather than a form of code switching.

What is more, the Muses themselves were objects of Roman cult by the time the *Annals* was published, given that Marcus Fulvius Nobilior built the temple of *Hercules Musarum,* presumably the common altar of Hercules and Muses mentioned by Plutarch (*q. Rom.* 59), after his campaign in Ambracia in 189 BCE. As many scholars have already noted, Fulvius Nobilior also brought back from Ambracia a series of sculptures of the Muses and Heracles that may be the partial inspiration for the invocation of the Muses in the opening of the *Annals* (Eumenius 7.3).[25] The Muse has therefore at least recently been nativized not only into the Latin language but also into Roman cult, just as I have suggested that the Oscan cult title Jupiter Versor was nativized during the Third Samnite War. Because there was a *Mouseion,* a temple of the Muses, as near as Croton in southern Italy, as Skutsch observes, the Muse may have been vaguely familiar, even if she was not nativized.[26]

If Alex Hardie's thesis that the Muses are implicated in the cult of Juno Regina as well as of Hercules is correct,[27] then the expression *pedibus . . . pulsatis* may not only lend a general ritual character to the *incipit* of the *Annals* but also refer to the specific connection between the cult of the Muses and Juno Regina. As I have noted above, Bettini observes that Livy mentions a song composed by Livius and performed in procession that ended at the temple of Juno Regina and was accompanied by a stomping of the feet, *pulsu pedum* (27.37.14–15), a collocation of the same two roots as *pedibus . . . pulsatis*. If the expression *pulsu pedum* was a collocation that denoted a dance performed in rituals honoring Juno Regina (and I stress the word *if*), then the opening line of the *Annals* may allude to the association of the cult of the Muses with the cult of Juno Regina by means of this ritual collocation.

Although *Musae* is likely not an example of code switching, the use of the Greek accusative *aera* is another matter:

> Et densis aquila pennis obnixa volabat
> vento quem perhibent Graium genus aera lingua (*Ann.* 139–40)

> and there came flying on thick-set wings an eagle, battling with the breeze
> which the Greek nation calls in its tongue "aer." (trans. Warmington)

Aera is a not a borrowing, because it is a Greek word that retains its Greek grammatical form. The final *-a* in *aera* must be an accusative singular ending, which exists in Greek but not in Latin, in order to place it in apposition with *quem*, since both are objects of *perhibent*.

Because Ennius tends to use the verb *perhibere* to gloss Greek words, however, it does not necessarily follow that these Greek words are all examples of code switching. The Greek word *sophiam*, for example, appears to be a borrowing:[28]

> Nec quisquam sophiam, sapientia quae perhibetur
> in somnis vidit prius quam sam discere coepit (*Ann.* 211–12)

> Nor has any man seen in his dreams Wisdom (a name given to knowledge)
> before he has begun to learn her secrets. (trans. Warmington)

The digraph *-ph-* for Greek -φ- might have communicated its Greek origin at the end of the second century BCE, but such spellings do not predate the mid-second century BCE. (The modern texts of the *Annals* employ the spelling *sophiam* to indicate its Greek origin.) It is therefore unlikely that Ennius spelled the word in any way other than *sopiam*. The spelling of the root and perhaps its pronunciation are therefore not unequivocally Greek. If the root is not unambiguously Greek or Latin, the accusative ending *-am* is definitively a Latin accusative ending, since Ennius transliterated the Greek accusative ending -ην for the name *Anchis<u>en</u>* (*Ann.* 28).

Nevertheless, *sophia* appears to be glossed in a manner that obscures the boundary between Greek and Latin. Because *sapientiam* is placed to the left of the relative pronoun *quae* in the fragment, even though it is part of the relative clause, it is placed alongside *sophiam,* an arrangement that may not be fortuitous. The phonetic similarity between *sophiam* (again, probably written *sopiam* in the original text) and *sapientia* is emphasized both by the similar meanings of *sophiam* and *sapientiam* and by word order. *Somnis* may also be an etymological gloss on *sophiam* analogous to the semantic and etymological connection between *somnus* and *sopor.* The image of someone seeing *sophia* in a dream may therefore be mimicked by "seeing" *sop-ia* in *som-nus,* or rather its underlying form *sop-nus.*

The archaic pronoun *sam* may be the instrument of an interlingual pun on how one learns *sophiam. Sam* resembles σάν, the name for sigma in the Doric dialect of Greek, according to Herodotus (Hdt. 1.139). By the time of Varro the letter in the Latin alphabet was almost certainly called *se,* but a fragment of Lucilius suggests that the letter was called by its name in the Ionic dialect of Greek, "sigma," by at least some Romans in the second century BCE:[29]

> S nostrum et semigraeci quod dicimus sigma nil erroris habet. (Lucil. 379)[30]
>
> Our "s" and what we call in our half-Greek way "sigma" has no fault in it.

If some Romans used the Ionic Greek name, then others could have used the Doric Greek equivalent, including Ennius, who likely learned Greek in Tarentum, a Dorian foundation. Whatever Ennius called this letter, it is certainly not possible for one to write of a dream of Greek ΣΟΦΙΑ before one learns the first letter of the word, a letter that some Greeks, and perhaps Ennius, called "san." The close resemblance of σάν to pronoun *sam,* "that one" (translated with poetic license as "her secrets" by Warmington above), may have been one of the reasons that Ennius chose to use it here in order to generate the interlingual pun on a dialectical name of the first letter used to spell ΣΟΦΙΑ.

Ennius' introduction of Greek wisdom into Latin poetry is characterized by a number of poetic refinements that are at least similar to those employed by the Alexandrian poets. If *sam* is in fact a pun on Greek σάν, then Ennius alludes to a Doric form. Callimachus employs dialectical forms as "dialectical glosses" in his poetry, such as Ἀριήδης, the Cretan form of the name Ariadne, an appropriate dialectical form of the name of the Cretan princess used by the Greek poet in his *Aetia* (fr. 67.13). The idea of *sophiam* as something one can see in the state of *sopor* may also be a motif borrowed from the poetry of Callimachus, who dreams that

Muses come to him and answer questions on recherché topics at the beginning of the *Aetia*. Moreover, the use of *perhibetur* may be yet another indication of the influence of Hellenistic poetics in addition to the dream motif, since it is similar to an "Alexandrian footnote," "the signaling of specific allusions by a poet through a seemingly general appeal to tradition,"[31] a technique used by Alexandrian poets like Apollonius of Rhodes.[32] Whether or not the Alexandrian poets have influenced Ennius' display of poetic virtuosity in this particular fragment, the mixture of Greek and Latin elements is characteristic of the *Annals* as a whole.

The two other surviving instances in the *Annals* where Ennius signals a gloss of a Greek word by means of the verb *perhibere* further problematize the relationship of Latin to Greek. These glosses speak of a Greek loan word as something from the language of mortals.

> Est locus Hesperiam quam mortales perhibebant (*Ann.* 20)
>
> There is a region, which mortals used to call the "Western Land." (trans. Warmington)

> Arcus ubi aspicitur mortalibus quae perhibetur (*Ann.* 399)
>
> When the rainbow is seen, which is called by mortals (Iris).[33] (trans. Warmington)

The expression *mortales perhibere* calls to mind the Homeric practice of giving something two names, one in the language of mortals and one in the language of the gods.[34] Given the view of Ennius as an enthusiastic philhellene, it is surprising that the language of mortals is Greek. If Greek is the language of mortals, it raises the question of whether Latin is the language of the gods. The equation of Greek with mortal calls into question the assumption that Ennius considered Greek to be superior to Latin and again illustrates how complex a relationship exists between Latin and Greek in the *Annals*.

Annals 1 and the Greek Tradition

The image of the Muses dancing on Mount Olympus punctuated by the borrowings *Musae* and *Olympum*, has both obvious and more subtle debts to the Greek poetic tradition in the first line of the *Annals*. Just as Ennius' Muses "beat mighty Olympus" with their feet (*pedibus magnum pulsatis Olympum*), the Muses "dance with soft feet" (ποσσὸ ἁπαλοῖσιν / ὀρχεῦνται) around a spring in the opening of the *Theogony* (*Th.* 3–4). It may not be coincidental that the

Theogony also begins with the proper noun Μουσάων. Homer also describes the dance of Phaeacian youth in a manner similar to Ennius' *incipit:*

> πέπληγον δὲ χορὸν θεῖον ποσίν (*Od.* 8.264)
>
> They pounded out the sacred dance with their feet.

Although the subject and context of the Homeric parallel differ more radically from Ennius than the Hesiodic parallel, the alliteration of πέπληγον . . . ποσὶν is a closer aural match to *pedibus . . . pulsatis.* Enrico Flores suggests another, much closer phonetic match from the *Iliad* that deploys the Greek cognates of *magnum* and *pedibus* along with the name Olympus:[35]

> ὑπὸ ποσσὶ μέγας πελεμίζετ' Ὄλυμπος (*Il.* 8.443)
>
> Under their feet great Olympus shook.

Because the phrase μέγας . . . Ὄλυμπος is deployed once more in the *Iliad* (*Il.* 1.530), the phrase may have also been perceived as an underemployed Homeric formula by Ennius, who translated it with the phrase *magnum . . . Olympum.*

Annals 1 and the Saturnian Traditions

The name *Musae* at the opening of the *Annals* is a statement that positions Ennius in relation not only to the Greek but also to the Saturnian tradition. Although the Greek Muses are an implicit correction of Livius' syncretism of the *Camenae* with the Muses, there is no direct evidence that Ennius is referring to the *Camena* of Livius until book 10:

> Insece Musa manu Romanorum induperator
> quod quisque in bello gessit cum rege Philippo (*Ann.* 322–23)
>
> Go on, O Muse, to tell what each commander of the Romans wrought with his troops in the war with King Philip. (trans. Warmington)

Ennius restores the original Homeric word order of ἔννεπε Μοῦσα and also its metrical shape. The verb *insece* is also a key verbal point of contact between Ennius, Homer, and Livius, These changes highlight Ennius' introduction of the Greek hexameter into Latin verse and the fact that Livius' Saturnians were unable to preserve the word order or metrical shape of the Homeric phrase.

The verb *insece* may also be an appropriation of the terminology of Italic ritual. If *insece* is, in fact, related to the Umbrian root of **sukatu,** "let him proclaim," and **prusikurent,** "they will have proclaimed," then *insece* may have the same ritual connotations as the Umbrian forms.[36] Whether or not Livius is using a "dialectical" form parallel to the Homeric use of the Aeolic form ἔννεπε, as George Sheets has suggested, the Latin word *insece* may have independently had ritual connotations for speakers of Latin or acquired them under the influence of Umbrian.[37] These connotations would then color the audience's understanding of *insece* in the *Annals* as much as its status as an allusion to the *Odyssey* of Livius Andronicus would for those who knew the latter poem.

Annals 1 and the Italic Tradition

Even in the invocation of the Greek Muses, who dance upon the Greek landmark, Mount Olympus, and resemble the *Camena* of Livius and the nine daughters of Jupiter (*novem Iovis concordes filiae sorores*) of Naevius, a traditional Latin collocation may be lurking just below the surface. The verb *pulso* can mean "to strike repeatedly or beat (a musical instrument) in order to produce sounds."[38] The striking of a drum or other musical instrument often presupposes that some beats are more pronounced than others in a manner reminiscent of the Latin stress accent rather than the quantitative accent of Greek. Moreover, the phrase *pedibus . . . pulsatis* may, in fact, indicate an engagement with Latin ritual. As Maurizio Bettini has noted, Livy's description of the *carmen* written by Livius for Juno Regina in 207 BCE has a chorus of virgins who begin their song with a stomping of the feet, *pulsu pedum* (27.37.14).[39] The parallels in the Greek epic traditions do not enable Ennius to efface the native Latin tradition but rather blend the Greek with Latin traditions and implicitly announce the invention of a hybrid form.

Livy may be alluding to Ennius or even to Livius, who in turn served as the inspiration for Ennius, but all three could be referencing something older. There are two more collocations of the roots of *pes* and *pulsare* that suggest that Ennius' *pedibus . . . pulsatis* is a traditional collocation. *Pedum pulsu* occurs not just in Livy but also in Ennius' *Thyestes:*

> Sed sonitus auris meas pedum pulsu increpat (*scen.* 341)
>
> But beats upon my ears a patter of footsteps. (trans. Warmington)

The "Cleopatra Ode" also collocates *pes* and the form *pulsare:*[40]

> Nunc est bibendum, nunc pede libero
> pulsanda tellus, nunc Saliaribus

ornare pulvinar deorum
tempus erat dapibus sodales. (*C.* 1.37.1–4)

Now let the drinking begin! Now let us thump the ground with unfettered feet! Now is the time, my friends, to load the couches of the gods with a feast fit for the *Salii*![41]

The collocation *pes pulsare* is not only a perfect match for *pedibus . . . pulsatis,* it also occurs in a ritual context. The *Salii,* the singers of the archaic *Carmen Saliare,* are involved in what appears to be a ritual banquet and a *lectisternium.*

Horace also collocates *pes* and *pellere,* a verb that is closely related to *pulsare,* in the dramatic setting of the *Faunalia,* a rural festival in honor of the god Faunus held on December 5th:[42]

Gaudet invisam pepulisse fossor
ter pede terram (*C.* 3.18.15–16)

The digger enjoys beating with his feet in triple time his old enemy, the earth.[43]

Although *pepulisse* is the perfect infinitive of *pellere,* not *pulsare,* the two verbs derive from the same root. *Pepulisse . . . pede* could be an ironic appropriation of the hyper-Hellenistic opening of the *Annals,* but a deeper sense of irony would arise from the implicit recognition that the poet who disparages the *vates* and the *Faunei* began his epic with a collocation that had close cultural connections to such entities. If the expression *pepulisse . . . pede* is a humorous allusion to the *incipit* of the *Annals* in the context of the worship of the *Faunei,* whom Ennius disparages, there does not appear to be any such motivation here, a circumstance suggesting that the collocation is not simply an allusion to Ennius.

Pedibus . . . pulsatis could also evoke the *tripudium,*[44] a sacred dance performed by the *Salii,* both through its expressive description of dancing and by means of a folk etymology. The vacillation between archaic forms that begin with *d-* and classical forms with *l-*, such as *dacrimas* and *lacrimas* and *dautia* and *lautia* (PAUL. *Fest.* p. 68M), allows the possibility that a speaker of Latin might make a connection between a root with the shape *pVl-* (i.e., as in *pulsatis*) and *pVd-* (i.e., as in *tri-pudium*), regardless of the historical validity of such a connection. Moreover, the obscure lexeme *puls,* "a kind of porridge,"[45] is also associated with the *tripudium* in Paulus ex Festo, a fact that may indicate a perceived etymological connection in a ritual context between yet another root with the shape *pul-* and the *tripudium,* even though Festus appears to have derived *tripudium* from *terripuvium,* a "thumping of the earth" (PAUL. *Fest.* 244M).

Pedibus . . . pulsatis could be understood as a *figura etymologica* that, in turn, may be etymologically connected to the *tripudium* by speakers of Latin, who had very different notions of etymology than modern historical linguists.

Whether or not speakers of Latin perceived an etymological relationship between *tripudium, pedes,* and *pulsare,* the proximity of *pes, pulsare,* and *-pudium* in a Plautine joke in the *Bacchides* suggests that there was a traditional association between the three:

> (PARASITUS:) Tu dudum, puere, cum illac usque isti semul
> quae harum sunt aedes, pulta. Adi actutum ad fores
> recede hinc dierecte. Ut pulsat propudium!
> comesse panem tris pedes latum potes,
> fores pultare nescis (*Bac.* 577–81)

> Boy, you came with her to this place not long ago. Whichever of these houses is theirs, knock. Go to the door now. Get away from there and be hanged! How the shameless rascal knocks! You can eat a loaf of bread three feet wide, but you don't know how to knock on a door.[46]

In mocking the boy's weak knock at the door, the parasite appears to be making a pun on *tripudium* and *pede pulsare.*[47] *Ut pulsat propudium,* a phrase that is phonetically similar to *pedibus . . . pulsatis,* could be read as "how he dances the *pro-pudium*!" If the audience were to miss the pun at first, the parasite follows it up with a mention of bread that is *tris pedes latum,* "three feet wide," a phrase that could be a grotesque pun on the word *tripudium.* The parasite may therefore be making a joke based on a traditional connection between *pes, pulsare,* and *tripudium.*

If the collocation *pedem pulsare* is a traditional expression for the performance of the *tripudium,* then the Greek Muses are, in fact, performing not only a native Latin ritual dance but also a dance known to Umbrian ritual. The verb *ahatripursatu,* "let him dance the *tripudium,*" (e.g., Rix Um1 VIIa 23), a nearly exact cognate of the Latin verb *tripudo,* occurs nine times in the Iguvine Tables in an explicitly ritual context. The Umbrian verb has an extra prefix, *aha-*, but otherwise the correspondence is exact, even to the conjugational class of both verbs. (The Umbrian phoneme that is spelled *-rs-* in the Latin alphabet corresponds to an intervocalic *-d-* in Latin, as can be seen in pairs such as Umbrian *persi,* "foot," and Latin *pede.*) The presence of the root in Latin and Umbrian in explicitly ritual context allows for a widespread Italic practice of *tripudium* that Ennius may allude to while he invokes the Greek Muses.

If *pedem pulsare* does not evoke the *tripudium,* it nevertheless appears to be a Latin traditional collocation that adds native ritual undertones to Ennius' Hellenizing *incipit* of the *Annals.* Even if *pedem pulsare* was not a traditional collocation in the lifetime of Ennius, it became a literary conceit with ritual connotations by the time of Horace. As I have said before, the difference between a literary conceit and a traditional collocation is not always easy to define. It is possible that Romans adopted the collocation in their ritual discourse even though it was not originally part of that discourse. If nothing else, the alliteration of *pedibus . . . pulsatis* invites the audience to see it as a native collocation, since alliteration was a marker of solemn language in common Italic ritual.

Because the alliterative pattern also matches that of the opening line of the *Odyssey,* however, it appears to have been inspired by a Greek literary model and Roman ritual.[48] The imitation of the sound pattern of the first line of the *Odyssey* also draws a subtle connection between the opening of the *Annals* and the opening of the *Odyssey* of Livius, who begins his epic with a word-for-word translation of the first five words of Homer's *Odyssey.* If the Plautine passage is an allusion to the collocation, moreover, then it has already made its appearance in a Greek literary genre. In sum, this traditional Roman ritual collocation in Ennius is as subject to the influence of Greek and Latin poetry as imitations of Homer and other Latin poets are subject to the influence of native ritual.

The Homeric Formula in the *Annals*

Even when Ennius ostensibly translates a well-known Homeric formula, he generates a hybrid of Greek poetry and Roman culture. Both Homer and Hesiod employ the formula πατὴρ ἀνδρῶν τε θεῶν τε, "father of gods and men," as an epithet of Zeus. Ennius deploys two variations of this formula: *divomque hominumque pater, rex* (*Ann.* 591), "father of gods and men, king," and *patrem divomque hominumque* (*Ann.* 592). The figure of Zeus-cum-Jupiter in these translations of the Homeric formula is not only a character in the Homeric poems but also the object of native Roman cult, as Denis Feeney has observed.[49] The use of *pater* in this quasi-formula in the *Annals* also partially etymologizes Latin *Iu-p(p)iter,* whereas no such etymological play is at work in the Homeric original.

Even when Ennius appropriates Homeric formulae, one of the basic structural principles of archaic Greek epic poetry, a cultural hybrid is the result.

Divomque in *pater divomque hominumque* may also be an etymological gloss of the first element of the compound *Iu-p(p)iter,* just as pater glosses *-piter.* It may be asking a bit much of Ennius and his audience to infer that *divomque* and *Iu-* in *Iuppiter* are derived from the same root based on the principles of historical linguistics, but no such knowledge is needed to make such an inference. The older forms of Jupiter beginning with a **D-* were still present in Latin inscriptions (e.g., *CIL* I^2 361 *DIOUIS,* 39 *DIUEI,* 558 *DIOUEM*). Moreover, Varro was aware that Jupiter was once *Diespater* more than a century after Ennius wrote the *Annals* (*L.* 9.77). In fact, Varro explicitly derives *dius* and *deus* from the first element of *Dies pater,* an archaic form of Jupiter:

> Nam olim Diovis et Di<e>spiter dictus, id est Dies pater; a quo dei dicti qui inde, et dius et divum. (*L.* 5.66)

> For, once, he (Jupiter) was called Diovis and Diespiter, that is father Dies, whence *dei* is derived, which in turn is *dius* and *divum.*

Because the similarity is obvious between *div-om(que)* and archaic spellings of *Iov-* (the oblique root of *Iuppiter*), especially the dative *DIU-EI,* it is possible that the etymological gloss of Latin *(D)Iu-pater* by means of a Homeric formula is deliberate. The existence of such forms in the epigraphic record would have also enabled the audience of the *Annals* to make the connection with Varro's learned pronouncements on the origin of the name Jupiter. Because Varro quotes *divomque hominumque pater, rex* (*Ann.* 591) almost immediately before he derives *divum* from *Diovis,* moreoever, it is likely that Varro understood *divomque* as a gloss of the first part of *Iuppiter.*

The addition of the word *rex* to *divomque hominumque pater, rex* (*Ann.* 591) may indicate that Ennius has conflated the formula πατὴρ ἀνδρῶν τε θεῶν τε with Δίι Κρονίωνι ἄνακτι, "to Zeus, the son of Cronus, the king" (e.g., *Il.* 2.102), another Homeric formula, or even with the Greek cult title Ζεὺς Βασιλεύς, "Zeus the King." It may, however, also be an example of native influence. The wording of a passage in the *Amphitruo* of Plautus raises the possibility that the root of *rex* was the basis of a cult title of Jupiter that is no longer directly attested:

> (MERCURIUS:) Nam quid ego memorem . . .
> . . . Quis benefactis meu' pater,
> deorum regnator, architectus't omnibus? (*Amph.* 41, 44–45)

For why should I mention all of the good deeds for which my father, the ruler of the gods, is the architect?

Pater deorum regnator refers to no other than Jupiter the father of Mercury. Plautus does not write *Iup(p)iter rex,* but he does collocate *pater,* the second element of *Iu-p(p)iter* and *regnator,* a word derived from the same root as *rex.* Naevius uses the noun *regnator* as an epithet of Neptune, but he also refers to Jupiter as *summi deum regis,* "the great king of the gods," in the same fragment:

Senex fretus pietatei deum adlocutus
summi deum regis fratrem Neptunum
regnatorem marum (*Bell. Poen.* 9)

The old man, relying upon his piety, addresses the god, the brother of the great king of the gods, Neptune ruler of the seas.

Although *fratrem regnatorem* must refer to Neptune rather than Jupiter, it may be a playful *paraprosdokian* for the expected *pater* or *patris.* Because *regis fratrem / regnatorem* closely resembles both *pater rex* in Ennius and *pater . . . regnator* in Plautus, there are turns of phrase in three archaic Latin authors that suggest a traditional collocation of *pater* with some form of the root of *rex* and *regnator,* a collocation that may actually have consisted of the roots of *Iu-p(p)iter* and *reg-*.

If *divomque, deorum,* and *deum,* all genitive plural forms of a single underlying root, are also part of the collocation, then the underlying root of the first member of the compound *Iu-p(p)iter* was part of the collocation in one way or another. As I have already observed, archaic spellings of the oblique form of Jupiter, especially *DIU-EI,* would have enabled the Romans of the second century BCE and later to infer that *deus, divus,* and *Iu-* in *Iuppiter* were all forms of the same root. For speakers of an older generation who prayed to *DIUEI,* no evidence for such an etymological connection was required except their own ears, a connection that may have originally made the first element of *Iu-p(p)iter* redundant. Even when the redundancy was no longer apparent, the custom of referring to *pater divom . . . rex* rather than *Iu-pater rex* may have persisted. It is even possible that collocations of the roots of *pater, deus,* and *rex* reflect a later misunderstanding of **PATRI DIUEI REGI* (or *REGNATORI*), an archaic inversion of *Iu-pater rex* that no longer survives in the written record.

Two Oscan inscriptions may indicate that the cult title of Jupiter based on the root of *rego,* "I rule," dates to the central Italian *koinê* period. The Oscan cult title **diúveí regatureí** from the Agnone Tablet (Rix Sa 1.12) collocates the Oscan cognate of Latin *Iovi* with a form that closely resembles *regnator.* If Lejuene's suggestion that the Oscan genitive plural ρεγο(μ) on another Oscan inscription from Lucania (Rix Lu 5 4) is a theonym that formally corresponds with the genitive plural of Latin *regum* and that refers to Jupiter and the Oscan goddess Méfitis,[50] then ρεγο(μ) is another indication that some form of the root *reg-* may have been a traditional ritual epithet for the common Italic god Jupiter. Although **regatureí** may not be a form of the root *reg-* and ρεγο(μ) may not even be an epithet of Oscan Jupiter,[51] it is possible that a collocation of Jupiter and the root *reg-* arose from a creative misunderstanding of the language of Oscan ritual by Latin speakers, or vice versa.

The audience of the *Annals* would likely understand the use of *rex* in a reference to Jupiter as a Roman element in the Greek formula. The evidence is not direct, but Jupiter may have been traditionally collocated with a form of *rego* in Latin. Even if there was never a cult of Jupiter Rex at Rome, the audience of the *Annals* could have also connected the epithet *rex* to Jupiter by analogy with Juno Regina, or the other instances of the epithet *regina* applied to a variety of goddesses including Diana, Salus, and Fortuna.[52] Moreover the use of the epithet *regnator* or *rex* to refer to Jupiter was already part of the Latin literary tradition. However the collocation became part of the tradition, and whether that tradition was ritual or literary, the simple word *rex* appears to lend native coloring to Ennius' appropriation of the Homeric formula πατὴρ ἀνδρῶν τε θεῶν τε, "father of gods and men."

An even subtler blend of etymological puns on Latin cult titles and Homeric diction may be in play in a word-for-word translation of a line from the *Iliad:*

> O genitor noster, Saturnie, maxime divom (*Ann.* 444)
>
> O son of Saturn, O our begetter, greatest of gods. (trans. Warmington)

Denis Feeney has already remarked upon the use of half of the cult title of Jupiter (Optimus) Maximus to translate the second half of *Iliad* 8.31:[53]

> ὦ πάτερ ἡμέτερε Κρονίδη, ὕπατε κρειόντων (*Il.* 8.31)
>
> Oh father of ours, son of Cronus, highest of the ruling (gods).

Feeney has also suggested that *genitor* may etymologize a perceived *sator* in *Satur-nus,* an example of wordplay that is possible only in Latin.[54] *Divom* may be both a translation of κρειόντων, "the ruling ones," and a gloss of the archaic form of Jupiter, *Diovis,* as I have already suggested. It is possible that a knowledgeable reader may even be able to go back to the Greek original and find the vocative πάτερ, a form that is identical to the Latin vocative and hence the second part of the vocative *Iu-p(p)iter* in Homer's Greek, but not in Ennius' Latin, where *genitor* has replaced *pater.*

The Language of Chthonic Ritual in the *Annals*

Although expressions like *divomque hominumque pater, rex* owe much to Homer, they are not allusions to a specific passage in the *Iliad* or the *Odyssey* that in turn invite a comparison between the Homeric and the Ennian context. I will now examine such a topical allusion in the *Annals* and put forth a radical hypothesis: Ennius' allusion to *Iliad* 2.489–90 (quoted below) appropriates a traditional collocation of the language of Latin curses. Moreover, the presence of this collocation, *lingua loqui saperet,* "my tongue could have the skill to speak," may not only explain the odd syntax of the Ennian passage, it may also foreshadow the fact that the gods of the underworld are particularly active throughout book 6 of the *Annals,* since the fragment may now be assigned to that book of the *Annals* with the discovery of the Herculaneum papyrus.[55] If my thesis is valid, then this blending of Greek poetry and Latin system reference captures the odd mixture of martial and chthonic ritual undertones that color many of the fragments of book 6.

The scholiast on *Georgics* 2.43 records Ennius' appropriation of one of the great Homeric *topoi:* the image of the poet claiming that, even if he had many tongues and a heart of metal, he could not do justice to a given subject:

> Non si lingua loqui saperet quibus, ora decem sint
> In me, tum ferro cor sit pectusque revinctum. (*Ann.* 469–70)

> Not if I had ten mouths in me with which my tongue could have the skill to speak and then my heart and breast were fast bound in iron.[56]

Specific verbal parallels in the Ennian fragment easily allow the identification of its Homeric source:

> οὐδ 'εἴ μοι δέκα μὲν γλῶσσαι, δέκα δὲ στόματ εἶεν
> φωνὴ δ̓ ἄρρηκτος, χάλκεον δέ μοι ἦτορ ἐνείη ' (*Il.* 2.489–90)

> Not even if I had ten tongues and ten mouths, an unbreakable voice and my heart was bronze.

If the spelling *at* in the manuscript conceals the word *quibus,*[57] the relative pronoun *quibus* has been postponed until the end of the clause. The unusual placement of the pronoun at the end of the relative clause may simply be an example of Ennius wrestling with a recalcitrant foreign meter, but it could also serve to highlight the phrase *non si loqui lingua saperet.*

If Flores has correctly joined Skutsch's line 164 to 469–70, then there may be further indications that the syntax of the phrase *lingua loqui saperet quibus* was meant to draw the attention of the audience. According to Flores, the opening of book 6 of the *Annals* reads as follows:[58]

Quis potis ingentis oras evolvere belli?
Non si lingua loqui saperet quibus ora decem sint
In me, tum ferro cor sit pectusque revinctum . . .

Who can unroll this great war from end to end? Not if I had ten mouths in me with which my tongue could have the skill to speak and then my heart and breast were fast bound in iron . . . (trans. Warmington, with adjustments)

The general syntactic and semantic counterpoint between *quis potis evolvere* and *loqui saperet quibus* generates a mirror image effect:

QuisRelative Pronoun ***potis***Modal Verb *ingentis oras* ***evolvere***Infinitive *belli?*
Non si lingua ***loqui***Infinitive ***saperet***Modal Verb ***quibus***Relative Pronoun *ora decem sint.*

The position of the interrogative pronoun *quis* in the first line of the newly constituted fragment would highlight the unusual word order of *lingua loqui saperet quibus.*

Before considering the possible appropriation of the language of curse tablets and its impact on the Ennian fragment, I would like to emphasize two things. In the first place, I am arguing for a possibility that will push the limits of system reference to the extreme. The fragment does not quote a traditional collocation found in any extant curse tablet but rather the phrase *lingua loqui saperet* is very similar to a number of formulations in curses that fixate on the victim's tongue and ability to speak, a similarity that some, but probably not all, members of the audience of the poem would notice. In the second place, Ennius is not cursing his audience but alluding to such curses without actually enacting such a ritual. If anything, the fact that it is the poet who is unable to say something would imply that he is the victim of a curse.

Two similar combinations of *lingua* and *loqui* in Plautus' *Truculentus* and in an epitaph that is attributed to Naevius, are the first indication that Ennius has imported a traditional collocation into his allusion to the *Iliad.* Astaphium, the maid of the *meretrix* Phronesium in the *Truculentus,* lists several traits necessary to be a successful *lena,* or procuress, among them:

> Bonis esse opportet dentibus lenam probam ad-
> ridere ut quisquis veniat blande adloqui
> male corde consultare bene lingua loqui (*Truc.* 224–26)

> The clever *lena* must smile with good teeth whenever someone comes, speak flatteringly, plan with evil intent, speak well with the tongue.

Although the epitaph of "Naevius" is likely not older than the *Annals,* it too collocates *lingua* and the archaic deponent infinitive *loquier:*[59]

> Immortales mortales si foret fas flere,
> Flerent divae Camenae Naevium poetam.
> Itaque postquam est Orci traditus thesauro,
> Obliti sunt Romae loquier lingua Latina.

> If it were right for immortals to weep for mortals the divine *Camenae* would have wept for the poet Naevius. After he was handed over to the vault of Orcus they forgot how to speak the Latin language at Rome.

All of these combinations of *lingua* and some form of the infinitive of *loquor* may be independent of one another. The possibility remains, however, that *lingua loqui* is a traditional collocation. If it is, then it has specific semantic connotations that give extra meaning to the literal combination of the Latin words for "speak" and "tongue." As it turns out, the contexts of *lingua loqui* in Plautus and *loquier lingua* in Naevius are not as dissimilar as they may first appear. A few lines before Astaphium expounds on the desirability of *bene lingua loqui,* "speaking well with the tongue," for a *lena,* she refers to the speech of her mistress Phronesium as "*naenia,*" an obscure word that can mean "charm" or "funeral dirge":[60]

> huic homini amanti mea era apud nos naenia dixit (*Truc.* 213)

> My mistress has sung a funeral dirge (the *naenia*) for this infatuated man in our presence.

The use of *lingua loquier* in an epitaph for a dead poet also may be an indication that the collocation has funereal connotations. If it does, the shift from its original context to the prologue of book 6 of the *Annals* is not as drastic as it may seem, since book 6 treats the Pyrrhic War, a conflict notorious for the loss of life on both sides of the battle lines.

Not only does the collocation *lingua loqui* occur in a funereal context that is assumed for "Naevius" and latent in Plautus, the expression *lingua loqui saperet* in Ennius is also similar to some expressions found in different curse tablets. If *lingua loqui* is not a collocation drawn from the language of curses, it is aurally similar to *linguas ligo,* "I bind (their) tongues," a collocation that appears on a number of curse tablets and that is semantically similar to Ennius' assertion that his tongue cannot speak. Audollent's collection of *defixiones* yields several examples: *al[li]go deligo linguas* (*DT* 217a.4), *adligate lingu[a]s* (*DT* 218.9–10), and *ligo o(b)ligo linguas* (*DT* 219.2–3). Moreover, the inability to speak, as in Ennius and "Naevius," is at least superficially similar to the effect of a binding spell that results in the loss of the ability to speak for a victim dedicated to the gods of the dead. Although *lingua loqui* appears to belong in the context of the funeral and *lingua loqui saperet* is more appropriate for cursing, both contexts are rituals that the gods of the dead, such as Persephone and Orcus, preside over.

The semantic similarity between *lingua loqui saperet* in Ennius and a variety of expressions of the same sentiment in Latin curse tablets increases the likelihood that Ennius is evoking the traditional diction of curses. There are also several expressions that consist of a verb of speaking, a modal verb that expresses the ability to speak, usually *posse,* in a negative proposition. One curse wishes that the victim lose the ability to speak:

> Quomodo mortuos qui istic/ sepultus est nec loqui nec sermonare potest seic Rhodine apud M. Licinum Faustum mortua sit nec loqui nec sermonare possit (*CIL* I^2 1012)
>
> Just as this dead person who is buried here is not able to speak or say anything so may Rhodine in the house of Marcus Licinus Faustus be dead and not able to speak or say anything.

A curse tablet from France yields a variant on *nec loqui . . . possit: loqui nequeat.*[61] Yet another variation may be seen in another *defixio: nei dicere possit,* "may she not be able to speak."[62] The verb *loqui* is also found in a context of a wish to deprive a victim of the ability to speak in still another curse tablet from Britain:[63]

> si vir si m-/ascel ne meiat/ ne cacet ne loqua- / tur ne dormiat /n[e] vigilet nec s[a]-/[1]utem nec sa-/ nitatem
>
> Whether man or male (*sic*), may not urinate nor defecate nor speak nor sleep nor stay awake nor (have) well-being or health.

The subjunctive with *ne* is semantically very similar to the *nec loqui . . . possit* and *loqui nequeat*, even if the verbal correspondences are not exact. Whether or not *loqui posse* was a traditional collocation from the language of curses, the use of a verb that signifies the ability to do something (*posse* or *nequere*) with a verb of speaking as a complementary infinitive (*loqui* or *dicere*) in a negative proposition occurs frequently in curse tablets. These same features are present in Ennius' claim that not even if he had ten mouths would his tongue be able to speak.

The use of the Oscan congeners of *nec posse* with a complementary infinitive that means "to speak" in a curse tablet may indicate that this configuration is characteristic of common Italic curses:

> **Nep fatíum. nep. deíkum. Pútíans** (Rix Cp 36 6)
>
> May they not speak or talk.

The similarity between the Oscan phrase and *nec loqui nec sermonare potest* in a Latin curse already discussed has led J. N. Adams to suggest that the Latin collocation *nec loqui nec sermonare possit* (*CIL* I^2 1012) has been influenced by the Oscan curse.[64] Moreover, the Latin phrase *ni dicere possit* from the Johns Hopkins *Defixiones* is cognate with Oscan **nep deíkum pútíans.** So there is evidence of a general pattern in Latin and common Italic found in the Ennian fragment that could recall the language of curses.

My hypothesis concerning the ritual coloring of *loqui lingua saperet* is based on the following demonstrable observations: the syntax of the (*non si*) *lingua loqui saperet quibus* (*ora decem sint*) is unusual; *lingua* and *loqui* are often used in curse tablets; *loqui* is also the infinitival complement of a modal verb (*possit* and *potest*) in at least two curse tablets. Moreover, the syntactic figure that deploys a verb of speaking with a modal verb in a negation is characteristic of curse tablets in Oscan and Latin. Even without specific verbal parallels, the inability to speak focalized on the tongue is so common that the phrase may have been evocative of the language of curses on purely typological grounds.[65] Because all of these characteristic features of curses are found in the Ennian fragment, it may not be going too far to suggest that some, if not many, readers of the *Annals* would note the syntactic and semantic parallels to Latin curse tablets.

The presence of the diction of curse tablets in the passage from the *Annals* could add layers of meaning that do not appear to be present in the original Homeric *topos*. The opaque syntax of *lingua loqui saperet quibus ora decem sint* is itself a self-reflexive demonstration of Ennius' poetic *aporia*. Although *lingua loqui saperet quibus* must eventually be parsed as an embedded relative clause, the placement of the relative pronoun at the end of this clause generates momentary confusion and obscures the meaning of the line. The effect is the appearance that Ennius has initially lost control of the syntax, or rather control of his tongue, something that is very often wished upon victims of curses. So there may be a fleeting impression that Ennius has come very close to cursing himself by using language that is typical of curses seeking to deprive a victim of the ability to speak.

The thematic patterns that emerge from book 6 of the *Annals,* or at least from what remains of book 6, may also have prompted the audience to connect the opening of the book to curse tablets after the fact. The gods of the dead, both Persephone and the unnamed chthonic addressees of Decimus Mus' *devotio,* the ritual dedication of oneself to the gods of the underworld (the same process applied to the victim in curse tablets), play crucial roles in book 6. The Herculaneum papyrus that contains fragments of book 6 yields few complete words and no entire lines, but there are two sequences, one that reads *ORC* and one that reads *RCI,* that could be the remnants of the name of the underworld god Orcus (or simply the land of the dead itself). In contrast to these papyrus fragments, Orcus is found once elsewhere in the other fragments of the *Annals* (*Ann.* 564). If the chthonic gods are significantly active in the narrative of book 6, as the evidence suggests, then the audience may have retroactively recognized similarities between the Ennian expression of Homeric *aporia* and the language of curse tablets, texts that are addressed to deities like Persephone.

Nor is *Annals* 479–80 the only allusion to the *Iliad* in book 6 that has funereal undertones. Macrobius (6.2.27) identifies the preparations for the funeral of Misenus in the *Aeneid* (6.179–82) as an allusion to a passage from Ennius describing the felling of trees in a forest:

> Incedunt arbusta per alta, securibus caedunt
> percellunt magnas quercus, exciditur ilex,
> fraxinus frangitur atque abies consternitur alta,
> pinus proceras pervortunt: omne sonabat
> arbustum fremitu silvai frondosai. (*Ann.* 175–79)

> Then strode they through tall timber-trees and hewed
> With hatchets; mighty oaks they overset;
> Down crashed the holm and shivered ash outhacked;
> Felled was the lofty fir; they wrenched right down
> Tall towering pines; and every woody tree
> In frondent forest rang and roared and rustled. (trans. Warmington)

Although the passage is based on Homer's description of the cutting of trees for the funeral pyre of Patroclus,[66] the context of the fragment of the *Annals* is unknown. The Homeric resonance, however, suggests that Ennius is also describing the preparations for burning the dead. Because the burning of the dead is a ritual that at least tangentially involves the gods of the dead, this allusion also supports the thesis that the gods of the dead play a significant role in book 6 of the *Annals*. If the language of curses colors the appropriation of Homeric *aporia* that opens book 6, as I have suggested, then both of the surviving allusions to the *Iliad* in book 6 specifically call to mind the cult of the gods of the underworld.

If the prominence of chthonic gods and rituals in book 6 is by design, it must have some narrative and thematic significance. Because book 6 contained the narrative of the Pyrrhic War, which was characterized by major battles with significant losses on both sides, the gods of the dead may symbolize the great loss of life in the conflict. It is also possible that the war between Rome and Pyrrhus was imagined as a war between the forces of order, represented by the gods of official Roman cult, and chaos, represented by gods to whom one could address curses and who ruled over the world of the dead, not the living. Even if a complete text of book 6 existed and the prominence of the chthonic gods in the narrative could be established without any reservations, however, this thematic thread would almost certainly give rise to more than one explanation of its significance.

There is, in fact, one fragment from book 6 that could indicate that the Pyrrhic War was imagined as a conflict between order and chaos personified by official Roman celestial gods and less official chthonic gods, whose rituals were at least sometimes not part of the state cult. If Flores has rightly joined a previously unattributed fragment to a fragment known to be from book 6, then we not only have an image of Jupiter speaking but also of Jupiter ranging a thunderbolt over the three regions of the universe:[67]

> Tum cum corde suo divom pater atque hominum rex
> ecfatur <quae iusserat. At>qui fulmine claro
> omnia arcet, per sonitus terram mare caelum. (*Ann.* 203–4 + 555–56)

> Then with all of his heart the father of gods and king of men spoke forth
> [what he had ordered. And then] with bright thunderbolt encloses all things
> with sound, [earth, sea, and sky.] (trans. Warmington, with adjustments)

The fragment is a description of Jupiter's rule over the universe and of his maintenance of order. *Arceo* means both "govern" or "control" and "keep apart, separate." The latter meaning of *arceo* as applied to the earth, ocean, and sky is suggestive of an image of an orderly universe where the earth, the domain of the chthonic gods, is kept separate from the sky, the dwelling place of the celestials. There may even be a hint of a recent restoration of an orderly separation of these regions after the inordinate amount of interventions in human affairs by the gods of the dead.

Whether or not the fragment is an image of Jupiter restoring or reasserting the ordered structure of the universe, it combines Greek and Italic features. Although it is not a topical allusion to the *Iliad,* the *divom pater atque hominum* (*rex*) is a close translation of the Homeric formula πατὴρ ἀνδρῶν τε θεῶν τε. As I have already suggested, however, the addition of *rex* at the end of the phrase likely lends it an Italic coloring. The division of the universe into land, sea, and sky may similarly have been characterized by hybridity. The separation of the universe into three regions by the agency of Jupiter recalls the division of the universe between Zeus, Poseidon, and Hades described by Homer in the *Iliad* (*Il.* 15.187–93). The phrase *terram mare caelum* may also evoke an Italic idea of the universe divided into three parts, and an equally Italic practice of assigning divisions of space to particular gods. The fragment is therefore a mixture of the foreign, in this case a translation of a Homeric formula, and perhaps a nod to the myth of Zeus, Poseidon, and Hades dividing up the universe, and the image of the familiar Italic god Jupiter, perhaps made more familiar by the addition of *rex* to the Homeric formula.

Although the prophecy of Vegoia is almost certainly neither a translation of an Etruscan document nor to be dated to the second century BCE,[68] there are similarities between the prophecy and the Ennian fragment suggesting that the audience could have understood the division of the universe into sea, earth, and air as an Etruscan idea. The prophecy's opening statement that the sea was separated from the sky (*mare ex aethera remotum*) followed by an image of Jupiter claiming the land of Etruria (*Jupiter terram Aetruria sibi vindicavit* [*grom.* 1.350]) is similar to the passage from the *Annals* in content and language. If the idea of the universe as divided between sky, sea, and earth in the Vegoia prophecy is based on an older source, then the contemporary audience of the *Annals* may have also understood the Ennian phrase as a reference to the *disciplina Etrusca.*

It is possible that the idea of the separation of the earth, sea, and sky is a distinctive Etruscan belief. It is certain that the Etruscans divided the liver of a sacrificial animal into discrete areas under the control of a single god. It is also likely that the Etruscans divided the sky in the same manner.[69] What is more, the assignment of particular regions of the sky to individual gods in ancient Bantia suggested by a series of *cippi* from an augural *templum* may indicate that such divisions of space existed in Roman culture as well.[70] The asyndetic phrase *terram mare caelum* may therefore be a mixed reference to Greek myth and Italic ritual.

Greek and Foreign Elements in the *Annals:* A Reassessment

Although my study emphasizes the Italic nature of the *Annals,* the shadow of Homer and other Greek poets looms large over the epic. No matter how old or how distinctly Roman a text may be, the system of writing is ultimately based upon the Greek alphabet. The profound influence of Greek culture on Roman and Italic culture is so deeply rooted as to exclude the possibility of a Latin text free of Greek influence. If any of the Latin texts appropriated by Ennius were written, as many surely were, then their "Italic" character has already been subject to mediation between Greek and Italic culture via the alphabet. These previous significant contributions of Greek culture to common Italic culture are therefore one reason why Ennius was able to transplant the Greek hexameter into Latin in the first place, and perhaps why Latin speakers were able to appropriate the idea of Greek literature itself.

If a given Greek cultural element was already appropriated during the central Italian *koinê* period, such an element was familiar from the point of view of Ennius and his audience. The invocation of the Muses introduces these Greek divinities into Roman literature along with the dactylic hexameter, but they may be dancing the *tripudium* to a Saturnian beat. Homeric formulae resonate with native cult when they are transplanted onto Italic soil. Even undeniable examples of Greek loan words problematize the difference between Greek and Latin, and perhaps even the implicit belief that the Greek language is culturally superior. The debt of Ennius to Greek literature and culture is undeniably and extremely significant. The hybrid nature of the *Annals,* however, can and does assert itself repeatedly, even in some of the most Homeric moments of the poem.

Ritual and Myth in the Augurium Romuli (Annals 72–91)

The language of the *Annals* does more than tell a story. Combinations of words and even individual words that belonged to important cultural contexts, such as ritual, continually emerge, if only partially, and then submerge, leaving semantic ripples on the surface of the narrative. Although the promise that Jupiter will not overturn but support someone does not imply a ritual context (*Ann.* 204, discussed in chapter 1), the cult title Jupiter Stator is implicitly present in the phrase *Iuppiter hac stat.* The hybrid of Greek and Roman elements in the Ennian adaptation of the Homeric formula πατὴρ ἀνδρῶν τε θεῶν τε (e.g., *Ann.* 591, discussed in chapter 2) is so seamless that the play between *pater* and *Iu-p(p)iter,* an impossibility for the Greek name Zeus, is almost wholly eclipsed by the Homeric source text. Because the native *figura etymologica* cannot be entirely eclipsed, however, the words *pater* and *divomque* in *patrem divomque hominumque* (*Ann.* 592) could evoke archaic dedications to *DIUEI PATRI as much as the Homeric formula. In addition to these two examples, I have suggested other fragments that may be characterized as a hybrid of Greek poetry and Roman ritual.

In contrast with the implicit ritual connotations of many of these fragments, Cicero quotes one of the longer fragments of the *Annals,* a passage that explicitly describes a Roman ritual, in his *De Divinatione.* Because Cicero, in the persona of his brother Quintus, quotes the passage in a discussion of augury (*Div.* 1.107–8), it is certain that some readers took the passage as a reasonably accurate description of the ritual. The passage is not only cited as an example of augury but is also explicitly termed an augury (*auguratus*) performed by Romulus who is an augur (*item augure*) and his brother Remus. Moreover, the passage is paired with another extended quotation of a poetic description of an augury, this time from Cicero's own *Marius* (*Div.* 1.106). If Quintus can cite this passage in this context, then it is extremely unlikely that Ennius took too much artistic license with the *realia* of Roman augury.

Although the beginning of the passage is corrupt, Romulus and Remus apparently take up different positions from where they will search the skies for birds that will indicate whether the gods wish the new city to be named after Romulus (Roma) or Remus (Remora). Ennius describes the intense interest of the crowd, who observe Romulus and Remus, by means of an extended simile that compares the crowd to spectators waiting for the consul to start a chariot race in Ennius' day. Soon after the simile, a single bird makes its appearance and then twelve more birds appear. Both are favorable omens that confirm that the new city will be named Roma and not Remora, but this clear sequence of events is obscured by the mention of a white sun, a bright light, and a golden sun over the course of the time it takes for the birds to appear. It is not obvious whether these suns represent the passage of time or some other phenomenon or are simply the result of textual corruption.

However corrupt the transmission of the fragment may be, Cicero preserves Ennius' entire description of the augury (*Div.* 1.107–8):

Curantes magna cum cura tum cupientes
regni dant operam simul auspicio augurioque.
In †monte Remus auspicio sedet atque secundam
solus avem servat. At Romulus pulcer in alto
quaerit Aventino, servat genus altivolantum.
Certabant urbem Romam Remoramne vocarent.
Omnibus cura viris uter esset induperator.
Exspectant veluti consul quom mittere signum
volt, omnes avidi spectant ad carceris oras
quam mox emittat pictos e faucibus currus:
sic exspectabat populus atque ore timebat
rebus utri magni victoria sit data regni.
Interea sol albus recessit in infera noctis.
Exin candida se radiis dedit icta foras lux
et simul ex alto longe pulcerrima praepes
laeva volavit avis. Simul aureus exoritur sol
cedunt de caelo ter quattuor corpora sancta
avium, praepetibus sese pulcrisque locis dant.
Conspicit inde sibi data Romulus esse propritim
auspicio regni stabilita scamna solumque. (*Ann.* 72–91)

Careful with great care, each also in eagerness for royal rule, they are intent on the watching and the soothsaying of birds on a hill. Remus is seated for the *auspicium*[1] and apart looks out for a favorable bird. But handsome

> Romulus makes his search on high Aventine and so looks out for the soaring breed. Whether they should call the city Roma or Remora—this was their contest. Anxiety filled all the men as to which of the two should be ruler. As, when the consul means to give the signal, all men look eagerly at the barrier's bounds to see how soon he will send the chariots forth from the painted mouths—so they waited. Thus were the people waiting, and held their tongues, wondering to which of the two the victory of right royal rule should be given by the event. Meanwhile the white sun withdrew into the depths of the night. Then clear shot forth, struck out in rays, a light: just when, winging to the left, there flew from the height a bird, the luckiest [by] far of flying prophets,[2] just then all golden there came out the sun. Thrice four hallowed forms of birds moved down from the sky, and betook themselves to places lucky and of happy omen. From this saw Romulus that to him, to be his own, were duly given the chair and throne of royalty, established firm by the watching of birds. (trans. Warmington)

Ritual system reference is universally acknowledged to be crucial in any interpretation of this passage, but literary interpretations tend to downplay the ritual elements, whereas philological treatments attempt to tease out the augural details from the poetry. A close examination of the literary structure, however, sheds light on the use of the language of augury in the passage, and vice versa. In other words, poetry and ritual work together to add layers of meaning, thereby revealing a conscious artistry that the Augustan poets, who considered Ennius to be rough and unpolished, would not have been ashamed to see in their own work.

Given the overt ritual content, it is not surprising to find many ritual collocations in the augural contest, even though many are not obvious at first glance. *Operam dare* is the only obvious quotation of a ritual collocation. There are, however, a number of allusions to the language of augury already noted by others. Skutsch unequivocally names the phrase *pulcerrima praepes* a "term of augural language."[3] *Remora,* the imagined name for the city if Remus wins the contest, recalls *aves remores,* an augural term for a bird that indicates that the *auspex* should defer his intended project, a connection already noted by Jerzy Linderski.[4] Moreover, the expression *cedunt de caelo* bears more than a passing resemblance to the phrase *de caelo cecidisse,* an expression used to describe prodigies in Livy (e.g., 22.1.9). I will also suggest that the relatively inconspicuous collocation *avem servat* is a traditional ritual collocation based upon its semantic and etymological equivalence with the Umbrian ritual collocation **aves anzeriates,** "after the birds have been observed." Moreover, this Umbrian collocation may not be unrelated to *avem specere,* yet another traditional augural expression that Ennius may allude to at the end of the fragment. Whether or not all of these collocations are, in fact, traditional, many of Ennius' word choices are drawn from the technical language of augury, including *praepes, conspicit,* and more obvious examples, such as *auspicium* and *avis.*

In addition to lending some verisimilitude to Ennius' description of the augury, the individual units of augural language also help to drive the plot of the passage and suggest meanings that are not apparent on the surface of the narrative. *Infera noctis,* the region where the "white sun" (*sol albus*) retreats, is reminiscent of the *avis infera,* a bird of unfavorable omen. The similarity between *cedunt de caelo* and *cecidisse de caelo* not only implies tension between sky signs (*signa de caelo*) and bird signs (*signa de avibus*), it also raises the possibility of a different outcome or interpretation of the events of the augural contest already implied by the alternate name of Remora for Rome. Although an alternative history of a city named Remora is intriguing, the idea that the founding of Rome could be viewed as something less than favorable is a much more salient possibility, given that many states and communities of the Italian peninsula came under Roman hegemony after losing to the Romans in an armed conflict. If nothing else, all of these collocations help to elide the difference between the specific augury that was performed by Romulus and Remus and the general practice of augury in the second century BCE familiar to the audience of the poem.

The power of the passage lies not only in the way that it draws attention to augural system reference but also in the appropriation of ritual phraseology, not unlike the way the Hellenistic poets utilize the language of archaic Greek poets. Because the contest is conducted according to the rules of contemporary augury, there is an anachronistic character to the narrative that is also characteristic of Hellenistic poetry. Callimachus, for example, refers to the *Deliades* before the island Asteria has changed her name to Delos.[5] Although the Ennian passage is not an aetiology of Roman augury, it still connects the present of the age of Ennius to the mythic past of Romulus and Remus by means of ritual. The passage is also a story that explains the origins and the name of the city of Rome, just as Apollonius wrote poems on the foundations of Alexandria and other cities. The allusions to ritual collocations in Ennius evoke the augural practice of the second century BCE in a narrative of the distant past in a manner consistent with the *arte allusiva* of Alexandrian poetry.

Because the augural rite is a form of narrative that can vary within the parameters of a fixed sequence of events, Ennius can choose one particular version of that sequence of events, much as Callimachus can elect to tell a particular variant of a canonical myth. In his *Hymn to Zeus,* for example, Callimachus considers two variant stories of the birth of Zeus and favors Arcadia as the god's birthplace, even though he continues to allude to the other variant.[6] Apollonius, another Alexandrian poet, has Jason as a resident at Iolcus, but alludes to a variant tradition that has Jason raised by Cheiron away from Iolcus.[7] These mythic variants are analogous to the variant outcomes of an augury that Ennius can allude to while narrating the inevitable outcome of the augural contest between Romulus and Remus, thereby heightening the suspense for his audience by subtly acknowledging that even the most traditional stories are malleable to some extent.

In spite of the similarities, it is important to acknowledge that the effect of the allusions to the ritual is not exactly the same as an allusion to a variant myth, since the narrative invites the audience to compare the story to a ritual rather than to another story. Augury in particular must allow for some variation of outcome that is not possible for a single version of a myth. The capacity for variant outcomes, however, may indicate that the audience should look for allusions to variants of the Romulus and Remus myth, a search that may yield a better understanding of the relationship of the passage to the larger tradition.

If augural system reference elides the difference between past and present, the extended simile that compares the augural contest to the start of a chariot race produces the same effect. The crowd of proto-Romans about the Aventine prefigures the crowd at the Circus Maximus in the lifetime of Ennius. The Circus Maximus was located at the foot of the Aventine, the setting of the *augurium Romuli.*[8] The difference between past and present is further elided by the repetition of the verb *exspectare,* which emphasizes the parallel actions of the pre-Roman herdsmen and the crowd at the chariot race. The phonetic similarity between *avidi spectant* and the various combinations of *avis* and *specere* in the main narrative may also serve to make the boundaries between simile and narrative more permeable.

The elision between past and present is, nevertheless, incomplete. Because the presence of a consul would only be possible after the regal period, the simile compares the augural contest to a future event. Although the chronological inconsistency between the narrative and the simile is not a true anachronism, the comparison of one event to another that will not happen for centuries serves as a reminder that Romulus and Remus lived in a different age that may very well have had different customs. The simile is therefore characterized by a tension between past and present as much as by a slippage between the ages of Romulus and Ennius.

Ring Composition and Ritual in the *Augurium Romuli*

The careful construction of the passage is evident in the complex ring composition that gives it structure. The last line of the fragment, for example, begins with the words *auspicio regni,* and the second line reads *regni dant operam simul auspicio augurioque.* Both of these instantiations of *regnum* are in the genitive case and dependent on *auspicio.* Moreover, *regni* is deployed a third time in, or close to, the center of the ring. The pattern therefore forms a ring bounded by (*auspicio*) *regni* with *regni* as the center. An inner ring also emerges upon recognizing that the compound forms *ex-spectant* and *ex-spectabat* form the boundaries of the extended simile with *spectant* as the center. The ring composition can be graphically represented thus:

. . . regni[a] dant operam simul **auspicio**[b] augurioque.
In monte Remus auspicio sedet atque secundam

Exspectant[c] veluti consul quom mittere signum
volt, omnes avidi **spectant**[c] ad carceris oras
quam mox emittat pictos e faucibus currus:
sic **exspectabat**[c] populus atque ore timebat
rebus utri magni victoria sit data regni.[a]

Conspicit inde sibi data Romulus esse propritim
auspicio[b] regni[a] stabilita scamna solumque. (*Ann.* 72–91)

Because all the elements of the ring composition—with the exception of *regni*—are compound forms of the root of *specere,* the ring composition draws attention to the key theme of sight in the passage. What is more, the repetition of *regni* calls attention to kingship, another key theme.

The etymological connection between the compound forms of *specere* and *auspicio* is not immediately obvious, but another, similar pattern of etymologically related words becomes visible once the connection is made between these forms. *Au-spicio* compounds a nominal form of *specere* and *avis,* yet another key word in the passage that occurs in lines 75 (*avem*), 87 (*avis*), and 89 (*avium*). Because the initial position of *avium* in 89 is also paralleled by *conspicit* in line 90, the arrangement is suggestive of an etymological gloss of *auspicio,* a word that, not incidentally, takes up the first position of line 91. The fact that *avium* must be pronounced *au-ium,* not *a-vium,* in order to fit the meter also suggests that *avium . . . conspicit* is a deliberate gloss of *auspicio.* If so, then it may be an etymological equivalent for the second use of *auspicio* in line 75, and another element in the ring composition:

. . . regni dant operam simul **au-spicio**[a] augurioque.
In †monte Remus **au-spicio**[b] sedet atque secundam
solus **avem**[c] servat. At Romulus pulcer in alto

. . . laeva volavit **avis.**[c] Simul aureus exoritur sol
cedunt de caelo ter quattuor corpora sancta
avium[b] praepetibus sese pulcrisque locis dant.
Con-spicit[b] inde sibi data Romulus esse propritim
au-spicio[a] regni stabilita scamna solumque. (*Ann.* 72–91)

Moreover, *avi-di,* the subject of *spectant* in the center of the ring composition, is phonetically very close to *avis* and suggests that the sighting (*specere*) of birds (*avis*) is the literal as well as the thematic center of the passage:

Exspectant[c] veluti consul quom mittere signum
volt, omnes **avidi spectant**[c] ad carceris oras
quam mox emittat pictos e faucibus currus:
sic **exspectabat**[c] populus atque ore timebat.

If *avidi* can be seen as a pun on *avis* (or better, *avem vidi*), then it can serve as the center of the ring formed by *avem* and *avis:*

Solus **avem** servat. At Romulus pulcer in alto 75
volt, omnes **avi**di spectant ad carceris oras 80
laeva volavit **avis.** 87

The passage is therefore united not only by theme and repetition but also by sound and etymology.

The etymological connection between the different elements of the ring composition can also extend to other words in the passage in a manner that unequivocally demonstrates how tightly Ennius constructed it. In addition to glossing *auspicium* with *conspicit avem,* Ennius implies a connection between *avem* and *Aventinus.* Varro (*L.* 5.43) tells us that Naevius claimed that the name *Aventinus* came from the birds that flew there from the Tiber,[9] a folk etymology of Aventine. The placement of *quaerit Aventino* preceded by *solus avem servat* and immediately followed by *servat genus altivolantum* sandwiches it between two glosses of *Aventinus:*

> . . . solus avem servat. At Romulus pulcer in alto
> quaerit Aventino, servat genus altivolantum

The placement of *Aventino* at the end of one phrase and *servat* at the beginning of the next yields the sequence *Aventino servat.* Even without any outside evidence for a derivation of *Aventinus* from *avem,* the aural similarity of *Aventino servat* and *avem servat* may not have gone unnoticed by a careful reader (or listener).

The ring composition informed by insistent etymological play communicates something more to the audience than the fact that the passage is carefully composed. Most of the elements of the ring composition refer to birds and sight and therefore continually remind the audience that an augury is taking place. *Avem servat* and similar phrases may not be immediately striking, but at least some, if not all, of these statements of searching for and sighting birds are traditional collocations in an augural context. The play on forms of *avem* and *specere* highlight the fact that *avem specere* is an attested augural expression. These appropriations of the language of augury, such as *dant operam . . . auspicio,* also color the passage. At the very least, these ritual collocations alert the audience that these auspices will be conducted according to the rules of contemporary augury.[10] Moreover, the two variants of a single collocation of *pulcer* and *praepes* in the passage, a collocation that appears once elsewhere in the fragments of the *Annals,* imply that the phrase is also a formulaic utterance by virtue of the repetition of the collocation, perhaps genuine or perhaps a creation of Ennius. The ring composition is therefore not only an arrangement of single words but also of traditional ritual augural collocations that Ennius appears to have taken great pains to emphasize.

Pulcerrima Praepes in the *Augurium Romuli*

The pairings of *praepes* and *pulcer* in the *Annals* demonstrate all the qualities of a ritual collocation, with one crucial exception: there is no direct evidence outside the *Annals* for the collocation. Although Gellius quotes two collocations of *praepes* and *pulcer* (7.6), both quotations of the collocation are from the *Annals.* Moreover, the context of these quotations in Gellius is a discussion of the augural connotations of the single word *praepes,* not the pairing of *praepes* and *pulcer.* Nevertheless, forms of *praepes* and *pulcer* form a syntagm three times in the *Annals,* a relatively high frequency of the collocations of the two roots that suggests a formulaic expression.

If *praepes pulcer* was not a traditional collocation, the repetition of the collocation of the two words in the *augurium Romuli* nevertheless gives the impression that there is an underlying formulaic expression that Ennius has transformed in two different instances within the passage. In the first pairing of forms of *praepes* and *pulcer,* the bird seen from the sky is not simply *pulcer praepes* but rather *pulcerrima praepes.* The second apparent transformation reverses the order of the *pulcerrima praepes* and inserts the pronoun *sese* between the two substantives: *praepetibus sese pulcrisque locis dant.* A single *-que* binds the two elements of the collocation, perhaps to offset the intrusion of *sese* into what is otherwise a unit. There is, in fact, a third instantiation of the collocation in the *Annals* used to describe the harbor in Brundisium (*Ann.* 457, discussed immediately below). The collocation of the roots *praepes* and *pulcer* therefore behaves like a traditional collocation in terms of frequency within the fragments of the *Annals.*

The collocation of the epithets *praepes* and *pulcer* is stable. This combination of adjectives, however, modifies three different but related entities. The first occurrence describes the bird, and the second, the place where the bird is sighted. If the shift is in keeping with the importance accorded to where the bird appears in augural practice, then the fact that Ennius transfers the epithet from an augural space to a geographical space in the third instantiation of an underlying *pulcer praepes(que)* may indicate that he is extending a traditional use of the collocation for a location in the sky to a less elevated space:

> Brundisium pulcro praecinctum praepete portu (*Ann.* 457)
>
> Brundisium belted by a beautiful fair haven. (trans. Warmington)

Because *praepes* seems to mean something like "of good omen" in the passage from the *Annals,* the meaning can apply to a bird or to where it appears to the augur without much change of meaning, but to call a harbor *praepes,* "fair" or "of good omen," is one remove from "favorable" (place to sight a bird). In order for such a semantic stretch to be effective, Ennius' audience would have had to be familiar with the phrase. Whether that familiarity comes from attending the taking of auspices or from seeing the phrase in the *Annals* is, at present, an open question.

Praepes in the Roman Augural Tradition

However traditional the collocation of *pulcer* and *praepes* may be, Festus and Gellius identify *praepes* as an augural term in its own right. Because *praepes* is collocated with *avis* in Gellius and Festus, *praepes / . . . avis* in Ennius is likely a traditional collocation. Moreover, the collocation may be amplified to three words: *avis praepes (praeter)volare,* a phrase with at least a passing similarity to *praepes / laeva volavit avis* in Ennius. *Praepetes aves* are the implied subjects of *praetervolant* in both Festus and Gellius. The latter cites the authority of Julius Hyginus:

> Nam "praepetes" inquit "aves ab auguribus appellantur, quae aut opportune praevolant aut idoneas sedes capiunt." (GEL. 7.6.6)
>
> "For *praepes* birds," (Hyginus) says, "are so called by the augurs because they fly by at the right moment or take up a safe position."

> Praepetes aves quidam dici aiunt quia secundum auspicium faciant praetervolantes. (FEST. p. 205M)
>
> Some say that these birds are called *praepes* because they make the augury favorable by flying by.

The placement of *praetervolare* in a relative clause and the plural subject in Gellius and in Festus may indicate that both authors obtained their information from a common source.

Because Festus and Hyginus agree that the *praepes* birds fly by (*praetervolare*), the verb *praevolant* may disguise a more traditional *praetervolant* in Apollonaris Sulpicius, another authority quoted by Gellius, who collocates *praepetes* and *aves* in an augural context:

> "praepetes" sibi videri esse alites, quas Homerus panypterygas appellaverit, quoniam istas potissimum augures spectarent, quae ingentibus alis patulae atque porrectae praevolarent. (GEL. 7.6.12)
>
> "*Praepes* birds" seemed to him to be those birds which Homer called *panyptergae,* since augurs looked for those especially that flew by straight and with great wings open.

Whether or not Sulpicius' *praevolant* is, in fact, to be understood as a mistake for *praetervolant,* Hyginus, Sulpicius, and Festus all collocate the same roots as Ennius' *praepes / laeva volavit avis* with the exception of *laeva.*

The discussions of augural terminology and *praepes / laeva volavit avis* not only collocate the same roots (*avis, praepes, volare*) but similar alliterative patterns, too. The sequence *praepes avis praetervolat* (or *praevolant*) contains the jingling collocation *praepes . . . praeter-*. Although it lacks the same sound effects, *praepes / laeva volavit avis* has its own pattern of assonance (*praepes / laeva volavit avis*), which is not far different from *praepes avis praetervolat*. There are other, more extensive alliterative patterns that manifest themselves in Gellius' discussion, including ***p**raepetes inquit aves ab auguribus appellantur, quae aut opportune **p**raevolant* and ***p**atulae atque **p**orrectae **p**raevolarent*. It is therefore possible that Ennius has appropriated both the individual roots from the traditional language of augury and the assonance that characterized this discourse by adding *laeva*, perhaps to soften the loss of an underlying *praetervolare* that traditionally alliterated with *praepes*.

More evidence, this time from Nigidius Figulus, another augural authority cited by Gellius, suggests that *praepes / laeva volavit avis* in Ennius is an allusion to a traditional augural collocation. According to Nigidius, *aves praepetes* are birds that *altius sublimisque volant*, "fly higher and elevated" (GEL. 7.6.11), a near match for the phrase condensed into the compound *altivolantum* in *Annals* 76. Furthermore, the phrase *ex alto* is separated from *praepes* by only two words in line 87, perhaps as a demonstration of the poet's control of his "source text." *Annals* 86–87 may therefore reflect an expansion of *avis praepes* (*praeter*) *volare: (Et simul ex) alto (longe pulcerrima) praepes / (laeva) volavit avis.*

Because the number of elements in the augural collocation and the Ennian expression also exceeds the usual two constituents of a traditional collocation, it strengthens the probability that the resemblance is not accidental. Ennius and Nigidius Figulus both use *praepes, avis, altum,* and *volare* together in an augural context. Neither *avis* nor *volare* nor *altum* is likely to attract much attention by itself, but the combination of the two words with *praepes*, a word that engendered discussion in later sources because of its augural connotations, may have triggered a recollection that all four roots occur together in the language of augury. The same principle holds for the correspondences between Ennius, Festus, Hyginus (*apud* Gellius), and Sulpicius (*apud* Gellius). The higher the number of correspondences, the more likely it is that the audience of the *Annals* would have perceived this combination of lexemes as an appropriation of an augural collocation.

If *alto . . . volavit* is, by itself, an allusion to an augural collocation of *altum* and *volare*, then Ennius may also be drawing attention to that fact by yet another ring bounded by *altivolantum* and *ex alto . . . volavit*. The word *alto* is also deployed at the beginning of the fragment in the line immediately preceding *altivolantum,* and the prepositional phrase *ex alto* then appears five lines from the end of the passage:

> . . . solus avem servat. At Romulus pulcer in **alto** 75
> quaerit Aventino, servat genus **alti-volantum**
>
> Et simul ex **alto** longe pulcerrima praepes
> laeva **volavit** avis. 86

Ennius not only adds another element to the ring composition, but the additional element also evokes the language of augury. If *praepes* and *altum volare* in fact constitute a ritual collocation, then this may be the motivation for two interlocking rings bounded by forms of *alto volare* and **praepes pulcerque:*

> . . . quaerit Aventino, servat genus **altivolantum**[a] 76
>
> Et simul ex **alto**[a] longe **pulcerrima praepes**[b] 86
> laeva **volavit**[a] avis. Simul aureus exoritur sol
> cedunt de caelo ter quattuor corpora sancta
> avium **praepetibus**[b] sese **pulcrisque**[b] locis dant.

The repetition of *avis* in a grammatical relationship with *pulcerrima praepes* and *praepetibus . . . pulcrisque* is a third element of the boundary of the ring; it is also suggestive of a formulaic connection between *avis, pulcer,* and *praepes.*

The Twin Suns of the *Augurium Romuli*

Because Nigidius identifies the opposite term of *praepes* as *infera,* another layer of meaning may be added to the passage. At *Annals* 84, Ennius describes the descent of a *sol albus* that returns *in infera noctis.* It may not be coincidental that Ennius uses the augural antonym of *praepes.* Although the primary meaning of *infera* in the passage must be "nether regions" (i.e., the underworld),[11] the augural "source text" implies a "ritual variant" that has a bird of Remus enter an unfavorable region of the sky rather than the sun descend into the nether regions. If *infera* refers the audience to an unfavorable omen, then the term may also index its outcome: the death of Remus.

In spite of its corruption, the manuscript tradition of the *De Divinatione* may add another layer of meaning to *infera noctis.* Skutsch's text reads *Remus auspicio sedet atque secundam* at the end of line 74, but the manuscripts of the *De Divinatione* (and the text of Flores)[12] all have a form of the verb *devovere* instead of *sedet,* a verb with specific associations with ritual and chthonic deities such as the *di manes* (LIV. 8.9.8) and the root of *devotio,* the act of consecrating oneself to the gods of the dead in exchange for the lives of others. If Skutsch's emendation is correct, *devovere* may have been added early in the manuscript tradition in anticipation of *infera noctis* (*Ann.* 84) and, in turn, may be an indication that someone, perhaps Cicero himself, understood *infera* as a reference to Remus' fated end.[13] T. P. Wiseman, who retains *se devovet* in his quotation of the fragment, asks in passing if there was a version of the story that had Remus "make a deal with the gods of the underworld," and if the answer is "yes"[14] then *infera noctis* and the presence of *devovere* in the manuscript tradition would suggest that the former expression is also an allusion to this particular variant of the myth.

The slippage between the expected *avis infera* and the sun that descends into *infera noctis* and, in turn, between Remus and his unfavorable bird may be grounds for equating Remus with the setting sun and Romulus with the rising sun that follows so quickly in the passage. Because the adjective *solus* is applied to Remus, and because Varro (*L.* 5.68) and Cicero (*N. D.* 2.68) derive *sol* from *solus,* one of the *soles* may be a symbol for Remus and the other for Romulus. This symbolism would not only explain the presence of a *sol albus* and a *sol aureus* in the same context, it would also forecast that only a single brother (i.e., *solus*) will be standing in the end. Moreover, Romulus recognizes that the auspices have confirmed his possession of *regni . . . scamna solumque.* In spite of the difference in vowel quality between the adjective *solus* and the noun *solum,* their phonetic similarity is patent. They would have looked identical save the endings in writing. In sum, given the obvious care that Ennius has taken in composing this passage, it is unlikely that two words so similar in sound have been accidentally deployed in association with each twin.

The two suns in the passage, the white (*albus*) and the golden (*aureus*), have troubled commentators for centuries.[15] Although the primary meaning of *sol albus recessit in infera noctis* could be taken as a setting sun, the rising sun that follows almost immediately creates a number of problems for such an interpretation. It is possible that the two suns in Ennius allude to an appearance of two suns in the sky, a prodigy that occurred from time to time.[16] The fact that the golden sun rises and the white sun moves to the lower regions, however, does not give the impression that both suns were in the sky at the same time. Even if such an interpretation could be sustained, it still leaves unanswered the question of why Ennius would have two suns in the passage. Whatever the two suns are doing in the narrative, the phonetic similarities of *sol—solus* in association with Remus and *solum* with Romulus—may indicate that the two suns are symbolic of the two *sons,* Romulus and Remus.

This slippage between the brothers and the twin suns is only one example of the semantic slippage that occurs elsewhere in the passage. Whether the phrase *auspicio augurioque* refers to a single ritual act or whether they express discrete practices, for example, *auspicium* and *augurium* are so similar semantically and phonetically that the two were "confused in everyday Latin," as Linderski observes.[17] The names of Romulus and Remus are also so similar that they suggest that it is difficult to distinguish the mythical twins from one another. This difficulty is given verbal expression in the potential names of the new city, each based on the name of a twin: *Romam Remoramne.* The individual collocations of *auspicio augurioque* and *Romam Remoramne* therefore reflect the central problem of the passage: how to decide between entities that are not identical but very similar.

Ennius also partially obscures the difference between Remus and another inauspicious augural term by hinting at an etymological connection between the name Remus and *remores aves*, a sign that indicates that the proposed action should be put off for another time by the auspicant. The potential name for the future city derived from Remus is Remora. The name of this hypothetical city implies a derivation of the name Remus from *remori,* "to delay," a derivation that, in turn, implies a connection between Remus and the *remores aves,* even though Ennius never uses the term *remores* in the passage. The similarity of Remus and Remora to *remores aves* may have invited the audience to make a connection between Remus and the *sol albus* that moves toward the *infera noctis.* Both *inferus* and *remores* are inauspicious augural terms in a passage where augury is the dominant mode of system reference. Moreover, Romulus is conflated with his own favorable birds. Because one of the birds that Romulus observes is *pulcerrima praepes,* not to mention the fact that the region where he observes twelve birds is also *pulcer praepes, Romulus pulcer* (*Ann.* 75) may also partially elide the difference between Romulus and his augural birds.

Signa de Caelo: Cedunt de Caelo and the Language of Celestial Prodigies

Although augury is the primary mode of ritual system reference in the passage, there are different forms of taking omens in the fragment besides the observation of birds (*de avibus*), such as the observation of prodigies (*de caelo*). A comment made by Servius Auctus identifies the phrase *de caelo* as an augural term that is different from *de avibus:*

> Servare enim et de caelo et de avibus verbo augurum dicitur (*ad Aen.* 6.198)
>
> For *servare* is said of the sky and the birds in the language of augurs.

Paulus ex Festo also lists augural signs that are *ex caelo* and *ex avibus* as two of five separate categories of omens (PAUL. *Fest.* p. 262M):

> Quinque genera signormum observant augures: ex caelo, ex avibus, ex tripudis, ex quadripedibus, ex diris.
>
> Augurs look out for five kinds of signs: from the sky, from birds, from *tripudii,* from quadrupeds and from ominous things.

The prepositional phrase *de caelo* in the Ennian fragment (*Ann.* 88) may therefore be a traditional collocation.

More often *de caelo* appears as the nucleus of another ritual collocation: *servare de caelo.*[18] The collocation occurs in Cicero and Gellius in the context of searching the sky for omens. Cicero employs several variations. He writes, for example, to Atticus: *Bibulus* <u>*de caelo tum servasset*</u> (*Att.* 2.16.2), and he asks in the second Philippic: *quisnamne divinare potest quid viti in auspiciis futurum sit nisi qui* <u>*de caelo servare*</u> *constituit?* (*Phil.* 2.81). Gellius explicitly states that the phrase *ne quis magistratus minor* <u>*de caelo servasse*</u> *velit* is written *ex vetere forma perpetua* (GEL. 13.15.1). Because Ennius employs *de caelo* and two forms of the verb *servare* in the passage, it is possible that he is alluding to the collocation *servare de caelo. De caelo* is, however, separated from the last *servat* by eleven lines, and it would take an extremely vigilant reader to collocate *servat* with *de caelo* across such a gulf. In sum, the audience could perceive an allusion to *servare de caelo,* even though the distance between *de caelo* and *servat* in Ennius did not likely encourage such an interpretation.

Cicero's *Marius* and the *Augurium Romuli*

If an allusion to *servare de caelo* is unlikely, *cedunt de caelo* may be an allusion to *de caelo delapsum,* a technical term used for divine epiphanies (CIC. *Har.* 62, CIC. *Man.* 41 11.24, and VERG. *A.* 5.772, etc.), prodigies that fall from the sky, like a torch (FRON. *Str.* 1.12.6), arms (LUC. 9.474–75), and a statue or *signum* (CIC. *Phil.* 11.24). Linderski has also noted the semantic similarity of *cedunt de caelo,* among other verbal parallels, to the verbal noun *lapsu* in Cicero's account of an augural sign observed by Marius in a fragment of his eponymous poem:[19]

> Hanc ubi praepetibus pinnis lapsuque volantem
> conspexit Marius, divini numinis augur
> faustaque signa suae laudis reditusque notavit,
> partibus intonuit caeli Pater ipse sinistris (fr. 17.9–12)

> When Marius, the augur of divine will, caught sight of it (the bird) with its feathers flying straight ahead and flying while gliding, he marked the favorable signs of his glory and return, the father himself thundered in the left quadrant.[20]

The fact that the Ciceronian fragment is followed immediately by the Ennian *augurium Romuli* in the *De Divinatione* (1.105–8) implies that Cicero perceived a relationship between the two passages, which may suggest in turn that Cicero's *lapsu* indicates that he understood *cedunt de caelo* in Ennius to be an allusion to the collocation *de caelo delapsum.*

If *lapsu* is an allusion to *cedunt de caelo,* it would not be the only one in the passage from Cicero's poem. *Volantem* could be a faint echo of *genus altivolantum* in the *Annals,* and *praepetibus pinnis* is a stronger echo of *pulcerimma praepes,* as implied by Linderski.[21] Cicero's *conspexit* also matches Ennius' *conspicit.* The arrangement of the key words *praepetibus, pinnis, volantem,* and *sinistris* may also be indicative of a literary debt to Ennius. *Volantem* at the end of the ninth and *sinistris* at the end of the twelfth line of the Ciceronian fragment may recall *laeva volavit avis* in Ennius, perhaps triggered by *praepetibus pinnis* in the first line. Given that *lapsu* is immediately preceded and followed by allusions to the diction of the *augurium Romuli,* a connection to *cedunt de caelo* in the mind of Cicero is possible.

It may be significant that the verbal echoes of Ennius in the *Marius* are all ritual terms and collocations that I have already discussed. The proximity of *praepetibus* to *volantem* and the repetition of the initial *p-* of Ennius' *pulcer* in Cicero's *pinnis* and of the initial *l-* of Ennius' *laeva* in Cicero's *lapsu* also suggests that Cicero had *praepes / laeva volavit avis* in mind when he composed this part of his poem. If Cicero is, in fact, alluding to the Ennian phrase, then he may also be alluding to the collocation of *avis praepes alt- volare* that I proposed above. Whether Cicero and Ennius are both alluding to these traditional collocations or Cicero is alluding to Ennius, however, must remain an open question. The parallels between Cicero and Ennius are therefore of a different order than those between Ennius and the augural experts like Hyginus and Nigidius Figulus.

The two explicitly separate omens in Cicero, a bird and thundering, or *signa de caelo* and *de avibus,* may also be a recognition of an implicit prodigy embedded in the augury in the *Annals.* Because *tacta de caelo,* "struck by lightning," is the most frequent extension of *de caelo* in the extant sources, Cicero may have understood the phrase *de caelo* as an allusion to a prodigy that accompanied the augury of Romulus. Whether or not Ennius is hinting that there was a lightning strike during the contest, three sources mention one in connection with the founding of Rome by Romulus, even though only the late antique *Origo Gentis Romanae* places the lightning strike during the augural contest. Moreover, the verbal echoes of Cicero in the *Origo* could reflect a traditional narrative of the *augurium Romuli* that included a lightning strike that Cicero alludes to and that the *Origo* simply appropriates in its proper place. If Cicero understood *de caelo* as a reference to *signum de caelo,* specifically a thunderbolt, then other readers of the *Annals* too may have understood *cedunt de caelo* as an oblique reference to a variant of the myth of Romulus and Remus.

If thunder or lightning was not a traditional element of the augural contest at the time of Ennius, it was part of the overall foundation story by the late Republic. Although Ovid implies that the augural contest took place some days before the setting of the boundaries of the new city,[22] he mentions that Jupiter gave his assent for the latter ceremony *tonitru . . . laevo,* "with thunder on the left," and with lightning (*F.* 4.833). Dionysius places a flash of lightning (ἀστραπή) after the *augurium* and after the boundaries are set in order to communicate divine approval of the kingship of Romulus (DH 2.5.1–2). The *Origo Gentis Romanae* actually has the thunder and lightning appear as the twelve vultures appear to Romulus (23.3). Even if the order of events in the *Origo* is a misreading of earlier sources, the phrase *cedunt de caelo,* appears to be a proleptic reference to the traditional presence of thunder in the foundation story of Rome.

In spite of its lateness, however, the *Origo Gentis Romanae* echoes Cicero's Marius in such a way as to raise the possibility that thunder and lightning were a traditional element of the augural contest. In the *Origo* a flash of lightning and thunder accompany the twelve vultures. The wording of the *Origo* (*caeli fulgore pariter tonitruque* [23.3]) is characterized by three of the same roots as the description of the thunder in Cicero (*partibus intonuit caeli Pater ipse sinistris*). Although the verbal parallels could be accidental, the *Origo* echoes a specific phrase from a poetic passage quoted in tandem with Ennius' version of the *augurium,* an arrangement that may not have been fortuitous on Cicero's part. If the anonymous author of the *Origo* has not chosen his words at random or intuited a connection between the Marius passage and the Ennian *augurium* because of their placement in the *De Divinatione*, then Cicero may be alluding to a phrase from a traditional narrative that served as the source of the version of events in the *Origo*. Even if such a hypothesis at present lies beyond verification, the thunderbolt is at the very least a misplaced traditional element of the story.

The reference to a different kind of divination in the narration of a specific form of divination such as augury is similar to an allusion to a mythic variant in the narration of another version of a myth, a characteristic feature of Alexandrian poetry that I have already discussed above. If *cedunt de caelo* is an allusion to the thunder omen, Ennius alludes to an omen that existed in other versions of the story, even though he does not incorporate it into his version. Moreover, the allusion to a different version of the story of Romulus and Remus imitates the Alexandrian practice much more closely than the play between variant outcomes of the augural rite.

Cedunt de Caelo and *De Caelo Cecidisse*

Cedunt de caelo also resembles the phrase (*de*) *caelo cecidisse* (LIV. 22.1.9, 41.9.5), a collocation that denotes *signa de caelo* in Livy twice, along with a variant *cecidere caelo* (1.31.3). Julius Obsequens, who collected omens from Livy's narrative of 249 to 12 BCE in a separate work, describes signs that fell from the sky in 140 BCE: *Praeneste et in Cephallenia signa de caelo cecidisse visa,* yielding a fourth example of *caelo cecidisse* from Livy. The fact that the phrase appears four times in similar contexts suggests that *caelo cecidisse* was part of the formulaic language of omens. Obsequens also employs the specific phrase *signa de caelo,* which has a technical coloring reminiscent of *genera signorum . . . ex caelo* in Festus (FEST. p. 262M, discussed above). Although stones are consistently the subjects of the verb in the phrase *caelo cecidisse* in Livy, the language of Obsequens suggests that the expression is appropriate for *signa de caelo* in general.

Cedunt in Ennius' *cedunt de caelo* is not, however, a finite form of the perfect infinitive *cecidisse,* "to have fallen," but rather of *cedisse,* "to have come." The substitution of *cedunt* for *cadunt,* the finite present form of *cecidisse,* could be due to metrical considerations, as the root vowel in *cedunt* is long, while that of *cadunt* is short (neither *cadunt de caelo* nor *cecidere de caelo* is possible at the beginning of a hexameter line). Because *cadunt de caelo* could be placed in other positions in the hexameter other than the beginning of the line, however, meter alone is not a sufficient explanation for the substitution of *cedunt* for *cadunt*. If *cedunt de caelo* is an allusion to *caelo cecidisse,* other circumstances must have prompted the decision to alter the traditional collocation. Whether or not the similarity of *cedunt de caelo* and *cadunt de caelo* is deliberate, the phrase has the appearance of an elegant and playful allusion rather than a simple appropriation of a traditional collocation, a pattern that has occurred time and again throughout my study.

Whatever the motivation for substituting *cedunt* for *cadunt* may have been, the phonetic and contextual similarity of *cedere de caelo* and *caelo cadere* suggests that Ennius is complicating the narrative by adding a "prodigal" variant from the discourse of sky signs to the *signa de avibus* and also by alluding to a type of omen that is not auspicious. In book 1, Livy uses *cecidere caelo* to describe stones falling from the sky that come before a plague (1.31.3). In book 22, the falling of stones precedes the loss of 15,000 soldiers in the disaster at Lake Trasimene (22.1.9). Because two Livian contexts of *caelo cecidisse* suggest that the phrase was used to describe troubling, if not dire, omens, *cedunt de caelo* may have added some extra semantic weight to the omen of the birds in Ennius by virtue of its close resemblance to *cecidisse caelo.* Such an expression encodes what every reader of the *Annals* already knows: even if auguries take place every day in Rome and Italy, this particular ceremony is not an everyday event. It is, in fact, the most important augury in all of Roman history. The particular slippage between *signa de caelo* and *signa de avibus* enables the addition of more ritual weight and perhaps some ambiguity to an already weighty passage.

The Meaning of *Cedunt de Caelo* in the *Augurium Romuli*

Given that the consequences of stones falling from the sky in Livy can be catastrophic, Ennius appears to have inserted into this most important augury a traditional collocation for a type of omen that could be as dire as it is important. An allusion to a potentially bad omen during the *augurium Romuli* may also imply some ambivalence toward the foundation of Rome analogous to similar attitudes detected by other readers in Vergil and other Augustan poets toward Augustus.[23] Because Ennius was not originally Roman but a citizen of Rudiae, a settlement located in Magna Graecia, a part of Italy that only within the previous century had come under Roman sway, there may have been some lingering resentment among its citizens pressed into military service. If ambivalence toward the foundation of Rome in the *Annals* on the part of Ennius is too radical an idea, it could be said that the ambivalence is toward the monarchy that

Romulus will found rather than Rome itself, or toward the civil strife that will emerge from the disagreement between Romulus and Remus over the omen.

If *cedunt de caelo* implies a negative omen, then the description of the omen in negative terms may also be a very subtle example of the "other voices" in the *Annals* posited by Jacqueline Elliott.[24] Although the Romans viewed the outcome of the augural contest between Romulus and Remus as favorable, other peoples like the Etruscans may have thought otherwise. As a native of a part of Italy that had been subject to Roman hegemony for not even two generations when he was born, Ennius himself may not have viewed the spread of Roman power as an entirely positive outcome. It is even possible that the verbal echo of *cecidere caelo* is something of a Freudian slip. The ambiguity of *cedunt de caelo* does not necessitate reading the *Annals* as a subversive text, but the presence of potentially negative augural language in an epic that ostensibly celebrates the achievements of the Roman people is a further validation of Zetzel's warning that Cicero may have oversimplified and distorted the nature of the *Annals.*[25]

It is also possible that some ambivalence toward the founding of Rome had been appropriated into the tradition from elsewhere. Because *cedunt de caelo* implies a *signum de caelo,* a type of omen that was an Etruscan specialty, it would be interesting to know how an Etruscan *fulgurator* might interpret such an omen.[26] It so happens that a Greek translation of a Latin translation of an Etruscan brontoscopic calendar, a list of interpretations of lightning strikes on different days of the year, made by Nigidius Figulus gives the *interpretatio Etrusca* for thunder on April 21st, the traditional day of the founding of Rome:

> Εἰ βροντήσῃ, τοῖς μὲν καρποῖς δεξιόν, τῇ δὲ πολιτείαι πόλεμον σημαίνει.
>
> If it thunders, it signifies good fortune for the crops, yet war for the state.[27]

In a sense, the Etruscan calendar predicts the outcome of the contest accurately, provided that the quarrel between Romulus and Remus qualifies as a civil war. It is possible that the Romans were aware of the Etruscan interpretation of a mythical thunderclap on the day of the foundation of Rome and made it a part of the tradition. If *cedunt de caelo* is suggestive of a sky sign such as thunder, and I think it is, it may foreshadow a number of things: the "civil war" between Romulus and Remus, the future prosperity of the Roman state, and, perhaps, an outcome that may not be a wholly positive result for those who came under the sway of Rome.

The significance of sky signs and their Etruscan character in the *Annals* is also implied in a fragment from book 3, perhaps a description of Tanaquil searching the sky for and receiving an omen to learn the significance of the flame above the head of Servius Tullius:[28]

> Olli de caelo laevom dedit inclutus signum (*Ann.* 146)
>
> The All-glorious sent down one day from the sky a favorable sign. (trans. Warmington)

The fragment reprises three other words from the *augurium Romuli: laeuum, dedit,* and *signum.* Because none of these words is especially rare or striking, however, these parallels may be the result of their common content rather than any perceived relationship. At the very least, the fragment gives an example of the technical term *signum de caelo* in Ennius. If Tanaquil is in fact the subject, then the fragment is also further testimony for the general reputation of the Etruscans as interpreters of *signa de caelo.*

To return to the placement of thunder and lightning in the overall foundation narrative of the city of Rome, even a proleptic allusion to such a *signum de caelo* changes the very meaning of the foundation in augural terms. In other words, even the merest hint that it thundered on the day of the augural contest would change the date of the thunder and thereby the meaning of the omen. If it had occurred any day after the contest, as Dionysius and Ovid would have it, then it would not mean war for the state but rather outcomes such as the destruction of flies or rain helpful for the sprouting time. To be clear, I am not claiming that Ennius had mastered the art of Etruscan brontoscopy. I am, however, suggesting that Ennius was aware of the traditional exegesis surrounding the foundation story that would have included what a thunderbolt would have meant on that day according to the Etruscans. Because thunder on the twenty-fourth of April predicts "discord among those in power," this prediction may also have been discussed in relation to Romulus and Remus.

Avem Servat: Ennius and the Umbrian Tradition

Although *servare* is an element of the Latin expression *servare de caelo,* it is also part of another collocation more appropriate to the augural context in Ennius: *auspicia servare.* Varro's use of the same phrase in an augural context the *De Lingua Latina* is the most salient evidence for the collocation:

> Ut nostri augures publici disserunt, agrorum sunt genera quinque: Romanus, Gabinus, peregrinus . . . Romanus dictus unde Roma ab Rom<ul>o; Gabinus

ab oppido Gabiis; peregrinus ager pacatus, qui extra Romanum et Gabinum, quod uno modo in his serv<a>ntur auspicia; (*L.* 5.33)

As our public Augurs discuss, there are five kinds of fields: Roman, Gabinian, foreign . . . The Roman was named after Romulus whence the name Rome, the Gabinian from the town of Gabii, a foreign field is one conquered and pacified, which is outside the Roman and Gabian territory, because in those fields the auspices are observed in one single way.

As is clear from the text, Varro is describing a technical discussion among augurs concerning the types of territories where auspices are taken. The phrase *auspicia servanto* also appears twice in Cicero's *De Legibus,* once in the context of the inception of public business by a magistrate and once as a quotation of Cicero's fictitious law (*Leg.* 3.11 and 3.43):[29]

"Auspicia servanto, auguri publico parento." (*Leg.* 3.11 and 3.43)

"They shall observe the auspices and obey the State augur."

In spite of the artificial nature of Cicero's proposed law, the similarities between Varro and Cicero are best explained by a traditional augural collocation of *auspicia* and *servare.* If *auspicia servare* is, in fact, a traditional augural collocation, then the proximity of *auspicio* and *servat* may have been enough to evoke *auspicia servare,* even though Ennius does not explicitly collocate the two roots.

Although *auspicia servare* is very likely a traditional augural collocation, there is, in fact, a striking similarity between *avem servat* and the Umbrian phrase **aves anzeriates,** "after the birds are observed," a similarity that may indicate that *avem servat* is also a traditional ritual collocation (as always, Umbrian forms in the native alphabet are written in bold, and Umbrian forms in the Latin alphabet in italics).[30] Out of the eleven occurrences of the Umbrian word **aves,** "birds," a root that is cognate with Latin *avis,* ten of them are collocated with a form of the Umbrian cognate of Latin *servare,* such as **anzeriates** above. *Avif* the accusative plural of Umbrian **aves,** is almost always the direct object of *anseriato* or, in one case, the simplex form *seritu* (both "observe"). Even in the one occurrence of *avif* without *anzeriato* or *seriato,* the verb is implied (Rix Um 1 VIa 18). In the remaining instantiations of the collocation, **aves,** the ablative plural form, is collocated with **anzeriates,** the ablative plural of the past passive participle of *anseriato.* There are therefore two basic variants on an underlying combination of the roots of **aves** and **anzeriates.** More importantly, the

Umbrian augural collocation is cognate with *avem servat,* a circumstance that may indicate that the phrase in Ennius is an instantiation of Latin traditional augural collocation that has not survived elsewhere.

In addition to the two basic variants of the Umbrian collocation, there is a longer form. The ceremony to purify the "Fisian Mount," an unidentified part of the territory of Iguvium, opens with a taking of the auspices that employs an expanded form of *avif anzeriato:*

> Stiplo. aseriaia. parfa. dersua. curnaco. Dersua / peico. mersto. peica. mersta. mersta. auuei. merst{.}a angla. esona. (Rix Um 1 VIa 2–3)

> Demand that I may observe a *parra* in the west, a crow in the west, a woodpecker in the east, a magpie in the east, in the east birds, in the east divine messengers.[31]

The longer and expanded variant that appears here in the sixth tablet stands in contrast to the terse instructions for the same ritual in the first tablet:

> **este: persklum: aves: anzeriates: enetu:** (Rix Um 1 Ia 1)

> Begin this ceremony after the birds have been observed.

However the relationship between the long and the short forms is explained, it is obvious that there is some relationship, since both forms occur in different versions of the same ritual.

Because the expanded Umbrian form is closely paralleled in Latin in two texts other than the *Annals,* one from the *Asinaria* of Plautus and one from Festus, the long form in Latin and in Umbrian may date back to the central Italian *koinê* period. Both Plautus and Festus collocate several species of augural birds so similar to the Umbrian list quoted above that these parallels are not likely to be accidental. Although the parallel long forms do not prove that *avem servare* is an augural expression in Latin, they are so close as to warrant further exploration of the possibility that *avem servat* and **aves anzeriates** are instantiations of a common Italic traditional collocation.

The first Latin parallel to the Umbrian long form is in the *Asinaria* of Plautus. The slave Libanus, who has been charged with the task of defrauding his master's rich wife of twenty *minae,* declares his readiness to undertake his assignment:

> Impetritum, inauguratumst: quovis admittunt aves,
> picus et cornix ab laeva, corvos, parra ab dextera
> consuadent; (*As.* 259–61)

> It is settled and confirmed. The birds allow it wherever I look. A woodpecker and a crow to the left, the raven and the *parra* on my right urge me on.

The sequence of birds is very similar to the series of birds in the expanded Umbrian expression quoted above. *Picus* and *parra* in Plautus and Umbrian *peico* (and *peica*) and *parfa* are reflexes of the same Italic roots. The resemblance of *curnaco* to *cornix* is also indicative of a common root.[32] Whereas *corvos* and *parra* appear on the right (*ab dextera*), the Umbrian *parfa* and *curnaco* are qualified with the directional adjective *dersua: parfa dersua curnaco dersua* (Rix Um 1 VIa 3). If *dersua* is equivalent to *ab dextra,* then *mersta* is very likely the Umbrian parallel to *ab laeva.*[33] Libanus sees a *picus* on the left and the Umbrian *peica* and *peico* are modified by a word that may mean left: *peico mersto peica mersta* (Rix Um 1 VIa 3).

Although Libanus does not observe a *pica* and a *picus, cornix* and *corvos* generate an alliterative pair that combines with *picus* and *parra* to form a chiastic arrangement of alliterative pairs (if the prepositional phrases are removed):

Picus,			parra
	et cornix,	corvos	
		ab laeva	ab dextera.
= (P + C)		+ (C + P)	

The alliterative pattern creates an impression that *picus* and *parra* and *cornix* and *corvos* are pairs, even though the *picus* is grammatically paired with the *cornix* and the *corvos* with the *parra,* a pattern not dissimilar to the Umbrian *parfa dersua curnaco dersua peico mersto peica mersta mersta* ***a****uuei mersta* ***an****gla esona.*

Poultney suggests that Plautus borrowed his list from the language of Umbrian augury,[34] but a similar passage found in Festus, also cited by Poultney, suggests that Plautus alludes to the language of Roman, not Umbrian, augury:

> Quod oris cantu significat quid portendi, cum cecinit corvus, cornix, noctua, parra picus . . . (FEST. p. 197M)

> Because (the bird) signifies that something is predicted by means of the song from its mouth, when the raven, the night bird, the crow, the *parra* or the woodpecker sing . . .

Because the order of birds in Festus differs from Plautus, and because a fifth bird is listed as opposed to the four birds in Plautus, it is unlikely that Festus is directly referring to Plautus. He is certainly not quoting him. All four birds named in the

Plautine passage are, nevertheless, present. Festus' arrangement of *corvus* and *cornix* and *parra* and *picus* in alliterative pairs may also indicate that Plautus' more complex chiastic arrangement is a transformation of an underlying arrangement of the birds into two alliterative pairs. Whether or not Plautus or Festus reflects the original configuration, the simplest explanation for the remarkable similarities between the two authors is a canonical list of augural birds.

The parallels between Plautus, Festus, and the Iguvine Tables appear to stem from a single list of augural birds of common Italic date. The fact that *picus* in Festus and Plautus matches two very similar terms in Umbrian, *peico* and *peica,* may indicate that *picus* is a conflation of *picus* and *pica* in the old Latin formulation. The *parra* and *cornix* of Festus and Plautus also recall the *parfa dersua* and the *curnaco dersua* of the Iguvine Tables. Moreover, the length of all three versions reaches four words at minimum, even though there is no agreement on the fourth bird. In the Plautine and Umbrian versions, the amplitude increases to six with the addition of words for left and right. In sum, accidental resemblance seems the least likely explanation for such extensive verbal echoes.

If there is a single origin for the augural long form in Umbrian and Latin, then the phrase *avem servat* in Ennius and its cognate expressions in the Iguvine Tables may also have a single origin. *Servat* is not a compound form, as it almost always is in Umbrian, but there are a number of ways to account for the missing prefix. If Cicero quotes these lines from memory, as most ancient authors were wont to do, he could have simply misremembered. Even if Cicero has not misquoted Ennius, the pronunciation of *avem servat* would not differ much from *avem asservat,* nor *Aventino servat* from *Aventino asservat.* The single use of *seriatu* with *avif* in the Iguvine Tables (Rix Um 1 VIb 48–49) may also indicate some wavering between the compound and the simplex form of the verb in the related collocation in Umbrian, and perhaps in common Italic. Because the language of Umbrian ritual is characterized by a tendency to create alliterative and assonant phrases, the alliteration of **aves anzereriates** and its various manifestations could also be an Umbrian embellishment of a common Italic ritual utterance that did not alliterate.[35] Whatever the differences between *avem servat* and phrases such as **aves anzereriates** may be, they are not as great as the similarities.

Because the parallels between Umbrian and Latin ritual language are not limited to these instances, the similarity between *avem servat* and **aves anzereriates** is not unique but rather part of a larger phenomenon. The Umbrian collocation *struśla* ficla, a common pair of sacrificial cakes (e.g., Um 1 VIa 59), for example, bears a striking similarity to collocations of two sacrificial cakes known as the *strues* and the *fertum* found in the *De Agricultura* (*Agr.* 141) and in Gellius (10.15.14), so much so that Brent Vine has suggested that the Umbrian and Latin expressions have a common origin.[36] Claude Sandoz connects the opaque Umbrian phrase **vestiçam** . . . **fiktu** (Um 1 Ia 28) to the phrase *panem depsticium,* "bread made by kneading," in Cato (*Agr.* 74).[37] In his prayer to Mars in the *De Agricultura,* Cato asks the god to "keep safe both shepherds and sheep" (*pastores pecuaque salva servassis* [*Agr.* 141]), an expression with more than a passing similarity to the Umbrian expression *viro. pequo . . . saluua. seritu,* "keep safe men and cattle" (e.g., Rix Um 1 VIa 42).[38] Not only are the semantic message and the context of both the Umbrian and Latin expressions the same; the Umbrian words *pequo, saluua,* and *seritu* are cognate with Latin *pecua, salva,* and *servassis.* Given that both the Romans and Umbrians were participants in the central Italian *koinê,* it is likely that these verbal parallels date to that era. If these parallels are, in fact, common Italic ritual collocations, it is possible that the relatively banal expression *avem servat* is another common Italic ritual collocation that is abundantly attested in Umbrian but not so in Latin.

Because so much effort has been exerted in adducing the Umbrian evidence for the traditional collocation of *avem* and *servat,* I emphasize that the audience of the *Annals* would have recognized *avem servat* as a collocation of *Latin* ritual. The audience of the *Annals* interpreted the ritual language in terms of its own horizons of expectation, not in terms of origins. In other words, it is possible that *avem servat* is a single survival of a phrase that at some point in the past was borrowed from Umbrian. It is equally possible that the Umbrian phrase was borrowed from Latin or that the phrase was generated in the ancestor of Umbrian and Latin and inherited into both languages. None of these possibilities, however, is relevant to my study. If *avem servare* had ritual connotations for the audience of the *Annals,* it is not important how the phrase became traditional, only that it was.

If the collocation *avem servat* is a traditional ritual collocation, then it would add still more layers of meaning to the *augurium Romuli.* In addition to adding to the already significant ritual coloring of the fragment, it would help elide the difference between the practice of augury in the second century BCE and the mythic foundation of Rome. Romulus and Remus would not simply be scanning the sky for birds but doing so in the same terms that augurs in the middle Republic would use for their own auguries. Moreover, *avem servare* may have been a specific step in the process of augury after the augur prepared for the ritual (*operam dare*) and before a bird was actually sighted. The use of specific terminology for consecutive actions in the augury may also have provided specific points for a plot map that could be followed in order to give some order to the passage.

Avem Specere, Auspicia Servare, and *Avem Servare* in the *Augurium Romuli*

Although I have identified the expression for beginning the ritual and suggested another for the scanning of the sky, I have yet to discuss the possible use of the terminology for sighting and interpreting the bird. Ennius employs the verb *conspicere* for this act. Linderski understands *conspicere* as an augural term that "denoted not only the act of observation but also the act of comprehension,"[39] an assertion that has some support in the ancient sources. Cicero employs the phrase *volantem conspexit* in an augural context in his poem on Marius (fr. 17.9–10). In the *Mostellaria,* Plautus also seems to be alluding to the use of *conspicere* in augury. Theopropides tells his slave Tranio: *nullam pictam conspicio hic avem* (*Mos.* 839). Moreover, verbs derived from the root of *conspicere* are employed twice more within five lines with *cornix* as an object (*Mos.* 835 [*conspicer*] and 837 [*conspicari*]). Although the context of this phrase is not the taking of auspices or divination of any sort, I have already suggested that the *cornix* as a bird of omen has a long history dating back to common Italic. Because the verb *auspicit* could have filled the same metrical slot as *conspicit,* and perhaps would have been a more elegant and emphatic commentary on the importance of *auspicium* to the passage, *conspicit* may have been the technical term for the sighting of the bird in the augural rite.

Whether or not *conspicere* had augural connotations, the simplex form *specere* explicitly did. Varro cites *specere* as an example of the survival of an older form of *spectare* "because the augurs even now say *avem specere*" (*L.L.* 6.82). The phrase *avem aspexit* in the fragments of Naevius (*Bell. Poen.* 25) may also be an allusion to the collocation *avem specere.* The object of *conspicit* in Ennius is not *avem,* but the acrostic arrangement that etymologizes *auspicio* (already discussed above) evokes the expected *avem* (*con*)*specere* without directly quoting it:

avium . . .
conspicit . . .
auspicio. . . .

If the phrase *conspicit inde sibi data Romulus esse* is an allusion to the phrase *avem* (*con*)*spicere,* then the audience likely expects *avem* to be the object of the line initial *conspicit,* only to be surprised by the indirect statement that follows instead.

Even if the acrostic *avium . . . conspicere . . . auspicio* is not an indirect allusion to the collocation of *avis* and *conspicere,* the *figura etymologica* is couched in an acrostic arrangement, a technique roughly parallel to the acrostic spellings of names and phrases in Hellenistic poetry. The first letters of lines 345–53 of Nicander's *Theriaca,* for example, spell out the name ΝΙΚΑΝΔΡΟΣ, but the *figura etymologica* in the *Annals* is not as sustained as in Nicander, nor does it spell out a name or phrase acrophonically. If *avium . . . conspicere . . . auspicio* is not a deliberate acrostic phrase, Ennius apparently did spell out his name acrostically in one of his poems. Cicero notes that he employed the acrostic Q. ENNIUS FECIT in *quibusdam Ennianis* (*Div.* 2.111). The use of etymological figures is a defining characteristic of the language of Italic ritual, as can be seen in phrases such as *bonas preces precor* in Cato (*Agr.* 139). The acrostic arrangement, however, could have been inspired by similar configurations in Greek poetry. If the acrostic phrase *avium . . . auspicio . . . conspicit* emulates Greek models, then it is also another hybrid of Greek and Italic elements, no matter how indirect the influence of the Greek practice of acrostic spellings may be here.

I acknowledge that I have adumbrated a number of possible traditional collocations rather than identified them and verified their existence, but my reading of the passage through an augural lens is based upon the combined weight of the evidence and not the individual collocations. Some of the collocations that I have discussed are demonstrably traditional ritual collocations, such as *operam dare . . . auspiciis* and *de caelo.* Many of the more hypothetical collocations consist of terms that also have demonstrably ritual connotations, such as *praepes* and *servare.* Moreover, forms of *specere* and *avis* are used to construct the ring composition that gives shape to the passage and were also the constituents of a traditional ritual collocation. However convincing or unconvincing any of the individual parts of my argument may be, the overall thesis that the language of augury colors and influences the interpretation of the *augurium* is supported by several features of the language of the text that are not hypothetical.

As I have demonstrated, the augural source text of the *augurium Romuli* seems to prompt, perhaps even compel, certain word choices in the passage to the point that they overpower, and occasionally obscure, the surface narrative of the mythical competition. One could object that a more skilled poet would have been able to negotiate such similar sequences without sacrificing the clarity of the story, but Ennius was perhaps not overly concerned with telling a basic story so well known to his audience. It is also possible that modern readers have missed the signposting by means of specific augural terminology for specific steps taken in the ritual that were the events of a different kind of story. Whether or not the language of augury has obscured some of the finer details of the story of Romulus and Remus, these traditional augural collocations, and even single signifiers with pronounced augural connotations, add new layers of meaning to an already meaningful Roman myth.

Although I emphasized the dialogue between the familiar and the foreign in the previous two chapters, a number of other negotiations take precedence in the *augurium*. The primary dialogue is between past and present. The most obvious manifestation of this negotiation is the extended simile that allows the middle Republican practice of chariot racing during annual *ludi* to intrude upon a contest between two mythical twins in the distant past. Because the passage is littered with traditional augural collocations of the middle Republic, the past and the present are mediated thematically and by means of diction. Most of these collocations point to a generally positive outcome for the foundation of Rome, but there are hints that the foundation of Rome will not bring welcome results to everyone, including Remus and the cities and peoples defeated in war and forced to submit to Rome, such as Ennius' own village of Rudiae.

If the mediation between past and present is central to the contest of Romulus and Remus, the encounter between the foreign and the familiar is still (re) enacted within the passage. The use of an extended simile is a characteristic feature of Homeric poetry that may have struck the audience of the *Annals* as foreign. Because Livius likely used extended similes in his translation of the *Odyssey*, however, the novelty of the extended simile may not have been as pronounced as other Greek elements such as the dactylic hexameter. Another element of the passage may evoke another culture that was at once familiar and foreign to the Romans. The hint of prodigies implies an interpretation of such omens, a form of divination that was still considered to be the province of Etruscan interpreters in the age of Ennius. Because the Roman *decemviri* and the Etruscan *haruspices* could disagree on the proper expiation after a storm overturned the *columna rostrata* in 172 BCE (LIV. 42.20.1–5), then this particular dialogue between Etruscan and Roman forms of divination must have been very current in the early second century BCE.[40]

Any Roman contemporary of Ennius would have known the story of Romulus and Remus and would probably be familiar with the basic sequence of events that took place during an augury. Although any Roman storyteller might import certain phrases that were uttered during the taking of auspices to impart some solemnity to the story and thus strengthen the connection between the past and present, Ennius has done more than simply adopt a phrase or two appropriate to the context. He has combined the various ritual and literary elements by means of simple formulaic phrases appropriate to an augural context (such as *dant operam* and *de caelo*) that lend a familiar but solemn ring to a passage that details a specific, if fictitious, performance of the augural rite. The effect is a temporary effacing of the differences between past and present and myth and ritual. It is inevitable that this superimposition of systems of meaning will call attention to their differences as much as to their similarities. The real achievement of the passage, however, is the general coherence and consistency of the message communicated by a variety of referential systems in order to ask how much one twin can really differ from another.

Ritual, Militia, *and History in Book 6 of the* Annals

To judge from the number and length of its fragments, book 6 of the *Annals* was especially popular with its ancient audience. Skutsch's edition assigns forty-two lines to book 6 distributed over nineteen fragments, a number of lines exceeded only by book 1 and book 8. Moreover, the only surviving papyrus of the *Annals* from Herculaneum contains fragmentary lines that are either assigned to book 6 of the *Annals* or to no particular book at all by the ancient sources. This discovery implies that the owner of the library, and possibly others, particularly enjoyed this part of the poem. Book 6 was so widely known that Cicero was able to quote its opening line to humorous effect while addressing a witness infelicitously named Sextus Annalis, "Sixth Annal" (QUINT. *Inst.* 6.3.86). If nothing else, as Elaine Fantham observes, the book was "obviously" the most read between the first book and the Punic War narrative.[1]

There is much in book 6 to recommend it to a Roman audience, and the reasons for its popularity may be observed even in its fragmentary state.[2] As Emma Dench suggests, Ennius' narrative of the struggle between Pyrrhus and Rome can be seen as an anti-*Iliad* that concludes with the satisfying defeat of a descendant of Achilles at the hands of the descendants of the defeated Trojans.[3] The narrative is populated with Roman *exempla* of every sort. Publius Decius Mus pronounces the dreaded ritual of *devotio* in order to save the lives of his soldiers (*Ann.* 191–93). Appius Claudius Caecus harshly berates the senate for considering peace with the enemy (*Ann.* 199–200) in a speech that Cicero has Cato the Censor quote from (*Sen.* 16). There is also Manius Curius Dentatus, the Roman commander who defeated Pyrrhus and who, according to Ennius, gave way neither to weapons nor money, *ferro . . . nec auro* (*Ann.* 456).

These *exempla* are not only stirring images of heroism in a defining moment of Roman history; they also represent the "distinctive moral and cultural values" of the Roman people, which Dench identifies as piety, austerity, and self-control.[4] Dentatus is a model of self-control, swayed by neither fear nor greed. Appius Claudius is austere in his refusal to negotiate a peace with the enemy. By consecrating himself as a sacrifice to the gods in exchange for victory, Decius Mus becomes the epitome of *pietas* toward the gods and the Roman people. Moreover, his decision to sacrifice himself in imitation of his father and grandfather may be seen as a form of filial piety. The actors in book 6 are therefore the living embodiment of the assertion made by Ennius in book 5 that the Roman state is founded upon *mores* and *viri: Moribus antiquis res stat Romana virisque* (*Ann.* 156), "On manners and on men of good old time stands firm the Roman State" (trans. Warmington). In sum, book 6 of the *Annals* was not simply a good story but also a morality tale that justified the eventual Roman victory in the Pyrrhic War.

As compelling as the deeds of the Roman collective must have been for the audience of the *Annals,* the character of Pyrrhus is the center of the narrative. Among the more substantial fragments of book 6 are his speech to a group of Roman envoys, the *devotio* of Decius Mus, an act performed in battle against Pyrrhus and a reference to his Pyrrhic victories expressed in the first person (*ego . . . vici victusque sum* [*Ann.* 182]). The two imitations of passages from the *Iliad* also center the action on the figure of Pyrrhus, who claimed to be a direct descendant of Achilles and who is called *Aeacida,* "descendant of Aeacus" (the father of Achilles), more than once in the fragments of book 6. As a descendant of Achilles, Pyrrhus is worthy of being the center of one of the most popular books of the *Annals.* The last word of the book is also apparently *Burrus,* the archaic Latin spelling of Pyrrhus.[5]

In a speech quoted and admired by Cicero (*Off.* 1.38), Pyrrhus expresses admirable generosity and unintentionally misuses the language of Roman ritual. The speech is charged with ritual suggestion that foreshadows Pyrrhus' eventual defeat and illustrates his inability to maintain the *pax deorum,* a key prerequisite for victory in the minds of the Romans. Even the seemingly innocuous reference to the "great gods" (*magnis dis*) displays an understandable but fatal ignorance of Roman ritual, since the collocation can refer to the Penates, who would certainly not be inclined to show favor to a hostile foreign power no matter how admirable. If the Penates were thought to have been carried by Aeneas from Troy to Italy in Ennius' day as in Vergil's, their attitude toward a descendant of Achilles and Neoptolemus would be especially negative. Pyrrhus' inadvertent collocation of two forms of *dare* both recalls the ritual collocation *donum dare* and highlights the lack of reciprocity in his speech, in contrast with the use of the *donum dare* in dedications to gods in exchange for help. Just as I have argued to be the case for the *augurium Romuli,* the language of ritual adds meaning and supports the thematic structure of Ennius' narrative of the Pyrrhic War.

If the use of ritual system reference was not enough to convince the audience of the *Annals* that Pyrrhus was doomed from the start, his misuse of the language of *militiae* in his speech further encourages such a conviction. The use of *accipere* and *dare* not only recalls the *deditio* the formal surrender of an enemy, yet another ominous sign for Pyrrhus, but also the collocations of *dare* and *cepere* that are sometimes found in the inscriptions of victorious Roman generals. Because Pyrrhus does the giving and the Romans do the taking in his speech, the "natural," reciprocal order of giving to a god in exchange for help after taking a city or territory by force is disturbed. Even worse for him, he gives to mortal men and not the gods, even as he acknowledges the "great gods." If his reference to *Era Fors,* "Mistress Fortune," in close proximity to *virtute* is an allusion to the collocation *vera virtus,* "true courage," as I hope to demonstrate, then Pyrrhus has misquoted still another traditional tenet of Roman *militiae.*

The language of Pyrrhus' speech misappropriates the language of Roman ritual and military service. It also resonates with the larger theme of proper exchange in book 6 of the *Annals.* His refusal to accept ransom for his Roman prisoners is one of two economic missteps that contrast sharply with at least two of the Roman generals he faces. Manius Curius Dentatus, the man who eventually defeats Pyrrhus on the field of battle, yields to neither iron nor gold, a phrase that invites comparison with Pyrrhus' references to gold and iron and subtly comments upon the latter's inability to strike a balance between commerce and war. The actions of Decius Mus, who consecrates himself to the gods of the dead in exchange for the safety of his army, on the other hand, contrast with Pyrrhus' inability to maintain properly the exchange of goods and services that is the *pax deorum.* In sum, Ennius marshals multiple forms of system reference in order to underpin the thematic structure of his narrative, including the language of ritual, *militia,* and even accounting.

As tempting as it may be to understand the Pyrrhic War narrative in the *Annals* as a simple series of binary oppositions between a single Greek and many Romans, the structure of the narrative complicates and problematizes such an interpretation. In the first place, later authors such as Cicero regarded Pyrrhus as a noble opponent, and there is no reason to assume that Ennius thought otherwise. The generous and brave tone of Pyrrhus' speech, for all its subtle verbal missteps, is admirable. Nor did the fact that he nearly defeated the Romans on the field of battle twice hurt his reputation as a military man. The Roman *exempla* are not without problems, either; if Decius Mus did, in fact, pronounce the *devotio* properly at Ausculum, the Romans still lost the battle. If he also survived his attempted self-sacrifice, as at least some evidence suggests, his behavior leaves something to be desired as an *exemplum* in two important respects. Book 6 of the *Annals* is therefore no unreflective celebration of the Roman victory over Pyrrhus.

Pyrrhus and Book 6 of the *Annals*

Pyrrhus is clearly an admirable opponent who nearly defeats the Romans, but his outmoded, Homeric code of conduct is both too rigid and too unbalanced to allow him to effectively negotiate the reality of third-century Italy. Pyrrhus himself outlines his code in one of the longer fragments from book 6, a speech that paints a picture of a man capable of great generosity but naïve in his understanding of the role of reciprocity in divine and mortal affairs:[6]

> Nec mi aurum posco nec mi pretium dederitis:
> Non cauponantes bellum sed belligerantes,
> ferro, non auro, vitam cernamus utrique.
> Vosne velit an me regnare, era quidve ferat Fors
> virtute experiamur. Et hoc simul accipe dictum:
> Quorum virtutei belli fortuna pepercit,
> eorundem libertati me parcere certum est.
> Dono—ducite—doque volentibus cum magnis dis. (*Ann.* 183–90)

> Gold for myself I ask not; no, to me ye shall not pay a price. Not chaffering war but waging war, not with gold but with iron—thus let us of both sides make trial for our lives. To see what Mistress Chance may bring, whether it be you or I she wishes to be king—let it be by bravery that we make the test. And withal hear this word of mine: of those warriors to whose bravery war's fortune has been kind, to the freedom of those same have I too planned to be kind. I give them to you, take them home—and with them I give you the blessing of the great gods. (trans. Warmington)

This speech establishes a simple binary opposition of peacetime commerce and wartime battle that allows no possibility of negotiation. In the opening line, Pyrrhus informs his addressees, presumably the Roman ambassadors who have come to negotiate for the release of prisoners, both what he will not do (*nec posco*) and also what they will not do: they will not give (*nec dederitis*).

Although war is not a time for equal commercial exchange, the Romans still sought to preserve the so-called *pax deorum,* a state of peace between the gods and men that needed to be maintained by means of ritual reciprocity. In all fairness to Pyrrhus, he could not enter into a relationship of *gratia* with his enemies, and a commercial exchange of money was as distasteful to the Roman aristocracy as it was to Pyrrhus. In Neil Coffee's terms, Pyrrhus was doomed either to prodigality, because the latter required a relationship of continued reciprocal exchange with the Roman state that was not possible for a *hostis,* or to the ignominy of commodity exchange, which was anathema to Roman aristocrats and avoided by the Homeric heroes whom Pyrrhus emulated.[7] A commercial exchange of prisoners for gold, no matter how distasteful, would have enabled the Greek leader to avoid acts of war against a goddess later on. As the audience knows, Pyrrhus will plunder the sanctuary of Persephone at Locri in order to obtain the gold he so despises in his speech. Pyrrhus' unconditional release is a noble and generous act, but it will later force an act of extreme impiety upon him that will violate the *pax deorum.*

In short, Pyrrhus' Homeric warrior code of conduct is too rigid and too simplistic to be successful in a complex and often contradictory world. This simplistic valuation of war over commerce may be the point of a rebuke, perhaps spoken by Appius Claudius Caecus, directed at the Aeacids, and presumably at Pyrrhus himself:[8]

> Stolidum genus Aeacidarum
> Bellipotentes sunt magis quam sapientipotentes (*Ann.* 197–98)

> That tribe of blockheads, stock of Aeacus are war-strong more than wisdom-strong. (trans. Warmington)

The contrast between *bellipotentes* and *sapientipotentes* is mirrored by the opposition of the participles *cauponantes* and *belligerantes* in the speech of Pyrrhus. If the implied equation between shopkeepers and those who are "wisdom-strong" is taken to its logical conclusion, then there are times when the shopkeeper proves to be wiser than the warrior. Moreover, if *sapientia* is the particularly Roman quality of "advisory competence," as Habinek suggests,[9] it may also be an inevitable conclusion that the Romans will prove to be wiser and superior to Pyrrhus.

The force of this criticism may be intensified by means of an allusion to Euripides, if Skutsch has correctly identified the fragment as an allusion to a remark made by Hecuba in the *Troades* of Euripides:[10]

> ὦ μείζον'ὄγκον δορὸς ἔχοντες ἢ φρενῶν . . . 'Αχαιοί (*Tr.* 1158–59)

> You Achaeans have larger sized spears than brains.

Here Hecuba accuses the Achaeans of relying on brute force rather than intelligence as she indignantly asks why the conquering Greeks are so afraid of her grandson Astyanax that they will murder him, even though he is still a young child. If Ennius is alluding to Hecuba's reproach, it undercuts any implied or begrudged admiration in *bellipotentes* in the *Annals.* The differences between Ennius and Euripides may also highlight the difference in context. Although the name Ἀχαιοί, the Achaeans, is aurally similar to Aecidae, descendants of Aeacus, the two are not the same.[11] The speaker in the *Annals* is not a captured foreign queen but presumably a male Roman citizen who can defend himself and his city, but who also understands that the warrior code is not always appropriate in every context. The fragment therefore creates temporal and cultural gaps by altering the setting, speaker, and wording of the source text, gaps that remind the audience that Pyrrhus is not the Homeric hero his ancestors were.

Annals 183–91 and Roman Ritual

Pyrrhus' actions are unsuitable because they are dated and lack nuance; they are also the antithesis of the core Roman values of self-control, austerity, and piety. His attack on the sanctuary of Persephone at Locri is an example of grave impiety. Although Pyrrhus' release of the Roman prisoners is generous and noble—as Cicero, who preserves the speech, remarks (*Off.* 1.38)—his action is not an expression of austerity. Nor does it give the impression of self-control. Moreover, as Ingo Gildenhard has observed, Pyrrhus assigns responsibility for the outcome of the war to courage and Fortuna, an opposition that is likely a Latin translation of the Greek pairing of ἀρετή and Τύχη,[12] whose behavior as a goddess is random and not governed by the bonds of *pietas.*[13] The lack of these distinctive Roman values of self-control, austerity, and piety in Pyrrhus is in pointed contrast with the collective strength of the Roman commanders, all of whom act according to these values. The Epirote Greek king is therefore a key figure in a "clash in how cultures construe the interface between the human and supernatural worlds."[14]

This contrast is not, however, a simple binary opposition. Although he is finally defeated, Pyrrhus is nearly equal to the task of defeating the Romans. The language of another fragment from book 6 highlights how close the contest was:

Qui antehac
invicti fuere viri, pater optume Olympi,
hos ego vi pugna vici victusque sum ab isdem (*Ann.* 180–82)

> Best father of Olympus, men as yet unbeaten, beat I them, by them was beaten. (trans. Warmington)

The paradoxical expression *vici victus sum* expresses a close similarity between Pyrrhus and the Romans, who are also *victores* and *victi* in the course of the war. The phonetic similarity of the Roman *viri* and the *vi* of Pyrrhus strengthens this impression. Moreover, the address to *Pater Optume* is a distinctly Roman note that harmonizes with the Greek *Olympi.* The connection is modulated by means of the common use of πατήρ in epithets of Zeus in Greek and the Latin name *Iu-p(p)iter,* as well as by the assonance of oPt**u**Me and Ol**y**MPi (at this time written, and perhaps pronounced Ol**u**mpi). Even if the context of the fragment is not a dedication at a temple, as Orosius claims (4.1.14),[15] the cult title *pater optume Olympi* still recalls the cult title *Iu-p(p)iter optimus maximus,* a traditional ritual collocation. Ritual system reference therefore helps to blur the already obscure distinction between Pyrrhus and his Roman enemies.

This play between difference and sameness is also mediated through ritual system reference in the speech of Pyrrhus in *Annals* 186–93. Pyrrhus unwittingly deploys the language of Roman ritual throughout in ways that signal to the audience that he does not understand the importance of the *pax deorum* even in times of war. He thereby forecasts his eventual defeat. The most obvious reference to ritual is the phrase *volentibus cum magnis Dis,* but *do* and *dono,* two of the verbs that immediately precede this phrase, bear a strong resemblance to the dedicatory formula *donum dare,* at least on the semantic and phonetic level. Because the expression *accipe dictum* recalls the pairing *accipe daque* from another fragment of the *Annals* (*Ann.* 32, discussed below), a single line that is itself characterized by ritual system reference, the collocation *accipe dictum* may have similarly solemn overtones. Once again, ritual system reference is not merely a source of poetic diction but also a means of enhancing the structure and meaning of the entire narrative.

Although *volentibus cum magnis Dis* resonates with common Greek expressions such as σύν γε θεοῖσιν (*Il.* 24.430), it appears to be an amalgam of two traditional collocations of Latin ritual. The variant *cum divis volentibus* is not only common in Latin literature (e.g., PL. *Per.* 332, SAL. *Iug.* 14.19, and LIV. 37.19.5), it also appears in the opening formula of the lustration of the fields in Cato's *De Agri Cultura* (*Agr.* 141):

> "Cum divis volentibus quodque bene eveniat, mando tibi, Mani . . ."
>
> "With the gods willing, and may it turn out well, I command you, Manius . . ."

Because the celebrated prayer to Mars, perhaps the most archaic of all Latin prayers in the manuscript tradition, is part of the same lustration, *cum divis volentibus* may be just as venerable.[16] Moreover, the phrase *magni di* can be a cult title of the Penates, a most Roman category of divinity.[17] Pyrrhus has inadvertently used a periphrasis for gods who are not likely to look upon a Greek general waging a war against Rome with any favor.

The metrical structure of the phrase also signals that it is at least a hybrid rather than a literal translation of a Greek proverb. The elision of *-s* in *volentibus* is a feature of the Ennian hexameter that is not permissible in Greek hexameters. Unlike Homer, Ennius elides final *-s* after short vowels and before consonants, even though final short syllables ending in *-s* are long by position if another *s-* follows. The final *-s* in Latin therefore appears to have been quite weak before consonants, as was final *-m,* a sound that is also elided before vowels, but not consonants even in Vergil. Under whatever circumstances Ennius elided final *-s,* it is a feature of Ennian prosody that differentiates it from Greek prosody. Because the elision of final *-s* is such a radical break with Greek practice and because it appears to reflect a feature of spoken Latin at the time of Ennius, *volentibus cum . . . dis* must have sounded very different from the Greek σύν γε θεοῖσιν. It is possible that the sound of *volentibus cum . . . dis* added an extra Latin coloring to the expression.

Dono—ducite—doque-, the second component of Pyrrhus' formal pronouncement of the release of the prisoners to the Romans, also bears a close resemblance to the traditional ritual collocation *donum dare.* Wolfram Euler lists several inscriptions with *CIL* numbers that deploy *donum dare* in his discussion of the phrase (e.g., *CIL* I^2 388, 394, 1805, 60, 61, 62, 756, and 2486)[18] and Vine lists more in his discussion of the forms *merito* and *meritod* (*CIL* I^2 31, 384, 386, 28, 32, 33, 27, 976, and 2675a).[19] Other examples may be cited (e.g., *CIL* I^2 26, 42, 47, and 399). Because these collocations repeatedly occur in the context of a ritual dedication, it is certain that *donum dare* is a traditional ritual collocation.

In spite of the insertion of the imperative, *ducite, dono,* and *do* clearly form a syntactic unit of two first-person verbs that are transparently derived from the same root as *donum* and *dare.* What is more, the use of *dederitis* in the final position of the first line of the speech and *do* and *dono* in the last line not only helps to mark off the speech as a unit but it also draws attention to *do* and *dono* because they form a ring composition. Given the ubiquitous nature of the expression *donum dare* and the repetition of *dare* in the ring composition, it is likely that some readers of Ennius would have noticed *do . . . dono,* recognized its resemblance to *donum dare,* and considered the impact of its ritual character in the passage.

Although *dono* is indisputably a verb in Pyrrhus' speech, the fact remains that in some inscriptions, and perhaps even in the spoken Latin of Ennius' day, *dono . . . do* and *donum do* would have been indistinguishable.[20] Two of the permutations of *donum dare* collected by Wolfram Euler deploy a form of *donum* without a final *-m:*[21]

Q. K. Cestio Q f Hercole donu [d]edero (*CIL* I^2 61)

Quintus and Kaeso Cestius the sons of Quintus gave this gift to Hercules.

. . . Hercole dono dat lubs merto . . . (*CIL* I^2 62)

(Lucius Gemenius) gave this gift to Hercules willingly and deservedly.

The unequivocal presence of *donum* in three other inscriptions suggests that *donu* and *dono* as they appear in the preceding inscriptions should also be read as accusatives, not datives or ablatives. Because accusatives are often written without a final *-m* in archaic inscriptions, the difference between *dono . . . doque* and the ritual collocation *donum dare* would not be immediately obvious in writing.

In addition to the relatively numerous Latin examples of *donum dare,* there are two Oscan examples, and one Umbrian example, that are cognate with Latin *donum dare.*[22] The first example is a dedication on a gold ring from Samnium to a female divinity, a goddess who was married, or related to, Jupiter:

Stenis. Kalaviis. G. Anagtiai. Diíviiai. dunum. deded. (Rix Sa 22)

Stenius Calavius G(avii? filius) gives this gift to Anagtia (Angitia?) of Jupiter.

The second Oscan example, from a statue base from Pompeii, is characterized by a more complex grammatical arrangement than the first. The simpler version, however, almost certainly underlies the odd usage of the genitive in the inscription:

. . . **ínim. m X. / ekík: se[g]únúm: Iúvei: Flagiúì / pr: Veriiad: duneìs: dedens** (Rix Cm 9)

. . . and ten Meddices Tutices gave this statue of a gift to Jupiter Flagius for Veria

The motivation for the transformation of an underlying **dunum dedens** is obscure, but the genitive **duneìs** that occurs in place of the expected accusative **dunum** is still cognate with Latin *donum.* There is at least one example of a cognate expression in Umbrian on a bronze statue from Tuder:

ahal trutitis dunum dede. (Rix Um 16)

Ahal Trutitius gave this gift.

Because the formula is so widespread in Latin and Oscan inscriptions, it is likely that the collocation was also traditional in Umbrian. Because there are cognate expressions in Latin, Oscan, and Umbrian, *donum dare* is almost certainly the Latin form of a traditional common Italic ritual collocation.

The parallel to the traditional ritual collocation *donum dare* in Ennius evokes a sense of solemnity but also of irony.[23] Pyrrhus seems to have misappropriated the dedicatory formula, since he uses it to refer to a gift to mortals rather than to the gods. Because exact wording was very important for Roman ritual, his misappropriation of its language, however accidental and however understandable, could not have been auspicious. The dedicatory inscriptions that employ the collocation *donum dare* imply that the expression identifies a gift given to a god *after* the dedicator has received something from that god.

An extension of *donum dare* in these same dedications provides evidence for its implicitly reciprocal nature. Out of a sample of twenty examples of the collocation *donum dare,* thirteen are qualified by *merito(d).*[24] Although *merito* is a fixed adverbial expression that somewhat obscures its economic nature, *merito* is derived from *meritum,* the fourth principal part of the verb *mereo,* a verb that primarily means to earn or receive pay and is related to more baldly economic terms such as *meretrix* and *merx.* If *donum dare* is an expression of reciprocal exchange, as implied by the frequent occurrence of *merito* in such expressions, then Pyrrhus' choice of words sounds a dissonant note in a statement that emphatically favors the warrior over the shopkeeper.

The expression *volentibus cum magnis dis* is not by itself an improper usage of a ritual collocation, but its placement immediately after *dono . . . doque* nevertheless lends it the appearance of a misquotation of a traditional expression of the reciprocal exchange with the gods. Without any other contextual clues, the audience could have understood *volentibus* to mean "for those [gods, perhaps two or more named divinities] who are willing," an interpretation that the conjunction *-que* with *do* initially implies. The line, however, continues with *cum* and thus, disambiguates ablative *volentibus* from the dative, a form that is otherwise impossible to distinguish from the ablative.[25] The syntax of the sentence does not allow the *volentibis . . . dis* to receive the dedication implied by the similarity between *dono . . . doque* and the formula *donu(m) dare.*

In contrast with the *gratia* between man and god implied in the collocation *donum dare,* Pyrrhus' negotiations with both men and gods are characterized by unconditional gifts to men and by plunder taken from a goddess without recompense of any sort. Although his release of the Roman prisoners is noble by almost any standard, it is couched entirely in commands and first-person pronouncements. The act is therefore indicative of his inability to negotiate with men and with gods. Instead of maintaining the *pax deorum* through proper ritual language, his use of *dono . . . doque,* a phrase that so closely resembles the dedicatory formula for offerings to the gods in recompense for aid already received, foreshadows the material and theological consequences of Pyrrhus' refusal to accept recompense for the prisoners.

Annals 183–91, *Annals* 32, and Roman Ritual

There is an echo of another fragment of the *Annals* in Pyrrhus' speech, a fragment that deploys at least one traditional ritual collocation:

> Accipe daque fidem foedusque feri bene firmum (*Ann.* 32)
>
> Give and take you plighted troth and make a treaty truly firm. (trans. Warmington)

The thematic relationship between the two fragments is obvious: they are both verbal expressions of a compact between two parties. Whoever the speaker of the line is, the fragment is almost certainly from a negotiation. Because Macrobius assigns the fragment to book 1 (6.1.13) and Vergil alludes to the same fragment in the negotiations between Aeneas and Evander in the *Aeneid* (8.150), it is likely that the two parties in the *Annals* are the newly arrived Trojans and the inhabitants of Italy whom they first encounter, perhaps the inhabitants of Alba Longa, as Norden suggests.[26] Even if the parties are Romulus and Titus Tatius, as one school of thought would have it,[27] the similarity of context invites a comparison between the treaty and Pyrrhus' speech. The two negotiations are also different in important ways. If the first negotiation involves proto-Roman Trojans who remain in Italy, the results of the negotiation are therefore permanent. In book 6 the Romans are negotiating with a Greek *condottiere* for a return of prisoners that will not end in a lasting treaty. The most striking contrast, however, is between the reciprocal character of the fragment in book 1 and the unilateral speech of Pyrrhus. The parties in book 1 exchange *fides,* while Pyrrhus does not exchange anything.

Both *Annals* 32 and the speech of Pyrrhus describe a similar situation by means of the verbs *dare* and *accipere.* Although they do not occur within the same syntactic unit, there are three forms of *dare* and one of *accipere* out of the twelve finite verbs in the speech of Pyrrhus:

> Nec mi aurum posco nec mi pretium **dederitis:** 186
> Et hoc simul **accipe** dictum: 190
> **Dono**—ducite—**doque** volentibus cum magnis dis. 193

The placement of *accipe* almost at the center of a speech that is framed by *dederitis* and *dono . . . doque* may have invited the audience to recall *accipe daque* in *Annals* 32. If the audience did, in fact, recall *accipe daque* when it came to the speech of Pyrrhus, the similarity to the language of the exchange of faith in book 1 would have sounded more than one ironic note.

It is also possible that the proximity of *accipe* and the various forms of *dare* in Pyrrhus' speech represents another misuse of a traditional ritual collocation that is used properly in *Annals* 32. If *foedus feri* was a collocation specific to a ritual performed by the Fetials in the sanctioning of treaties, as the evidence suggests, its traditional ritual connotations would have at least given the impression that *accipe daque* had similar overtones. If Pyrrhus has inadvertently evoked such a traditional collocation, then another level of irony is at work: the Greek leader nearly utters the words that will lead to a balanced and ritually sanctioned treaty that would end the war.

Annals 32 and the Fetial Prayer: *Foedus Ferire*

The most compelling evidence for a traditional collocation of *foedus* and *ferire* may be found in Livy, who employs variants of *foedus ferire* three times in the context of the rites conducted by the Fetial priests. For example, he describes the striking of a treaty ratified by the Fetials, in which the head of the college asks the king if he orders the priest *foedus ferire:*

> "Iubesne me, rex, cum patre patrato populi Albani foedus ferire?" (LIV. 1.24.4)

> The fetial asked King Tullus, "Dost thou command me, King, to make a treaty with the *pater patratus* of the Alban People?"[28]

As it is described by Livy, the rite deploys some other examples of traditional phraseology, including *pater patratum* (quoted above), that indicate the passage is constructed of traditional collocations, even if the Fetial rite as presented by Livy is an antiquarian reconstruction or his own invention. In addition to this description, the Fetials travel to Carthage at the end of the second Punic War *ad foedus feriundum* in Livy (30.43.9), and in the same passage the Senate orders the College *in haec verba,* "according to the formula,"[29] to ask the praetor for *sagmina* when he orders *ut foedus ferirent.*

Livy's use of *foedus ferire* could be a literary allusion, perhaps directly dependent on the *Annals,*[30] rather than a traditional collocation, but the context of another instantiation of the phrase in Plautus suggests otherwise. In the *Mostellaria,* the slave Tranio realizes he can no longer maintain the elaborate deception by which he convinces his master that his house is haunted. He decides *foedus feriam* (*Mos.* 1061), "I will strike a treaty." Moreover, the expression occurs within a speech that features other bits of ceremonial language, including *ut senatum . . . convocem,* "in order to summon the senate" (*Mos.*1049), and *eduxi omnem legionem* "I led forth the whole legion" (*Mos.*1047). The context of *foedus feriam* in the *Mostellaria* implies that the collocation is one more bit of solemn language distorted for comic effect.

Whatever its date or ultimate source may be, by the time of the mid-Republic, if not earlier, *foedus ferire* was very likely an established formula. It is unlikely that Plautus, who died in 184 BCE, is alluding to the *Annals.* Although Ennius could have appropriated the phrase from the *Mostellaria,* there is no good reason to posit a borrowing of a comic coinage to describe a solemn ceremony. Nor is Livy likely to have borrowed the phrase from Plautus. Because Livy consistently deploys the collocation in a single context that does not match the *Annals* in multiple points in his history, it is equally unlikely that he borrowed the expression from Ennius. The simplest explanation is that *foedus ferire* was a traditional collocation expressing the striking of a treaty, a collocation that became associated with the Fetial rite some time before Livy, and perhaps before Plautus and Ennius.

Accipe Daque and the Latin Tradition

In contrast with *foedus ferire,* it is harder to tease out compelling examples of pairings of such common words as *accipere* and *dare* in order to argue for the existence of a traditional ritual collocation. Sallust does pair the two words, however, once in the *Bellum Jugurthinum* and once in the *Bellum Catilinae:*

> . . . ut Allobroges . . . cum Catilina data atque accepta fide societatem confirmarent. (*Cat.* 44.3)

> . . . so the Allobroges, a pledge of faithfulness having been given and taken, might affirm their alliance with Catiline.

> Ibi fide data et accepta Iugurtha Bocchi animum oratione accendit (*Iug.* 81.1)

> Then after pledges of faith were given and taken, Jugurtha roused the spirit of Bocchus with a speech.

Sallust could have arrived at the collocation of *fides* with *dare* and *accipere* independently in the context of describing exchanges of faith, but its repetition in Sallust in the context of a solemn pact may indicate that collocations of *dare* and *accipere* are traditional in striking treaties just as *foedus ferire* are. Moreover, a sequence of three words is less likely to be repeated at random. Because there are no obvious allusions to the *Annals* in the entire corpus of Sallust, a fact that is all the more striking because the historian's style is demonstrably archaic, it is likely that the expression is another example of Sallust's penchant for archaic language. In other words, the instantiations of the collocation of *dare* and *accipere* in Sallust appear to be traditional and to belong to the ritual context of solemnizing a treaty.

Annals 183–91, *Annals* 32, and the Language of *Deditio*

Whether or not *accipe dictum* is an allusion to a collocation of the roots of *dare* and *capere* that concluded a treaty, *accipere* and *dare* are collocated in the record of a *deditio,* the formal surrender of a conquered people to a Roman commander. A bronze tablet recording the *deditio* of a people whose name is no longer legible begins the description of the surrender after naming the consuls of the year (Gaius Marius and Gaius Flavius Fimbria for the year 104 BCE) and the commander (Lucius Caesius) thus:[31]

> . . . populus Seanoc [. . .] / dedit L. Caesius C. f. imperator postquam [—] / accepit . . .

> The people of the ? gave (themselves?) . . . Lucius Caesius son of Gaius the imperator after he accepted (it?) . . .

The inscription appears to be a record of a *deditio* that not only collocates *accipere* and *dare* but also places them at the beginning of two consecutive lines in an acrostic arrangement:

> dedit . . .
> accepit . . .

The collocation and arrangement of *dedit* and *accepit* in the context of the *deditio* therefore suggest that the collocation could evoke the context of a formal surrender.

If the collocation of *accipere* and *dare* can evoke an unconditional surrender to a Roman commander, then it adds yet another layer of meaning to Pyrrhus' speech. By applying the verb used of the defeated party in the *deditio* to himself (*do*) and the verb used of the victorious Roman imperator (*accipe*) to the Romans, Pyrrhus has inadvertently predicted his defeat at the hands of the Romans at the battle of Beneventum at the end of the war. The collocation even implies that Pyrrhus will surrender, even though he, in fact, fled from Italy without ever formally surrendering to the Romans. Whether or not the presence of *dare* in close proximity to *accipere* in Pyrrhus' speech could be construed as an accidental declaration of surrender, the use of the two verbs in a single speech would have struck the audience of the *Annals* as an inauspicious choice of words for the Greek leader.

Although the impact of a collocation from the *deditio* in *Annals* 32 is more difficult to gauge, there are two points that can be made. Regardless of who spoke the line, *accipe daque* and the use of *dare* and *accipere* in Pyrrhus' speech are connected not only by repetition of these two verbs but also by an evocation of the language of the *deditio,* a connection that would intensify the foreshadowing that permeates Pyrrhus' speech. In addition to this intensification, a comparison between the two fragments emphasizes the reciprocal and balanced character of *accipe daque* in the earlier fragment, a balance that cannot be achieved with an enemy of the fully formed Republic.

Annals 183–91, *Annals* 32, and the Language of Military Victories

In addition to the collocation of *dare* and *accipere* in the *deditio* from Spain, there is also evidence for a traditional pairing of *dare* and *capere,* the simplex form of *ac-cipere,* in the language of inscriptions set up by victorious military commanders. In his discussion of these inscriptions, Andrew Riggsby notes that these dedications almost always feature some form of *capere.*[32] Of the inscribed dedications collected by Riggsby, the inscriptions that deploy forms of *capere* or *dare* constitute a small subset of the collection. Three of the twenty-five inscriptions[33] deploy a form of *dare* and *capere,*[34] two have a form of *dare* without *capere,*[35] and the majority have a form of *capere* without *dare.*[36] The bare underlying formula suggested by the evidence of the inscriptions may be seen in a fragmentary inscription probably set up by Lucius Quinctius Flamininus, the brother of the more celebrated Titus:

> L Quinctius L f Le]ucado cepit
> Eidem conso]l dedit (*CIL* I² 613)

> Lucius Quinctius the son of Lucius took this from Leucadus. The same one gave it as consul.

Miraculously, the only two complete words on the stone are *cepit* and *dedit* because of their placement at the end of the two lines of the inscription. If *capere* and *dare* are the elements of a traditional collocation, this fact may have led the stonecutter to place them at the end of the lines to emphasize the parallel.

The oldest and most elaborate of the texts that collocate *dare* and *capere* in a military context is an epitaph of the son of Lucius Cornelius Scipio Barbatus, an epitaph that makes use of a number of other traditional expressions from a variety of registers:[37]

> Honc oino ploirume consentiont R[omani]
> Duonoro optumo fuise viro
> Luciom Scipione. Filios Barbati
> Consol censor aidilis hic fuet a[pud vos]
> Hec cepit Corsica Aleriaque urbe
> Dedet tempestatebus aide merito (*CIL* I² 9)

> Very many Romans consider this one man to have been the best of the good, Lucius Scipio, son of Barbatus. He was consul, censor and aedile among you. He captured Corsica and the city of Aleria. He dedicated a well-deserved temple to the Storms.

Because the phrase *Consol censor aidilis hic fuet a*[*pud vos*] corresponds almost exactly to *consol censor aidilis quei fuit apud vos* in the epitaph of his father (*CIL* I² 7.4), even to the point of serving as the fourth line of both epitaphs, it may be a traditional collocation. Cicero gives the impression that the opening line of the *elogium* of Aulus Atilius Calatinus, the consul of 258 BCE is unique, but it bears a close resemblance to the opening of the epitaph of *filius Barbati,* and he cites it twice (*Sen.* 61 and *Fin.* 2.116):

> Hunc unum plurimae consentiunt gentes
> Populi primarium fuisse virum (*Sen.* 61)

> Very many families consider this one man to have been the first of the people.

Although the orthography of the epitaph of Calatinus has been modernized, the only significant differences are the use of *gentes* instead of *Romani* and *populi primarium* instead of *duonoro optumo.* Because the close parallel cannot be explained as a result of the influence of one of the other *elogia* in the tomb of the Scipios, the opening of the *elogia* may also be a traditional way to begin a Roman epitaph.

In addition to the arrangement of *cepit* and *dedet* in a parallel syntactic structure, the collocation of *dedet* and *merito* in the epitaph of *Barbati filius* is one element short of the dedicatory formula *donum dare merito.* The verb *dare* is common to both *donum dare merito* and *dare capere,* and this shared root perhaps indicates that some speakers may have perceived the expression *urbem cepit . . . dedit* as a conflation of *donum dare* (*merito*) with the pairing of *dedit* and *cepit.* The dedicatory context that celebrated military achievement, and sometimes specifically marked a ritual exchange with a divinity (as in the case of the Scipionic epitaph), enables such a perception. The lexical and contextual overlap between *donum dare* and *capere dare* would therefore have suggested a connection between these expressions in other texts, a suggestion that perhaps led Ennius to deploy the verb *accipe* and the expression *do . . . donoque* in the speech of Pyrrhus.

Three collocations of *capere* and *dare* may seem like a meager yield, but there are other inscriptions from Riggsby's list that suggest the combination of *capere* and *dare* was formulaic in this context. An underlying pairing of these verbs seems to inform two different inscriptions set up by Marcus Claudius Marcellus:

> M. Claudius M. f. consol Hinnad cepit (*CIL* I^2 608)
>
> Marcus Claudius, consul, son of Marcus took [this] from Enna
>
> Martei (M.) Claudius (M. f.) consol dedit (*CIL* I^2 609)[38]
>
> Marcus Claudius, consul, son of Marcus gave [this] to Mars.

Because both inscriptions have the same wording for their subject, they may have been meant to stand together in order to complete the formula. If so, then four of twenty-five inscriptions pair *capere* and *dare.*

An inscription set up by Lucius Mummius is similarly divided into two halves in one continuous inscription. The first part describes his triumph after the sack of Corinth, the second his dedication of a statue and a temple to Hercules in celebration of his victory:

> L. Mummius L. f. cos. duct(u) auspicio imperioque eius Achaia capt(a) Corinto deleto Romam redieit triumphans. Ob hasce res bene gestas quod in bello voverat hanc aedem et signu(m) Herculis Victoris imperator dedicat. (*CIL* I^2 626)

> Once Achaea was taken and Corinth destroyed under his leadership, auspices and command, Lucius Mummius, son of Lucius, the consul, returned to Rome in triumph. On account of these fine deeds, the successful commander dedicates this temple and statue of Hercules Victor, fulfilling his vow during the war.[39]

Although there are no finite forms of *dare* or *capere* in the inscription, the alliterative ablative absolute construction *Achaia capta Corinto deleto* seems to allude to the first half of the more traditional *cepit dedit* formula. *Dedicat,* the final word of the inscription, is semantically and phonetically similar to *dedit,* the third-person perfect of *dare.* The placement of *capta,* the past passive participle of *capere,* toward the beginning of the dedication, and *dedicat* at the end, is an indication that the dedication is structured around an underlying collocation of *capere* and *dare* that the writer is attempting to evoke without quoting the actual collocation. Moreover, the two halves of the inscription expand upon the act of taking a city (*Achaia capta*) and making a dedication after the victory (*dedicat*). If there is no collocation of *capere* and *dare* in Mummius' triumphal notice, the essential idea of the collocation underlies the bipartite structure of the text as a whole.

Another allusive use of the collocation may be seen in a tablet that Livy quotes and ascribes to Titus Quinctius:[40]

> Iuppiter atque divi omnes hoc dederunt ut T. Quinctius dictator oppida novem caperet (LIV. 6.29.9)

> Jupiter and all the gods granted that Titus Quinctius, the dictator, should capture nine towns.

Here the commander takes a city (*caperet*), but the gods give (*dederunt*), an arrangement that gives expression to the unspoken reciprocity that is assumed when a victorious general gives a gift (*donum dare*) to the gods because they have given him the victory.

Another text that deploys forms of *capere* and *dare* together comes from Isaura in Cilicia and is dated to ca. 75 BCE:[41]

> Serveilius C f imperator
> hostibus victeis, Isaura Vetere

> capta, captiveis venum dateis,
> sei deus seive deast quoius in
> tutela oppidum Vetus Isaura
> fuit . . . votum soluit (*CIL* I^2 2954)

> Servilius son of Gaius Imperator after the enemies were defeated, after old Isaura was taken, after the captives were sold, if there is any god or if there is any goddess under whose protection old Isaura once was, he fulfilled his vow.

Given that P. Servilius Vatia Isauricus, the author of the inscription, was a *pontifex* (CIC. *Har.* 12), as Edward Courtney observes, it is not surprising that at least one traditional ritual collocation is quoted in the inscription, the phrase *sei deus seive deast.* Courtney describes *si deus si dea est* as "a typical formulation in Roman cult."[42] The fact that the inscription celebrates a Roman military victory and co-opts the language of ritual emphasizes how difficult it is to assign the traditional collocation of *capere* and *dare* to a single cultural sphere, since the Roman general-cum-*pontifex* proclaims his victory by means of a prayer.

The phrase *sei deus seive dea* is a "typical formulation," but the parallelism between *capta* and *dateis* in the inscription of Isauricus is an atypical twist on a traditional formulation. *Dateis,* the archaic past passive participle does not refer to a temple or part of the booty from a campaign dedicated to a god. Instead the idiomatic expression *venum dateis* informs the reader that slaves (*captiveis*) were put up for sale. Because *capta* is placed next to *captiveis,* it is a reminder that *captiveis* is derived from *capere.* The expression *captiveis venum dateis* therefore appears to be a reconfiguration of the traditional collocation of *capere* and *dare,* with a noun derived from *capere* as the passive subject of the participle *dateis.*

The inscriptions of Mummius, Quinctius, and Servilius Isauricus playfully evoke the traditional collocation of *capere* and *dare* in a manner that parallels the use of the language of ritual in the *Annals.* Because the collocation of *capere* and *dare* is attested in other inscriptions in similar contexts, it is likely that these permutations of the expression are deliberate allusions. The same may be said for the use of the language of augury in the *augurium Romuli* (as discussed in chapter 3). Ennius often alludes to and plays with augural phraseology in the context of an augury, just as the inscriptions of Mummius, Quinctius, and Isauricus allude to the traditional collocation of *capere* and *dare* without actually collocating the two roots. Such wordplay suggests that Ennius' practice of alluding to traditional ritual collocations is itself traditional. Moreover, the ambiguity between ritual and military discourse that characterizes the inscriptions of the Roman generals is not dissimilar to the use of ritual language in contexts that do not apparently belong to the ritual sphere. The slippage between military and ritual language in the inscriptions is, in fact, a close parallel to the allusion to the cult title of Jupiter Stator (as discussed in chapter 1).

If the collocation of *capere* and *dare* originally belonged to a single traditional matrix, by the time it appeared in the written record it was not possible to determine which matrix that may have been. The collocation *accipe daque* in *Annals* 32 is characterized by a similar contextual overlap of ritual, military, and political contexts. Even if the collocation *capere dare* was not previously perceived as belonging to ritual, the overlap in the traditional language of both ritual and *militiae* would have given this expression an incipient ritual status that Ennius could exploit. The expression adds yet more semantic weight to the collocation *accipe daque* in *Annals* 32, and perhaps *accipe dictum* in the speech of Pyrrhus. If the parallel between *accipe dictum* and *accipe daque* is salient, then Pyrrhus has misused another traditional expression of reciprocity.

If *accipe dictum* does not specifically recall *accipe daque,* the traditional collocation of *capere* and *dare* does underlie the structure of the speech. As I have already observed, variant forms of *dare* frame the passage and *accipere,* a compound form of *capere,* sits approximately at the center of the pronouncement. Because this arrangement appears to be an expansion of typical formulations found in the dedications of victorious Roman generals, the speech would come across as a perversion of such inscriptions to anyone who could perceive the parallel. The most serious deviation is the use of *dare* to express a nonreciprocal gift to men rather than a state of *gratia* between the general and the gods. It would also not escape a knowledgeable audience that such a collocation is appropriate for the *end* of a war and the final defeat of the enemy, not after a single battle. If the audience recognized the traditional collocation of *capere* and *dare* as the underlying structural principle of the speech of the Greek general, a great deal of latent and culturally specific meaning could be communicated.

Vera Virtus or *Era Fors*?: Pyrrhus and Roman *Virtus*

The same play between sameness and difference in a traditional collocation may also be found in the deployment of two constituents of another expression in the speech of Pyrrhus that appears to have had some currency in discussions of Roman military conduct. Matthew Leigh observes that the prologue of Plautus' *Casina* ends with the following phrase:[43]

vincite
virtute vera, quod fecistis antidhac (*Cas.* 87–88)

Conquer with true courage as you have done before.

The same phrase in the *Cistellaria* again enjoins the Romans to conquer with true courage, *vera virtute,* as they have done before (*Cist.* 197–98). On the basis of the repetition of *vera virtute* in Plautus and in other authors, Leigh suggests that *vera virtus* is an expression of a quality that may be directly opposed to *Punica fides.*

It may be significant that two other instantiations of the phrase have direct connections with Pyrrhus; the first comes from *Phoenix,* a tragedy written by Ennius:

sed virum vera virtute vivere animatum addecet (*Trag.* 254)

But it behooves a man to live a life inspired with virtue true.

Not only is Ennius the author of *Phoenix,* but also in the Greek tradition, the eponymous protagonist has close ties to the Aeacids, the family of Pyrrhus. The second occurs in Livy's description of the negative attitude that some senators took toward the deceit employed against the Macedonian monarch Perseus, a position that is justified by the *exemplum* of the senate's refusal to use such tactics against Pyrrhus:

Nec ut astu magis quam vera virtute gloriarentur, bella maiores gessisse . . . eadem fide indicatum Pyrrho regi medicum uitae eius insidiantem; (LIV. 42.47.5)

And (they said that) their ancestors waged war not in order to boast of their cunning more than their true courage . . . with the same good faith, the doctor plotting against his life was made known to king Pyrrhus.

Pyrrhus' doctor, presumably a Greek, was apparently happy to offer to poison Pyrrhus, a tactic that was not in keeping with the values of the Roman aristocracy. The *exemplum* carries the suggestion that the expedition of Pyrrhus was doubly doomed, because the Greeks who served under overvalued deceit (*astu*) and because he overvalued *virtus.*

Because Pyrrhus nearly "quotes" the collocation *vera virtute* in his speech from the *Annals,* he again appears to be a noble enemy who is similar to the Romans but deficient in understanding the subtleties of the Roman character that allowed them to win the war:

> Vosne velit an me regnare, era quidve ferat Fors
> Virtute experiamur. (*Ann.* 186–87)
>
> To see what Mistress Chance may bring, whether it be you or I she wishes to be king—let it be with bravery that we make the test. (trans. Warmington)

Virtute, the second part of the collocation, is clearly present and is emphasized by beginning its line. It is also in the ablative, the same case of *virtus* in the other collocations of *virtus* and *vera* cited above. Not only does the word *era* closely resemble *vera* phonetically in spite of the two short vowels of *era* and the two long vowels of the ablative form of *vera,* the repeated use of *v-* at the beginning of the line *vosne velit* and the conjunction *-ve* may also have prompted the audience to connect *era* with *vera* once *virtute* appears at the beginning of the next line. As in the case of *doque . . . dono,* Pyrrhus has nearly quoted a traditional collocation.

The "accidental" paronomasia of *vera virtute* again invites a comparison of the worldview of Pyrrhus and his Roman opponents, just as the "inadvertent" misquotations of the language of Roman ritual raise the same questions. Although both sides accept the importance of *virtus* for the outcome of the battle, Pyrrhus highlights the importance of random chance in the persona of a mistress (*era*).[44] Ingo Gildenhard formulates the distinction as one between the view of Pyrrhus that an outcome is "ultimately up to chance" and that of the Romans who "developed a means of rendering the future more certain" by means of ritual.[45] In other words, the Romans rely upon both *virtus* and the maintenance of the *pax deorum,* a condition that lies within human agency rather than divine chance. The alphabetic overlap between *era . . . Fors* and *(v)era . . . virtute* is all the more meaningful because it iconically represents how near Pyrrhus came at times to the ideal of Roman behavior and yet how far he diverged from the worldview that would allow his enemies to extend their empire around the Mediterranean.

The pattern of ironic near quotation is consistent throughout the speech of Pyrrhus and demonstrates the use of traditional system reference in the *Annals* for generating meaning. The phrase *dono . . . doque* is a virtual quotation of the traditional collocation *donum dare.* The use of forms of *dare* combined with the single form *accipere* may also allude to a ritual collocation of *dare* and *accipere,* a collocation that occurs in book 1 of the *Annals* and in the *deditio* from Spain. Moreover, the proximity of *dare* and *accipere* may recall the traditional pairing of *capere* and *dare* in the dedicatory inscriptions of victorious generals. In addition to these misquotations, Pyrrhus appears to conflate *era Fors* with *(v)era virtus,* a traditional expression of the Roman code of conduct in war. Although *dis . . . volentibus* is the only outright quotation, the weight of evidence here suggests that some, if not all, of these verbal echoes were designed to communicate something to the audience that lies outside the noble sentiments of Pyrrhus' speech.

It is also possible that Pyrrhus' misquotations of traditional ritual collocations, however accidental on his part, would have been ominous as well as ironic. The language of ritual in many ancient societies requires precision in order to be efficacious. The Romans were no exception. Pliny the Elder describes in detail the elaborate precautions that were taken to ensure that a prayer be recited correctly (*Nat.* 28.11). Pyrrhus is not performing a ritual, but his misquotations of traditional ritual collocations could still recall mispronunciations of the same collocations that must have occurred from time to time in the rituals familiar to the audience of the *Annals.* If these mistakes were bad omens, perhaps the same could be said for Pyrrhus' unintentional misuse of the language of Roman ritual.

The use of traditional collocations that are appropriate for ritual or military action in a military setting without regard for their ritual connotations is also symptomatic of Pyrrhus' inability to wage war and maintain the *pax deorum.* The near quotation of so many expressions of ritual reciprocity with military connotations is an ironic reminder that in spite of his admirable qualities, Pyrrhus is unaware of the importance of the *pax deorum.* Pyrrhus lacked not only the distinctive Roman values of austerity, self-control, and *pietas* but also an understanding of the subtleties of Roman ritual language, something that the audience of the *Annals* presumably did not lack and that allowed them to perceive the subtle use of ritual system reference to foreshadow the defeat of an enemy no matter how admirable.

Iron and Gold: The Symbolism of Metals in Book 6 of the *Annals*

Although *aurum* and *ferrum* do not appear to be constituents of a traditional collocation, Pyrrhus' expression *ferro non auro,* "not with gold but with iron," would be infelicitous in the eyes of the Romans and also, potentially, of his fellow Greeks. As I have already suggested, Pyrrhus' refusal to accept gold in favor of fighting yet another battle against the Romans (with iron weapons) likely foreshadows his sack of the shrine of Persephone. The decision to fight another battle itself also calls to mind the results of the battles Pyrrhus has already fought and will fight with the Romans, a series of victories that were nearly as costly for the victor as for the vanquished and that eventually forced Pyrrhus to abandon Italy. Pyrrhus can be forgiven for his failure to predict the future or to grasp the subtleties of Roman culture. His preference for iron over gold, however, is a preference for the least desirable of the metals that designate Hesiod's five ages in the *Works and Days.* Moreover, according to Hesiod, the Golden Age was a time when commerce was not necessary and the Iron Age was a time of toil and greed. If Ennius had read Hesiod, and there are indications that he did, Pyrrhus' choice of words may be an invitation to anyone who knew the poetry of Hesiod to interpret *ferro non auro* as an unfortunate choice of words on the part of the Greek *condottiere.*

Ferro non auro forges a thematic connection with the rest of book 6, since the frequency of *auro* and *ferro* is very high in the fragments of book 6 relative to the fragments of the other books. The noun *aurum* appears to be especially frequent in book 6, where it appears at least three times, once in the fragmentary papyrus from Herculaneum and twice in the speech of Pyrrhus. Although *ferrum* is apparently more evenly distributed throughout the *Annals,* it is not explicitly collocated with *aurum* outside of Pyrrhus' address to the Roman envoys and in an epigram about Curius that likely belongs to book 6. The opposition of gold and iron is symbolic of the balance between commerce (including ritual exchange) and warfare, a balance that is necessary, in the Roman worldview, to defeat an enemy. The frequency of *aurum* and *ferrum* is another indication that the near quotations of ritual expressions of reciprocity between gods and men in the speech of Pyrrhus, such as *donum dare* and possibly *accipere dare,* are also elements that contribute to a larger thematic structure within Ennius' narrative of the Pyrrhic War.

At least one Roman was able to manage his own exchanges better than Pyrrhus, even if he did so by means of disdain for both iron and gold, assuming that Flores is right in assigning this single line to book 6:

> Quem nemo ferro potuit superare nec auro (*Ann.* 456)

Whom none could overcome with iron or gold.[46] (trans. Warmington)

Skutsch calls the pairing of *aurum* and *ferrum* a "natural contrast,"[47] but it is significant that Curius cannot be overcome by either iron or gold. Although Pyrrhus relies solely on iron in his speech to the Roman emissaries and disdains gold (*ferro non auro*), he fails to spurn gold in spite of his earlier claim when he plunders the sanctuary at Locri. Pyrrhus, who overvalues iron when he releases his Roman prisoners without ransom and who overvalues gold when he violates the shrine of Persephone, is therefore contrasted verbally and thematically with Curius, who remains indifferent to gold and iron until his death.

The epitome of Livy's second decade is quite terse, but it preserves a curious story that may reflect the importance of exchange in book 6:

> Curius Dentatus cos. cum dilectum haberet, eius, qui citatus non responderat, bona primus vendidit; iterum Pyrrhum ex Sicilia in Italiam reversum vicit et Italia expulit. (*Per.* 14)

> Curius Dentatus the consul, when he was holding a levy, first sold the goods of someone who failed to report. He defeated Pyrrhus, who had returned to Italy from Sicily for a second time, and drove him out of Italy.

The sale of goods appears to have taken place during the levy for the final campaign against Pyrrhus and is thus consistent with the context and the thematic structure of book 6 as I have outlined it. If Ennius narrated this episode in the *Annals,* it would have served to contrast Curius, who demonstrates an understanding that the sale of goods is appropriate in some circumstances, even while at war with a foe who adamantly refuses to engage in commerce when given a legitimate opportunity. A picture emerges of Curius as someone who can strike a balance between warfare and exchange, in contrast with Pyrrhus, who overvalues warfare sometimes and money other times. If the source of the anecdote is not the *Annals,* it may, however, still reflect the influence of a thematic contrast between Curius and Pyrrhus.

The inability to achieve reciprocity is also manifest in the final episode of Pyrrhus' career in Italy, when he plunders the sanctuary of Persephone before losing the entire crew of his ship at sea. It is very likely that Ennius treated this episode. A fragmentary papyrus from Herculaneum from book 6 of the *Annals* that speaks of *mors, reges,* and *vi mari*[*s*] appears to confirm this intuition:[48]

> o]RCI[
>]NUMQU[.]M[
> fer]RTUR IN ORA[s

]NT ET MAGIS I[p]S[e
]C[o]NTRARI[a] I[u]RA[
]AUERUNT AUR[um
]REGES SUD[asse
necan]NTUR NE FRAT[res
ia]M MORS EST ES ET A[
]ERUNT INDUP[
    ] ET UI MAR[is
        ]AT[r]A

. . . of Orcus . . .
. . . never . . .
. . . goes in(to) the beaches
. . . they? . . . and he himself more . . .
. . . contrary(?) Oaths . . .
. . . they . . . ed gold . . .
. . . kings sweat . . .
. . . let brothers not be killed . . .
. . . now death is at hand for them(?) And . . .
they . . . ed . . . the commander (?)
    . . . and the might of the sea . . .
    . . . . black . . .

If the fragment does indeed narrate the consequences of the plundering of the sanctuary at Locri, then it also connects this act to Pyrrhus' speech to the Roman ambassadors by means of verbal repetition. If the root *aur*[*um*] can be restored in line 6, then it may remind the audience of the consequences of Pyrrhus' decision not to accept *aurum* for his Roman prisoners, a result that I have suggested is foreshadowed in the misquotations of ritual collocations and the phrase *ferro non auro* in Pyrrhus' speech. *Reges* may also recall *regnare* in the speech of Pyrrhus and therefore his intention to rule or to be ruled at the whim of Fortuna as well as his tendency to command rather than to communicate. The repetition of the roots *aur-* and *reg-* are not in themselves very striking, but the thematic connection in this episode, only hinted at in the tattered remains of the papyrus, may have been buttressed by other verbal repetitions in the lacunae. If the verbal parallels are not salient enough to recall the speech of the Greek general to the Roman ambassadors, the presence of *aurum* in the papyrus is one of several occurrences of the word in book 6 that may be another indication of the importance of equal exchange.

The *Devotio* of Decius Mus and Economy of Ritual in Book 6 of the *Annals*

There remains another less obvious example of exchange in book 6 of the *Annals* that provides a mirror image of Pyrrhus' inability to maintain the *pax deorum* through reciprocal exchange with the gods. In this case, the language of exchange is employed in a true ritual context, as opposed to the accidental use of ritual language in the context of a failed exchange such as I have suggested in the speech of Pyrrhus:

> Divi hoc audite parumper
> ut pro Romano populo prognariter armis
> certando prudens animam de corpore mitto (*Ann.* 191–93)

> Ye gods, hear my prayer for a little while; just as from my body I breathe my last for the Roman people's sake, with foreknowledge and awareness, in arms and battle . . . (trans. Warmington)

The language of the prayer must have had a solemn tone, given the content; Decius Mus consecrates himself as ritual capital to be exchanged for a Roman victory, since by performing this ritual he has sacrificed himself to the gods as the price of the safety of the Roman army. In Gildenhard's words, the rite is the "starkest articulation of the 'contractual' outlook of Roman religion."[49] The *devotio* may therefore be an example of a ritual performed correctly and intentionally in an appropriate setting, serving as a counterexample to the accidental but significant misuse of the language of ritual exchange by Pyrrhus.

Because Decius Mus appears to have lived after the battle, however, the proper use of the language of ritual exchange in the *devotio* appears to be even more important than the successful completion of the exchange. If the suffect consul Decius in 265 is the same Decius Mus,[50] then the *devotio* was either not completed or never took place at all.[51] Even if it is a poetic fiction, it testifies to the centrality of ritual exchange for Ennius' narrative of the Pyrrhic War. If the *devotio* did actually take place, or if it was already part of an established tradition, then Ennius may have "quoted" the *devotio* of the third Decius Mus because it served the thematic structure of the narrative of the Pyrrhic War.[52]

There are, nevertheless, a number of complications that arise when discussing the proper formulation of the pronouncement of the *devotio*. It cannot have been pronounced often, if at all, during the lifetime of any Roman citizen or ally and thus is very different from an augural pronouncement. If there was a traditional wording for the ritual, and it is far from certain that there was, even the transmission of the ritual from one generation to another would be liable to corruption, because it was performed so seldom. Although literature likely influenced the performance and language ritual as much as the performance and language of ritual influenced literature, a rarely performed ritual such as the *devotio* would be even more susceptible to the depictions of poets and historians.

The instability of the wording of the *devotio* can be seen clearly in Livy's version of the same ritual as performed by Publius Decius Mus, the grandfather of the Decius Mus at the battle of Vesuvius during the Latin War:

> Iane Iuppiter Mars pater Quirine Bellona Lares Divi Nouensiles Di Indigetes Divi quorum est potestas nostrorum hostiumque Dique Manes vos precor venereror veniam peto feroque uti populo Romano Quiritium vim victoriam prosperetis hostesque populi Romani Quritium terrore formidine morteque adficiatis. Sicut verbis nuncupavi ita pro re publica (populi Romani) Quiritium legiones auxiliaque hostium mecum Deis Manibus Tellurique devoveo (LIV. 8.9.6–8)

> Janus, Jupiter, Father Mars, Quirinus, Bellona, Lares, divine Novensiles, divine Indigites, ye gods in whose power are both we and our enemies, and you, divine Manes,—I invoke and worship you, I beseech and [bear] your favour, that you prosper the might and the victory of the Roman People of the Quirites, and visit the foes of the Roman People of the Quirites with fear, shuddering, and death. As I have pronounced the words, even so in behalf of the republic of the Roman People of the Quirites, and of the army, the legions, the auxiliaries of the Roman People of the Quirites, do I devote the legions and auxiliaries of the enemy, together with myself, to the divine Manes and to Earth.[53]

The lack of specific verbal parallels between the *Annals* and Livy raises the possibility that both *devotiones* are literary concoctions rather than descriptions of an actual ritual. It is unlikely, however, that these *devotiones* were invented without regard for the conventions of ritual language. In other words, Ennius and Livy likely reconstructed their versions of the ritual from various traditional expressions that seemed appropriate to them, perhaps due to a lack of familiarity with the actual *devotio*.

One possible source for the wording of the personal *devotio* may be a variant of the ritual performed on the enemy rather than by the Roman general on himself, as described in a lengthy passage written by an unidentified Furius.

The antiquarian Serenus Sammonicus, who cites Furius, is the direct source of Macrobius' quotation:[54]

> Dis pater Veiovis Manes, sive vos quo alio nomine fas est nominare, ut omnes illam urbem Carthaginem exercitumque quem ego me sentio dicere fuga formidine terrore compleatis quique adversum legiones exercitumque nostrum arma telaque ferent, uti vos eum exercitum eos hostes eosque homines urbes agrosque eorum et qui in his locis regionibusque agris urbibusque habitant abducatis, lumine supero privetis exercitumque hostium urbes agrosque eorum quos me sentio dicere, uti vos eas urbes agrosque capita aetatesque eorum devotas consecratasque habeatis ollis legibus quibus quandoque sunt maxime hostes devoti. Eosque ego vicarios pro me <meaque> fide magistratuque meo pro populo Romano exercitibus legionibusque nostris do devoveo, ut me meamque fidem imperiumque legiones exercitumque nostrum qui in his rebus gerundis sunt bene salvos siritis esse. si haec ita faxitis ut ego sciam sentiam intellegamque, tunc quisquis votum hoc faxit ubiubi faxit recte factum esto ovibus atris tribus. Te Tellus mater teque Iuppiter obtestor. (Macr. 3.9.10–11)

> Father Dis, Veiovis, Manes, or by whatever other name it is right to call you: may you all fill that city of Carthage, and that army of which it is in my intention to speak, and those who will bear arms and missiles against our legions and army, with the urge to flee, with dread, with panic; and may you lead away that army, that enemy, those people who dwell in these places and regions, fields and cities, deprive them of heaven's light; and the enemy's army and the cities and fields of those people of whom it is my intention to speak, may you consider those cities and fields and the people's lives and lifetimes cursed and execrated according to those laws under which enemies have at any time been cursed. In place of myself, my duty, and my office, I dedicate and curse them in place of the Roman people, our armies and legions, that you might vouchsafe the wellbeing of myself, my duty and command, our legions and our army on this campaign. If you do these things so that I know and understand them, then whoever has made this vow, wherever he has made it, may the appropriate action be performed with three black sheep. I call on you, mother Earth, and you, Jupiter, as witnesses.

There is some overlap in the names of the gods addressed at the beginning and the end of the *devotio* of Livy, in addition to the use of *devoveo,* even though the Macrobian version expands *devoveo* into the alliterative doubling figure *do devoveo.* Moreover, there is a partial overlap between *terrore formidine morteque* in Livy and *fuga formidine terrore* in Macrobius. The expression *pro populo Romano exercitibus legionibusque nostris* in Macrobius matches the only obvious point of contact between Livy and Ennius.

Even if the text in Macrobius is an antiquarian reconstruction rather than a genuine ritual text,[55] it is colored by traditional ritual phraseology that would add illocutionary force to any pronouncement. *Pro me fide magistratuque* is a variant of a traditional formula from the wording of the *lustratio* ceremony quoted in Varro that I have discussed in chapter 1—*mihique collegaeque meo fidei magistratuique nostro* (*L.* 6.86)—and perhaps alluded to in *Annals* 102 (*mihi reique fidei regno*). Varro, Ennius, and the *devotio* all deploy the expression in an extension of the traditional wish for things to turn out well for the speaker and the *fides* of the speaker, whereas in Varro—or rather the *Tabulae Censoriae*—and in the *devotio* the speaker's *magistratus* is also a beneficiary. Although *bene salvos siritis esse* is not a close verbal parallel to Ennius' *fortunatim feliciter ac bene vortat* (*Ann.* 103) or Varro's *bonum fortunatum felix salutereque siet* (*L.* 6.86), the expression *grandire beneque evenire siris* in Cato's prayer to Mars (*Agr.* 141) confirms that the phrase *bene* VERB *siri(ti)s* is traditional for Roman prayer. Whether or not the entire *devotio* of Macrobius dates back to the third century BCE, at least some of its elements appear to be traditional.

Although no frozen verbal form of the *devotio* may have existed, the general rules of Roman prayer are not abandoned in Ennius, Livy, or Macrobius. The traditional building blocks of prayer are present in all three authors, such as the address to the chthonic gods, even though *divi* in Ennius is much less impressive than the roll call that begins the utterance in Livy or *Dis pater Veiovis Manes* in Macrobius. All three *devotiones* employ an illocutionary verb, either *devoveo* or *mitto.* The listing of the beneficiaries is not only a traditional feature of Roman prayer, but it is also the one point where the language of all three authors is similar enough to suggest a common source. These elements may have been all that was necessary to signal to the audience that a *devotio* was taking place. If the ritual had no fixed prayer, the *devotio* of Ennius would then be as legitimate as the other examples of the rite preserved by Livy and Macrobius.

In addition to the general principles of Roman prayer, the language of the cult of the dead would have been a natural source for some of the features of the seldom spoken utterance and would have served as a somewhat stable point of reference. Franz Bömer elucidates the use of *mitto* as a "Terminus des Totenkultus," for example, in a number of texts, and its status as a verb of the cult of the dead would have indicated a close engagement with the rituals performed for the dead and underworld deities.[56] Ennius' *mitto,* therefore, was appropriate for a chthonic rite such as the *devotio,* even though it was not as obvious a choice as *devoveo.* Furthermore, the use of *animam* in the *devotio* of Ennius is also consistent with the use of its Oscan congener as an object that can be offered to the deities of the underworld. A curse tablet from Cumae (Rix Cm 13) devotes the **anamúm,** the Oscan cognate of *animus,* of one Stenius Kalavius to an unnamed underworld entity. Perhaps not incidentally, the same Oscan curse devotes the victim's **aitátum,** the Oscan cognate of *aetatesque* one of the enemy's possessions that are devoted in the Macrobian *devotio.* The phrase *animam mitto* may not be a genuine ritual collocation, but its elements are legitimate signifiers in the language of chthonic ritual.

The use of *prognariter* and *prudens* in the Ennian formulation may be a reference to the collocation *prudens sciens,* as Skutsch suggests, a collocation that has connotations that make it appropriate for the *devotio.*[57] The collocation may be found in a reference to Amphiaraus in a letter of Cicero to Aulus Caecina:

> Ut in fabulis Amphiaraus sic ego "prudens et sciens ad pestem ante oculos positam" sum profectus. (*Fam.* 6.6.6)
>
> Just as Amphiaraus in the plays, I set out "well aware and knowing toward the death placed before my eyes."

Amphiaraus did not perform the Roman ritual of *devotio,* but the Argive hero, who was one among the first seven against Thebes, did go to Thebes knowing he was destined to die there and then was swallowed by the earth whole, a fitting parallel to a ceremony where a Roman general consecrates his body to the gods of the dead. The use of this phrase in the context of the story of Amphiaraus therefore suggests an association with death, if not the *devotio,* for someone who is *prudens et sciens.* Death is also the subtext of the collocation in Phaedria's exclamation in the *Eunuchus,* although not in a serious way:

> . . . et prudens sciens
> uiuos uidensque pereo . . . (*Eu.* 72–73)
>
> Well aware and knowing, alive and seeing, I am dying!

If Cicero's use of the same collocation may be located in the context of a tragic figure willingly accepting his fate, the use of *prudens* and *sciens* in Terence could be either a joke based on the unknown tragedy or a paratragic trope, because Phaedria is expressing a loss of honor rather than a loss of life.

Another passage from a letter of Caelius preserved in the correspondence of Cicero, does, however, invite a comparison to the *devotio* of Decius Mus in the *Annals* by means of several verbal echoes, including *sciens* and *prudens:*

> Etiam atque etiam, Cicero, cogita, ne te tuosque omnes funditus evertas, sciens prudensque eo demittas, unde exitum nullum vides. (*Fam.* 8.16)

> Again and yet again, think, Cicero, before you bring utter ruin on yourself and your family, before you plunge yourself with your eyes wide open into a situation from which you see there is no escape.[58]

The situation from which there is no escape (*unde exitum nullum*) is death, here an intimation that if Cicero joins Pompey, the result would be a death that Cicero would knowingly accept, a situation similar to that of Amphiaraus. The verbal echoes recall the *devotio* in Ennius. *Prudens sciens* is at least a partial echo of *prognariter . . . / . . . prudens* in Ennius. Moreover, the use of a form of *mitto* with the preverb *de* and *prudensque* parallels the climax of the *devotio* in Ennius closely: *<u>prudens</u> animam <u>de</u> corpore <u>mitto</u>.*

At some point, *prudens sciens* appears to have been associated with the *devotio* in the manner that it is conceptualized in the *Annals.* It is difficult to determine, however, whether the phrase was originally a literary coinage or was borrowed from ritual, even though there are indications that *prudens sciens* was associated with voluntary death as early as Terence. Either the Ennian *devotio* was so influential that later authors could collocate *prudens* and a verb of knowing in order to evoke the *devotio,* or Ennius is the first to record a traditional ritual collocation that was a natural fit because of its association with a voluntary sacrifice of one's life. Whatever the cause may have been, *prudens sciens* is an independent collocation attested in multiple texts in the context of a willing acceptance of death.

To return to the phrase *animam de corpore mitto* in the *Annals,* there are at least two collocations of a form of *mitto* and *animam* in the context of a loss of life outside of the *Annals,* even though the Ennian expression is no more likely to represent the "exact" wording of a traditional collocation than *prognariter . . . prudens.* The use of *demittas* in Caelius' letter and *de . . . mitto* in Ennius already suggests that *animam mitto* is a traditional idiom for death. This intuition finds some confirmation in Plautus' description of the battle against the Teleboans in the *Amphitruo:*

> Animam amittunt prius quam loco demigrent (*Am.* 240)

> They lost their lives before they left their posts.

A second, similar collocation is found in a joke of Strobilius, a slave in the *Aulularia,* who explains to two cooks just how miserly his master Euclio is:

> STROBILIUS: Quin, quom it dormitum follem opstringit ob gulam.
> ANTHRAX: Qur? STR: Ne quid animae forte amittat dormiens.
> AN: Etiamne opturat inferiorem gutturem,
> ne quid animai forte amittat dormiens? (*Aul.* 302–5)

> STROBILIUS: Indeed when he goes to sleep he ties a bag to his mouth.
> ANT: Why? STR: So that he doesn't lose any breath while he's asleep!
> ANT: Does he stop his nether orifice to prevent losing any air while he's asleep?

The literal understanding of *quid animae forte amittat,* an idiomatic expression for death, gives the joke its punch. The semantic relevance of *animam (de)mitto,* if not its frequency, suggests that it is a particularly Roman periphrasis for death.

A fragment from a play by Accius suggests that a similar expression had an association with the *devotio:*[59]

> Patrio exemplo et me dicabo atque animam devoro hostibus (*Praet.* 15)

> Following my father's example, I too will dedicate myself and devote my soul to the disadvantage of my enemies.

This utterance, apparently of the father of Decius Mus in his own *devotio* at the battle of Sentinum during the Third Samnite War, combines the object *animam* and a future form of *devoveo,* the verb used by Livy. Although the evidence vacillates between *mitto* and *devoveo,* the consistent use of *animam* suggests that it was, at least, the second root in the central expression of the rite as it was conceived in Rome in the second century.

Because the evidence for *devoveo* is later than that for *(de)mitto* and because *devoveo* is an obvious choice for the illocutionary verb in the rite, it is more likely that *animam . . . mitto* was the traditional core for the pronouncement of the ritual, provided a traditional core existed at all. The lack of such terminology and phraseology in Livy, with the exception of *Di Manes* and perhaps *devoveo* as a technical term, may be an indication that the Ennian version is closer to what a speaker of Latin in the second century might expect from a *devotio.* It is also possible that the differences between Ennius and Livy are the result of changes in Roman culture over a century and a half that led to different ideas of how *devotio* should be performed or that there never was a single idea because the ritual was very rarely performed.

Even if a fixed formula for the *devotio* existed, it would be surprising if Ennius had quoted the ritual verbatim. Ennius treats his ritual material in an allusive manner and often alters his source material for literary reasons, such as the near quotations in the speech of Pyrrhus and the play on augural phraseology in the description of the augury of Romulus and Remus. Moreover, if correctly performed, the *devotio* necessarily meant the death of the one who utters the formula, a circumstance that would encourage variation as a form of taboo deformation and discourage any direct quotation in order to pass it on to the next generation. If Pyrrhus has indeed endangered himself by the accidental misuse of ritual language in the wrong context, one can only imagine what would happen to the reader who uttered the exact wording of a ritual phrase that compelled him to die as a chthonic sacrifice.

Whether the notional climax of the *devotio* was *animam mitto, animam devoveo,* or something completely different, the verb *mittere* may, in fact, have been especially appropriate in a ritual that amounts to an exchange of one's life, or *anima,* for the safety of an army in peril. The archaic verb *mitat* appears in two inscriptions, at least one of which is ritual in nature. Moreover, recently proposed etymology for *mitat* suggests that *mitto* may be a misreading of a verb that meant "to exchange," not "to send," that may have been a constituent of an archaic Latin ritual collocation semantically parallel to *donum dare.* It is even possible that the phrase *animam . . . mitto* in Ennius is a misreading of this collocation, lending ritual weight and venerability to the already weighty Ennian *devotio.*

This verb *mitat* occurs in the Duenos Bowl, one of the oldest of all Latin inscriptions:

> Iovesat deiuos qoi med mitat nei ted endo cosmis virco sied . . . (*CIL* I^2 4)
>
> The one who *mitat* me swears by the gods if the girl is not friendly to you . . .

Although much of the inscription is far from transparent,[60] the portion under discussion here is fairly easy to understand in spite of the archaic spellings, prerhotacisms (the presence of an *-s-* between vowels where an *-r-* is found in classical Latin) and uncontracted forms. The archaic spelling *iovesat,* for example, indicates that the form contracted at some point to *iusat* (from an earlier form *iousat*) and that the *-s-* in *iusat* became the *-r-* in *iurat,* or "rhotacized."

Because *mitat* occurs in a second archaic inscription of a ritual nature, the verb may also have ritual connotations. The so-called Tibur Pedestal commemorates a gift on behalf of the dedicator's son:

. . . med mitat kauios [. . .] monios qetios d[o]num pro fileod (*CIL* I² 2658)

Kavius Cetius *mitat* me as a gift on behalf of his son.[61]

The expression *donum pro fileod* in the Tibur Pedestal suggests a ritual context, since a gift in exchange for one's son implies the fulfillment of a vow to a god to save the life of one's offspring. It is therefore likely that a votive offering once stood upon the pedestal. If the Tibur Pedestal is a ritual text, then *mitat,* the central action described on the pedestal may indicate that the Duenos Bowl is a parody of a ritual dedication or simply a ritual dedication with a playful inscription.

The use of *mitat,* a verb that closely resembles *mittit,* in these archaic inscriptions suggests that the audience of the *Annals* might readily consider *mitto* an acceptably solemn verb for the *devotio.* Because geminate consonants are often spelled with a single consonant in archaic Latin inscriptions, such as *anua* for *annua* in *CIL* I² 366 and *Apolenei* for *Apollini* in *CIL* I² 368, *mitat* gives every impression of being an archaic spelling of the classical Latin form *mittit.* The use of *mitto* in the language of chthonic ritual may therefore be a more recent narrowing of the wider ritual connotations of the verb in archaic Rome.

Nevertheless, there are formal and semantic problems with such an equation. In the first place Paulus ex Festo (PAUL. *Fest.* p. 67M) cites *cosmittere* as an archaic form of *committere.* If *cosmittere* is genuine,[62] then the archaic form of *mittere* would almost certainly be spelled **smitere.* If Paulus ex Festo is incorrect, *mitat* could be a subjunctive of *mittere* in a relative clause of characteristic in the Duenos Bowl, but such an interpretation is untenable for the Tibur Pedestal, because *mitat* is the main verb in the inscription. Because the form in the Tibur Pedestal is apparently indicative and belongs to the first conjugation, it is very likely that *mitat* in the Duenos Bowl is another occurrence of the same first conjugation verb. If *mitat* is a first conjugation form of *mittere,* it must be an "intensive" form, just as *dictare,* "to say repeatedly," is an intensive form of *dicere,* "to say." It is not at all obvious, however, what such a verb would mean, as Brent Vine observes.[63] It is not unthinkable that the *mitat* of the Duenos Bowl implies sending something repeatedly, but the dedication of the Tibur Pedestal must be a one-time act.

Vine sidesteps these formal and semantic problems by understanding the verb as a factitive verb formed from a completely different root like the one seen in a form like *mutare* (originally *moitare*). If *mitat* is a Latin reflex of an Indo-European verbal root that means "to exchange,"[64] as Vine suggests, then *mitat* would mean "he exchanges" rather than "he sends," a much more appropriate meaning for the Tibur Pedestal. Although "he sent" is not obviously the wrong meaning in the Duenos Bowl, neither is "he exchanges."

Mitat may also have been a member of a traditional collocation that referred to ritual exchange similar to the ritual collocation *donum dare*. Vine argues that *mitat . . . donum* on the Tibur Pedestal is an alteration of an archaic **mitat meinom,* "he exchanges an exchange," a semantically weightier phrase that co-existed with *donum dare*. This collocation may, in fact, underlie the overall structure of the inscription on the Duenos Bowl, if the expressions *mitat . . . donum* and *feced . . . meinom* in the third line of the inscription are variants of **mitat meinom:*

> Iovesat deiuos qoi med mitat nei ted endo cosmis virco sied . . .
> Duenos med **feced** en mano(m) **<u>meinom</u>** duenoi ne med malos tatod

> The one who exchanges me swears by the gods if the girl is not friendly to you . . . A good man made me as fine (exchange-)gift for a good man, let an evil person not steal me.[65]

The fact that a repetition of a single underlying root of *mitat* and *meinom* would also form a loose, interlocking ring composition with the repetition of the root *duenos* may also be an indication that *meinom* and *mitat* are derived from the same root:

> . . . mitat[a]. . . . (intervening conditional clause)
> duenos[b]. . . . meinom[a] duenoi.[b]

The combination of *mitat* and *donum* in the Tibur Pedestal also implies that *mitat* is an acceptable variant for *dare* in the traditional collocation *donum dare,* another indication that *mitat* had ritual connotations.

These ritual connotations may explain why Ennius chose *mitto* as the illocutionary verb of his *devotio*. Once the verb *mitat* became obsolete, the vague similarity between the semantics of "send" and "exchange" and the phonetic similarity of *mitat* and *mittit* likely led to a reinterpretation of **mitare* as a form of *mittere*. The form *mitat* may have been especially susceptible to reinterpretation as a form of *mittit* in the context of chthonic cult, where the difference would not have been great between sending things to the dead and to underworld entities and exchanging the one's life or the life of another. Along this line of reasoning, the use of *mitto* as a "Terminus des Totenkultus" may have its origin in a reanalysis of *mito* as an archaic spelling of *mitto* without *geminatio*. It is also possible that Ennius, or his audience, perceived *mitat* as an archaic form of *mittit* in expressions on dedicatory inscriptions such as *mitat donum*. Whether or not the "archaic spelling" of *mittit* meant "he exchanges" to Ennius, its appropriateness for a ritual exchange in archaic dedications would have been manifest, another condition that may have prompted him to use the verb *mitto* in the pronouncement of the *devotio*.

If **meinom mitare* was in fact, a traditional collocation, as Vine proposes, then *animam mitto* in Ennius may even be a reintrepretation of this archaic ritual formula. If there were instantiations of *meinom mitare* in other archaic votive inscriptions, then the context of these inscriptions would suggest that the phrase was an expression of the latest in a series of reciprocal exchanges, or in Roman terms a state of *gratia*, between a mortal and a god. Because *meinom* would have been incomprehensible to a speaker of Latin in the second century BCE, any direct quotation of **meinom mitare* would be meaningless when recited, even if **mitare* could easily be understood as *mittere*. *Animam* would have been a particularly attractive reanalysis of *meinom* in the context of the *devotio*, on semantic and phonetic grounds, since the consonantal skeletons of both words were very similar. It is possible that Ennius has adapted **meinom mitare* in his version of the *devotio*, an adaptation that could lend the semantic weight of an archaic ritual collocation to an already charged context. The verb *mitat* may therefore be not only a philological curiosity but also a word choice that was meaningful to Ennius and his audience.

The underlying concept of the *devotio* as a reciprocal exchange with the gods of the underworld resonates with other fragments of book 6 in more than one way. I have already noted that these chthonic gods seem to be especially active in book 6. I have also demonstrated that reciprocity is a central theme of book 6 that plays itself out in the actions and words of Pyrrhus and Decius Mus. The language of Pyrrhus' speech and Decius' *devotio* is colored by allusions to, and quotations of, various ritual collocations that invite comparison between the two speakers and also betray the attitudes of both speakers toward ritual reciprocity, attitudes that augur for the success of Decius Mus and the eventual failure of Pyrrhus.

Parallel Lives: Decius and Pyrrhus in Book 6 of the *Annals*

As is the case with any contrast, the differences between the *devotio* of Decius Mus and the speech of Pyrrhus imply sameness. Although the Epirote leader is concerned more with war than the *pax deorum*, and although the Roman general is remembered more for a ritual than the battle he lost, the use of ritual system reference in the speeches of Decius and Pyrrhus provides a common frame of reference. The difference in the intentionality of ritual language is similarly marked by sameness. Pyrrhus closes his speech with a formulaic nod to the gods, *volentibus cum magnis,* a closing that cannot be unintentional. Moreover, the explicit ritual of the *devotio* is no more effective than the implicit, accidental ritual elements in Pyrrhus' speech, because both passages ultimately fail *qua* ritual (if Decius Mus did indeed survive his attempted self-sacrifice). If the *devotio* and the speech of Pyrrhus are meant to be read against one another, these similarities are necessary to draw attention to what initially appear to be unrelated acts in the drama of book 6, since there are no verbal correspondences in the two passages.

In addition to the pointed use of ritual system reference in the words of Pyrrhus and Decius, there are other points of similarity between the Greek and his Roman opponent that defy easy categorization. Pyrrhus' victory against Decius at Ausculum complicates a simple equation of proper performance of Roman ritual with success against the foreigner who fails to observe such protocols. Moreover, the relationship between Decius and Pyrrhus becomes very complicated in the larger tradition of the Pyrrhic War. The massacre of the leading citizens of Rhegium by another commander named Decius, who then installs himself as a tyrant (*Per.* 12, D. H. 20.4), blurs the distinction between pious Roman general and despotic Greek king by virtue of their shared *nomen* Decius.

The sources agree that a Campanian named Decius Vibullius was sent at the head of a legion to the Greek city of Rhegium. Dionysius says that his purpose was to protect the inhabitants from the Lucanians, Bruttians, and Tarentines (D.H. 20.4.2). Instead Decius massacres some portion of the population, among other outrages, and makes himself tyrant (D.H. 20.4.3–8). (In the epitome of Livy's history, the so-called *Periochae,* the action is described by the ablative absolute construction *occisis Rheginis,* "after the citizens of Rhegium were killed" [*Per.* 12].) At some point the Romans besieged Rhegium and beheaded the legion that occupied the city. What is most interesting for the theme of exchange in the Pyrrhic War is a detail in the story of the death of Decius reported by Dionysius (20.5.5). The Campanian prefect bribed the guards in order to escape beheading (only to commit suicide). The namesake of Decius in this story sets himself as a monarch and then participates in an illicit commercial transaction. Such thematic parallels beg the question of whether the last detail was taken from book 6 of the *Annals.*

Other details in the historiographical tradition that are concerned with commerce may also reflect the influence of the thematic structure of book 6.

Although these details are not attested for the *Annals,* the mention of the pernicious influence of a king's gold in another fragment of book 20 of Dionysius resonates with the thematic importance of gold and kings in the fragments of book 6 (20.6.3).[66] Nor is there any mention in the fragments of a tradition that at the end of the Pyrrhic War the Romans began to use silver coins for the first time, an event described in the extremely terse *Periochae* (*Per.* 15). Any connection between these historical details and book 6 of the *Annals* would be tenuous, but there does seem to be a common emphasis on commercial exchange in the fragments of the poem and the historians of the Pyrrhic War, either because the historians have been influenced by Ennius or because an older tradition influenced Ennius. In either case, it seems that the poet's narrative of the Pyrrhic War was as much a meditation on commercial and ritual exchange as it was a historical account of a war.

Because Pyrrhus had become familiar to Roman audiences, the negotiation between foreign and familiar in book 6 is something that takes place in the past rather than in the present. Perhaps it is possible for Ennius to imagine the original encounter between the foreign and the familiar in the *Annals* because Pyrrhus defamiliarized Greek culture for the Romans so profoundly that there was a historical memory of the experience of marching to southern Italy to encounter something that was beyond Roman expectations. For the first time, a Roman army encountered elephants and a charismatic Greek leader who did not hail from Magna Graecia and who claimed descent from the Homeric hero Achilles.[67]

Pyrrhus is analogous to Jupiter Versor in my discussion of Jupiter Stator, a figure who was symbolic of a different culture but was, in turn, appropriated into a discourse of Roman identity. Because he was both a familiar figure in the Roman tradition in the lifetime of Ennius and an agent of defamiliarization in the early third century BCE, Pyrrhus is at the center of the mediation between the foreign and the familiar, on the one hand, and the past and the present on the other.

The use of history in the *Annals,* and the use of the traditional language of ritual, a recognizable and specialized form of language that must have been heard daily in the lives of real Romans, invites some thought about another common binary opposition: life and literature. Pyrrhus in many ways embodies this tension as both a historical and epic figure who himself elided the gap between epic and reality, both because of his claim of descent from Achilles and because of his status as a king in an era when the difference between royalty and divinity was not always easily perceived. History, another Greek invention, implies historical truth about real people whose motivations and characters cannot be easily known or reduced to an epic prototype. The difficulty in accurately representing history in an epic form must have been all the more obvious to anyone who had at least known a participant of the Pyrrhic War, as Ennius likely did.

The confrontation between recent history and epic is exactly the combination that drives the action of much of Athenian tragedy, a genre similar and dissimilar to epic, much as Pyrrhus is to his Roman opponents. The tragic elements of the story of Pyrrhus in the *Annals* may superimpose yet another literary model over the already complex mix of history and epic that forms the generic template of the *Annals*.[68] Ritual system reference is as implicated in the few allusions to tragedy in the *Annals* as it is in the allusions to Homer discussed in chapter 2. At the risk of stating the obvious, a binary opposition between history and poetry cannot be maintained in a poem that treats history, let alone between history and a specific poetic genre.

Although Pyrrhus is part of a discourse of what it means to be Roman, he is himself a discourse that can raise larger issues concerning the relationships between Roman and Greek culture, man and god, and literary genres. In sum, Pyrrhus is "good to think with" for Ennius, just as ritual is in the *Annals*. When the two are combined, the result is a narrative of the Pyrrhic War so compelling that it still had at least one reader in Herculaneum in the first century CE.

CHAPTER 5

Ritual, Kinship, and Myth in Book 1 of the Annals

If the number of lines preserved by other sources for a particular book is any indication, then book 1 of the *Annals* was even more popular than book 6. One hundred and twelve of 623 extant lines are assigned to book 1 in Skutsch's edition, including two fragments that exceed 18 consecutive lines. There are also a number of *testimonia* for parts of book 1 that attest to its significance for later readers: the division of the Romans into tribes by Romulus and several details of the narrative of the rape of Ilia and the subsequent exposure of her twins, for example, are credited to Ennius by several sources, such as Servius, Porphyrio, who wrote a commentary on Horace, and the *Origo Gentis Romanae.* Because the first book of the *Annals* was a definitive statement of the myth of the origin of the Roman nation, no Roman author who came after Ennius—even the fourth-century CE author of the *Origo Gentis Romanae*—was able to approach the beginnings of the city without engaging the *Annals.*[1]

The number of quotations and references to book 1 of the *Annals* not only suggests that this part of the epic was widely read; it also provides a clearer glimpse of its thematic structure than any other part of the poem. Book 1 presents early Roman history as a family history over three generations—Aeneas, his daughter Ilia, and her son Romulus—which would have resonated with various traditions about different aristocratic families and their contributions to the Roman state. The *Aeneidae* are not a typical *gens nobile* of the middle Republic, though, since they all become immortal. Nor are they distant descendants of gods like the Fabii, who claimed Hercules as their ancestor; rather they are the immediate offspring of Venus and Mars. In spite of their close genetic relationships with the gods (and the fact that they don't die), the three generations of the *Aeneidae* are a family of mothers, fathers, sons, and a daughter, who interact with each other as an ordinary family under extraordinary circumstances. Although it is never easy to piece together a narrative from scattered fragments, Ilia appears to have less difficulty communicating with her grandmother Venus than with her father, for example, an indication that gender roles play an important role in the first book of the *Annals*. Because gender, family, and mortality are a means of placing an individual in the larger social (and cosmic) structure, these three elements of the narrative are all subthemes of a larger concern with social hierarchies.

The exploration of these hierarchies in book 1 cannot be studied in precise detail because of the fragmentary state of the text. The great majority of the fragments, however, provide glimpses of constant negotiation of social position. The augural contest of Romulus and Remus (discussed in chapter 3) is, among other things, a means of determining which twin will be subordinate to the other in the society of their future city. Although little can be said of the details, the rape of the Sabine women and the co-optation of the Sabines into the Roman state integrate various individuals into a new and all-encompassing social structure. Moreover, the incorporation of the Sabines into the Roman state resonates with Ennius' own experience as a native Italian who took up residence in Rome and was granted citizenship. In sum, these negotiations between different characters of different social standing in the *Annals* would not have differed very much from the navigation of the network of unequal relationships familiar to its Roman audience.

The mythic origin of Rome in the *Annals* is not, however, a monolithic expression of the power relationships or of the ideology behind the system; it is a series of narratives that are "good to think with" about Roman society. The narratives explore the weak points of Roman social structure and the space between the fixed points on the hierarchical continuum, an exploration that should not be surprising, given the limited social mobility at Rome. Ennius himself, as well as manumitted slaves, became citizens. Nor is the use of literature to think about the social hierarchy of the middle Republic confined to the *Annals*. The comedies of Plautus invert social positions, if only to restore and reaffirm them, as Kathleen McCarthy has demonstrated.[2] If the *Annals* is not a monoglossic encomium of Roman society, any more than Ennius was a "groveling national epicist,"[3] then the same is true of book 1 of the epic, only more so. Just as in the comedies of Plautus, Ennius interrogates, problematizes, and, ultimately, affirms the Roman social order in the mythic context of book 1.

The diction of the fragments can also be "good to think with" about the social relationships in the story and, by extension, the same relationships in contemporary Rome. The ambiguity of the single signifier *pater,* for example, becomes manifest in a mythological narrative that details the birth of children fathered by gods and born to mortal women. Because *pater* has one meaning when used in the context of kinship (e.g., *paterfamilias*) and another in ritual (*Iu-p(p)iter* < *Dies pater*), these meanings are in dialogue with one another but maintain their separate meanings. The signifier *pater* is one point of contact between two forms of system reference, which can recall one form of system reference when the other is the primary mode. Although some overlap between forms of system reference or registers is natural, the pattern of system reference in book 1 is characterized by a consistent overlap between ritual and kinship. When Ilia calls upon her *pater* Aeneas, kinship is the primary mode of system reference, even though her father is an immortal who could in theory be addressed as *Aeneas pater* in a ritual context. When Ilia makes use of ritual collocations while addressing her *pater,* the potential for slippage becomes greater. The slippage between ritual and kinship reference is not unique to Ilia's experience with her father; it is endemic to all of book 1.

In addition to the augural contest between Romulus and Remus, there are several other substantial fragments from book 1 of the *Annals.* The longest of these describes an impressionistic dream narrated by Ilia, the mother of Romulus and Remus, that seems to indicate she was raped by the god Mars. This fragment of seventeen lines is one of eight fragments of two or more entire lines of hexameters and one of fifteen of more than one line in Skutsch's edition of the *Annals.* The content of the shorter fragments includes a portrait of Anchises, a description of the actions of the she-wolf who nursed Romulus and Remus, and several prayers and invocations. The amount of material that survives from book 1 is extensive and allows a surer glimpse of Ennius' narrative technique and his use of more than one form of system reference.

Because of its length, the dream of Ilia is the most tractable for a standard literary analysis, as can be seen in the extensive bibliography on the fragment, but also for a study of system reference in the *Annals.* The primary mode of system reference is not ritual, however, but kinship, since the content of the dream deals with the relationships between sisters, father, daughters, and mothers and the language of the fragment naturally includes some kinship terms, the basic unit of any kinship system. Kinship is the primary mode of system reference, but the use of ritual collocations throughout the passage engages in just as lively a dialogue with ritual system reference as military and ritual system reference in the already-discussed speech of Pyrrhus from book 6 (see chapter 4). As I have demonstrated, this dynamic conversation between two culturally meaningful spheres of language adds layers of meaning to the narrative of the *Annals.* The most striking effect of this particular passage is the reminder that Ilia is a mortal lost in the world of immortals, like Mars and even her recently apotheosized father in her dream.

In the fragment there are single kinship terms and collocations that lend weight and meaning to Ilia's various familial relationships. The unnamed daughter of Eurydica is not simply her sister but her *germana soror,* a traditional and weighty expression of their relationship. Moreover, the sequence contains both constituents of the traditional collocation *patre prognatus,* yet another formal expression of kinship, even though *pater* and *prognata* are not actually collocated in the passage. The yield of collocations of kinship is much more meager than the yield of ritual collocations in the other fragments I have already discussed, but the impact of this form of system reference on readers of the *Annals* would still have been meaningful, since kinship systems tend to consist of single words rather than phrases and because the content of the passage is so focused on the relationships between Ilia and members of her immediate family (not to mention the mysterious man who is likely Mars, the father of her twin boys).

Kinship system reference is in dialogue with ritual system reference in the passage and can be seen in a number of traditional ritual collocations therein. When Ilia addresses her father, the now immortal Aeneas, she raises her hands to him and describes her posture with a traditional collocation that signals an attitude of prayer: *tendebam manus.* Yet another expression in the interchange with her father parallels a traditional ritual collocation in Umbrian so closely that it is likely to be another traditional expression of prayer in Roman ritual. Because her narrative opens with an expression that closely resembles an Oscan phrase from a curse tablet, this phrase too may be a traditional ritual collocation. Moreover, these collocations do more than add solemnity to the narrative. They implicitly comment on the dynamics of the relationship between Ilia and her immortal father, who can now be a figure of cult addressed in prayer.

Nor is the use of ritual language to problematize a family relationship between mortals and immortals unique to the dream of Ilia, since there are at least three other fragments that generate tension between familial and ritual *pietas* from book 1 of the *Annals.* Whereas Ilia strikes an attitude of prayer when she addresses Aeneas, an unidentified speaker, presumably Jupiter, speaks of raising someone to the skies (*tu tolles in caerula caeli / templa* [*Ann.* 54–55]). Because this expression recalls Ilia raising her hands to the sky, the lifting of hands in Roman prayer and the formal recognition of one's offspring as legitimate, it generates still more tension between ritual and kinship system reference. The collocation *genetrix patris* (*Ann.* 58) "mother of my father," also sounds odd in Ilia's prayer for divine aid from Venus, even though the goddess is, in fact, her grandmother. Nor does the use of the same collocation to refer to Romulus later in book 1 help to separate the ritual meaning of the collocation of *pater* and *genitor* from its literal meaning as a kinship term. Although the details are not entirely clear and much of the text is missing, Ennius appears to put constant pressure on the connotative instability of these signifiers throughout book 1.

The insistent use of traditional ritual and kinship collocations where slippage is almost bound to occur reveals something both about the Latin language and Roman culture and also about Ennius as a poet. In the first place, the deconstruction of the binary opposition between mortal and immortal by means of implicitly calling attention to the metaphors of kinship employed in ritual, in a single passage as well as across a larger narrative, suggests that Ennius had a sophisticated understanding of the limits of language. Nor does Ennius ever seem to lose control of his own diction, since the two systems never completely collapse into one another or into pure chaos. Instead, Ennius is able to raise implicit questions about the familial and ritual structures that give meaning to Roman society while simultaneously affirming them.

Annals 34–51: The Dream of Ilia

Gender, family, and mortality, three of the key themes of book 1 of the *Annals* are all in play in a well-known fragment from book 1 quoted by Cicero in his *De Divinatione* (1.40–41). This extended passage from the *Annals* that treats the dream of Ilia, the daughter of Aeneas, and the mother of Romulus and Remus. The beautiful stranger (*homo pulcer*) must be Mars, the father of her twins:[4]

> Et cita cum tremulis anus attulit artubus lumen,
> talia tum memorat lacrimans, exterrita somno:
> "Eurydica prognata pater quam noster amavit,
> vires vitaque corpus meum nunc deserit omne.
> nam me visus homo pulcer per amoena salicta
> et ripas raptare locosque novos: Ita sola
> postilla, germana soror, errare videbar
> tardaque vestigare et quaerere te neque posse
> corde capessere: semita nulla pedem stabilibat.
> Exim compellare pater me voce videtur
> his verbis: 'o gnata, tibi sunt ante gerendae
> aerumnae, post ex fluvio fortuna resistet.'
> Haec ecfatus pater, germana, repente recessit

> nec sese dedit in conspectum corde cupitus,
> quamquam multa manus ad caeli caerula templa
> tendebam lacrumans et blanda voce vocabam.
> Vix aegro cum corde meo me somnus reliquit." (*Ann.* 34–50)[5]

> When the old woman roused up, had with limbs a-tremble brought a light, then the maid, frightened out of sleep, spoke thus in tears:—"O Daughter of Eurydica, you whom our father loved, now strength and life too leave all my body. For a man of beautiful looks seemed to hurry me away among pleasant sallow-thickets and banks and places strange; so, my own sister, after that did I seem to wander alone, and slow-footed to track and search for you, but to be unable to catch you in my senses; no path made sure my stepping. Then it was father who seemed to lift up his voice and speak to me in these words:—; 'O daughter, first there are hardships to be borne by you; but after that, your fortunes will rise again from the river.' With these words, my own sister, did father suddenly withdraw, and no longer gave himself to my gaze though my heart longed for him; no even though many a time and with tears did I keep holding out my hands toward the blue precincts of the sky, and called and called him with caressing voice. Then did sleep scarcely leave me all sick at heart." (trans. Warmington)

The importance of gender in the passage has been the subject of much discussion, since Ilia's voice is feminine and therefore an alternative to the traditionally masculine voice of epic.[6] Such a focus also implicitly recognizes the importance of the family, including the relationship between Ilia and her father, her sister, and the father of her twin sons. The dream is also an account of the interaction between Ilia (a mortal woman who will become immortal), an Olympian deity, and her once mortal, but now immortal, father. Because gender, family, and mortality are means of positioning an individual in the overarching hierarchical social structure of Roman society, Ilia's dream is an exploration of the web of relationships between Ilia, her father, her sister, and Mars.

To begin at the level of the single signifier, kinship appears to be the primary mode of system reference. Several signs belonging to the Roman kinship system are repeated in the space of twenty lines. *Pater* is deployed three times within eleven lines. Although Ilia's sister is without a name, her relationship to Ilia is explicitly illustrated by the vocative *germana soror,* and to Aeneas by the title *Eurydica prognata.* The pronoun *noster* in the relative clause *pater quam noster amavit* also indicates that Ilia and her addressee are sisters begotten of the same father. *Prognata* and *germana* are both at least partially repeated. The relationship between sisters, father, and (step)mother is therefore relatively easy to map onto the kinship system of Republican Rome, a subtle collapse of the distance between the past and the present.

The fact that Ilia, her sister, and Aeneas are never named in the fragment also gives an impression of a system of signifiers defined by opposition rather than an actual family of individuals. The only name in the fragment is Eurydica, which had little weight of tradition. The name Aeneas, on the other hand, would have evoked not only this story but also other episodes, both in the larger mythic tradition and within the *Annals,* a tradition that is partially effaced by the generic signifier *pater.* The name Ilia alone may not have been enough to evoke the mythical foundation of Rome, since it is not the only name of the mother of Romulus and Remus that is attested in the tradition. The similarity between Ilia and Ilium, an alternate name for Troy, would also recall the story of the larger Trojan war narrative within the *Annals.* The narrative context of the dream does not enable total slippage between the family of Aeneas and a typical Roman family in the age of Ennius. The poet nevertheless foregrounds kinship system reference within the larger mythic narrative by referring to the actors within the fragment by means of generic kinship terms.

These generic terms of kinship also imply a hierarchy of gender. Because *germana, soror,* and *(pro)gnata* are not gender neutral, they signify a position of subordination to masculine relatives, especially the *paterfamilias.* The use of gendered signifiers in the passage also overlaps with and reinforces the emphasis on structural opposition over individuality. The lack of names again leaves the impression of a system of male and female signifiers opposing one another in a way that is unexceptional for the age of Ennius.

The fragment narrates a key mythological moment in the foundation of the Roman state, but on the level of word choice it does not differ much from a Roman comedy in terms of plot and character. A *gnata* is raped by an unknown *homo* and must appeal to her *pater* for protection. Moreover, the *homo* turns out to be someone the family "knows," although the characters of the drama are not yet aware of the fact. This similarity to the generic plot of a Roman comedy is not just another indication of the emphasis on structure over the individual; it also calls attention to the gender dynamics of the passage.

The narrative of the dream differs from the typical comic plot, because the focus is on the female instead of the male characters. The *homo pulcer,* a jarring intrusion into a decidedly feminine world, is the analogue to the comic *adulescens,* but he has no voice, while Ilia is the primary speaker. Ennius has here created a private feminine space that gives an alternative point of view toward situations and characters that are typical of comedy, rather than the usual masculine view of these events played out in a public space, as is usual for Roman comedy.

This system of familial relationships is not entirely commensurate with the great majority of Roman comedies, or the kinship system of Rome in the second century BCE, since Mars is a god, Aeneas is immortal, and Ilia and her unborn son Romulus are destined to achieve immortality. In other words, kinship overlaps with ritual system reference, even though kinship is the dominant mode of system reference in the passage. Because he is never mentioned by name, Mars is drawn into the ambiguous semantics of *pater;* he is both the god addressed as *Mars pater* in Cato's prayer and the actual sire of Romulus and Remus. Aeneas is both father to Ilia and apotheosized hero, much as Romulus will be both son to Ilia and apotheosized hero. The opposition between mortal and immortal that was a constant in the experience of the audience of the *Annals* is unstable in book 1, to say the least. This instability is a natural product of the mythic nature of the narrative, but Ennius appears to exacerbate the relative mobility between mortality and immortality by means of ambiguous word choices such as *pater.*

Kinship system reference is operative not only on the level of the single, generic signifier but also on the level of the traditional collocation. The side-by-side placements of *prognata pater* and *pater germana* do not constitute true collocations, but the semantic associations between these lexemes are very strong, all the more so because they operate within the kinship system that colors the passage. Moreover, the force of tradition helps to bind two of these implied doubling figures, if *prognata pater* and *germana soror* are transformations of underlying traditional collocations in the language of kinship—and the evidence suggests they are. If *prognata pater* is, in fact, an allusion to the collocation *prognatus patre,* the feminine form is unusual, though not unattested. The predominance of the masculine form *prognatus patre* outside of the *Annals* therefore indicates that Ennius has changed the traditional gender of the collocation, and it resonates with the slippage between immortal and mortal in signifiers like *pater.*

Traditional ritual collocations are also present in the fragment. Ilia deploys the expression *manus . . . tendebam,* a ritual collocation that demonstrably indicates an attitude of prayer in Latin poetry and prose after Ennius. The expression *voce vocabam* has a cognate expression in Umbrian, and it can also be found in a ritual context in later Latin poetry. The close semantic and phonetic parallel between Ilia's *vires vitaque* and the Oscan expression **biass biítam** may indicate that the Latin phrase is another allusion to a traditional ritual collocation. Whatever meaning it may have had, it seems likely that the audience of the *Annals* would have recognized the ritual coloring of the passage.

Although these traditional collocations do not overlap in their original context in the same manner as *donum dare,* the slippage between kinship and ritual system reference is implied by juxtaposition rather than inherent ambiguity. The mere presence of ritual language in a passage where kinship is the dominant mode of system reference invites an exploration of the overlap between the two modes. If the ambiguity endemic to the single signifier *pater* is not immediately obvious, the use of ritual collocations that specifically index the act of prayer may alert the audience to the fact that the meaning of *pater* is especially unstable in the case of Aeneas in relationship to Ilia. The larger pattern of apotheosis in three successive generations within the same pattern may also encourage the audience to consider the gray area between kinship and ritual system reference and between mortal and immortal.

Kinship System Reference in Ilia's Dream

The combination of *germanus* and *frater,* and occasionally *germana* and *soror,* is common enough in early Latin to warrant the suggestion that *germana soror* in Ilia's account is a reference to a traditional collocation. In the *Menaechmi* of Plautus, the slave Messenio expresses his belief that the two Menaechmi are *fratres germanos (Men.* 1102). The *Fasti Consulares Capitolini* also employs the phrase *HEI FRAtRES GERMANI FUERUNT* (*Fast. Con. Cap.* 18b). In addition to these examples, there are more in Cicero (*Ver.* 1.128) and Livy (35.10.8). The use of *hermano,* the Spanish reflex of *germanus,* as the generic word for "brother" implies that the expression *germanus frater* was shortened to *germanus* sometime before Spanish became a distinct language from Latin. Terence also employs the phrase *in germani fratris . . . loco* (*An.* 292).

The collocation is not limited to the masculine gender. There are numerous examples of *germana soror* in one form or another in Plautus, including *germana mea sororcula* (*Cist.* 451). Variants of *germana soror* may be found at *Aulularia* 122 (*germanam sororem*); *Miles Gloriosus* 238 (*sororem geminam germanam*), 383 (*mea soror geminast germana*), and 441 (*geminam germanam meam hic sororem*); *Trinummus* 690 (*germanam meam sororem*), and *Truculentus* 438 (*germanae quod sorori non credit soror*). The audience of the *Annals* almost certainly would have recognized *germana soror* as a traditional collocation of kinship.

Although *prognata* and *pater* in the sequence *prognata pater* belong to different syntactic units, the placement of both signifiers one after the other is reminiscent of the traditional kinship collocation *prognatus patre,* a phrase that appears in a number of texts from the second century BCE, including one of the epitaphs of Cornelii Scipiones. The second oldest of the collection features a pristine example of this traditional expression of kinship:[7]

Cornelius Lucius Scipio Barbatus
Gnaivod patre prognatus fortis vir sapiensque
quoius forma virtutei parisuma
fuit, consol censor aidilis quei fuit apud vos
Taurasia Cisauna Samnio cepit
subigit omne Loucanam opsidesque abdoucit (*CIL* I² 7)

Lucius Cornelius Scipio Barbatus
son of his father Gnaeus, a brave and wise man,
whose appearance was very much equal to his courage,
who was consul, censor and aedile among you,
captured Taurasia and Cisauna in Samnium,
subdued all Lucania, and brought back hostages.

The epitaph tends to allude to rather than to quote the traditional language of triumphing generals, but its traditional character is not in question. The conclusion of this inscription, for example, evokes the traditional collocation of *capere* and *dare* in other texts of this nature. Moreover, as Friedrich Klingner notes, *sapiens et fortis* in Horace's *Epistle to Augustus* (2.1.50) parallels the phrase *fortis vir sapiensque* in the epitaph,[8] an expression that Horace uses while describing the poetry of Ennius and other archaic texts. The resemblance of the two phrases may be fortuitous, but given the other plays on traditional phraseology in the inscription, *fortis vir sapiensque* is also likely to be a traditional expression, perhaps germane to the *laudatio funebris* rather than the inscriptions of victorious commanders. The context of *Gnaivod patre prognatus* therefore implies that it too is a traditional expression.

It is not likely to be accidental that three instances of *prognatus patre* occur in the *Menaechmi,* a play that is very much concerned with paternity. When the man whom the *meretrix* Erotium believes to be her client, but who is actually the brother of her client, fails to recognize her, she asks, exasperated, whether she does not know Menaechmus, the son of Moschus:

EROTIUM: non ego novi Menaechmum, Moscho prognatum patre . . . ? (*Men.* 407)

I do not know Menaechmus, the son of his father Moschus . . . ?

The fact that both Erotium's client and the man who does not know her are both named Menaechmus and are, in fact, born of the same father, becomes known to the characters only much later in the play, when Messenio, the faithful slave of the Menaechmus who does not know Erotium asks the other Menaechmus for the name of his father. The other Menaechmus responds thus:

MENAECHMUS 1: Me esse dico Moscho prognatum patre.
MENAECHMUS 2: Tun meo patre es prognatus? (*Men.* 1078–79)

M1: I declare I am the son of my father Moschus.
M2: You are the son of my father?

The two other collocations of *prognatus* and *patre* in the Plautine corpus come from the *Amphitruo,* another play that is concerned with paternity, and one that features characters who look so much alike that the other characters cannot tell them apart. Sosia, the slave of Amphitruo identifies himself twice as the son of Davus:

SOSIA: Sosiam vocant Thebani Davo prognatum patre (*Am.* 365)

The Thebans call me Sosia the son of his father Davus.

SOSIA: Davo prognatum patre eodem quo ego sum . . . (*Am.* 614)

The son of the same father Davus from whom I was (born).

All the instances in Plautus occur when the identity of a character is questioned, a context suggesting that *prognatus patre* had illocutionary force. To state that one is the *prognatus* of a particular *pater* in Plautus amounts to a speech act that guarantees the identity of the speaker, even in the face of doubt over one's identity and paternity. If the same connotations applied in Rome in the second century BCE, then the use of *Gnaivod patre prognatus* is not merely a collocation but a solemn affirmation to all that the *laudandus* is indeed a member of the *gens* Cornelia and the son of Gnaeus. The statement that the sister of Ilia is the *prognata* of Eurydica may also be a representation of a speech act that formally recognizes the status of the sister. Moreover, the fact that formal recognition of the paternity of the sister is in proleptic contrast with the doubts concerning the paternity of Ilia's twins may have added an edge to Ilia's speech act that the individual meanings of *prognata, Eurydica,* and perhaps *pater* by themselves could not.

It is also possible that *patre prognatus* has some connotations of ritual solemnity, and specifically of divine birth, if its use in Caesar is not atypical. In his ethnography of the Gauls in the *de Bello Gallico,* Caesar reports a claim by the Gauls concerning their divine progenitor:

> Galli se omnes ab Dite patre prognatos praedicant idque ab druidibus proditum dicunt. (*Gal.* 6.18.1)

> The Gauls claim they are the offspring of father Dis and they say that it (i.e. this belief) is promulgated by the Druids.

The use of *patre prognatus* also occurs once in the context of divine parentage and once of a mythical father and son relationship in Roman tragedy. It therefore suggests a solemn connotation for the expression.

> Iove patre prognatus est (*Inc. trag.* 101)

> He is the offspring of father Jove.

> Dryante regem prognatum patre (NAEV. Trag. 49)

> The king, the offspring of his father Dryas.

Because tragedies often feature the recognition of a long-lost son, like Ion or Oedipus, these fragments may also be representations of speech acts that transform a stranger into legitimate offspring. It is possible that Caesar has here been influenced by recognition scenes of sons of gods in Roman tragedy or that he is hinting at the seriousness of the claim on the part of the druids. Whether or not *patre prognatus* attained ritual connotations primarily or secondarily, it seems to be a well-established expression that could be used to intimate some type of divine parentage in some contexts.

In spite of the fact that *prognata* and *pater* are divided by the common boundary of their respective syntactic units, a number of conditions would enable the two roots to retain the connotations of the traditional collocation without actually being a collocation. In the first place the semantic difference between "one begotten from her father" (*prognata patre*) and "one begotten whom our father loved" (*prognata pater quam noster amavit*) is not great. If the reader or reciter pronounces the syllables slowly, as Servius recommends for *Aeneid* 4.19 (*ad Aen.* 4.19), then the first four syllables of *prog-na-ta pa-* could deceive the reader into expecting *prognata patre.* The impression would be especially strong in the short time it takes to pronounce the onset of the fifth syllable: *prog-na-ta pa-t-*. *Pater* also has been moved to the left of the relative pronoun instead of occupying the usual position to the right, even though it is a constituent of the relative clause governed by *quam,* a syntactic transformation that generates the sequence *prognata pater.* Such a movement is not uncommon in Latin, but it does draw attention to the word *pater.* The leftward movement of *pater* and the resulting sequence *prognata pater* also preserves the binding alliteration of *prognata patre.* Ennius may have arranged these two words in order to allude to this traditional pairing for the purpose of emphasizing the importance of kinship and family in Ilia's story.

If *prognata pater* is mistakenly taken at first to be *prognata patre,* then it is similar to a phenomenon known as the "garden path sentence," whereby the expectations of the reader prompt an initial misreading.[9] Sometimes, as is the case for *prognata pater,* a formula is the basis for the reader's false expectation. Michael Fontaine suggests, for example, that the line *heus! manedum, Astaphium, priu' quam abis!* (*Truc.* 115), "Hey, wait, Astaphium before you go!" could initially be read *heus! manedum asta-*, "Hey, wait, stop!" because it is phonologically similar to the common collocation of *mane* and *asta* in Plautus.[10] The correspondence between the expected and the actual sentence need not be exactly the same phonetically, either. Fontaine suggests that the clause *qui fana ventris caussa cirumis* (*Rud.* 140), "you who haunt shrines for the sake of your belly," may have been pronounced in such a way that the difference between *ventris* and *Veneris* was obscure. The sentence could therefore be understood as *qui fana Veneris caussa circumis,* "you who haunt the shrine(s) of Venus for this reason," rather than the intended insult, a fact that would explain why Plesidippus, the addressee, does not take offense at the remark.[11]

There are several features of the potential confusion between *fanum ventris* and *fanum Veneris* that are directly applicable to a potential misreading of the sequence *prognata pater* as a quotation of the formula *prognata patre.* Fontaine suggests that repeated use of the phrase *fanum Veneris* would have enabled a misinterpretation on the part of Plesidippus. Although there are no repetitions of *prognata patre* in the fragments of the *Annals,* the collocation was apparently heard repeatedly in certain contexts. In other words, Ennius would have no need to repeat the phrase to create this condition for confusion. If the oral delivery of these lines would have enabled the Plautine puns, as Fontaine suggests, then it is also possible that a reader, pronouncing the line in the *Annals* slowly, could have unconsciously shortened *-ter-* to *-tr-* or even mistakenly metathesized *-er* to *-re*. Liquids such as *-n-* and *-r-*, as in *ter-* in *pater* and in *-ntr-* in *ventris*, may have been particularly susceptible to garden path misinterpretations. For that matter, it is not impossible, albeit not verifiable, that the susceptibility of a cluster like *-tr-* to reanalysis may have led to a corruption of *patre* in the original text to *pater* in the later manuscripts, especially in light of other textual problems in the passage.[12]

Neither the grammatical nor the natural gender of the collocations *germana soror* and *Eurydica prognata pater* is fixed, but these feminine versions of traditional kinship collocations invite some thought on the possible spaces where male and female could overlap. Because the overwhelming majority (if not all) of the literary instances of the collocation of the root *prognat-* and *patre* are masculine, it raises the question of how often the audience of the *Annals* heard *prognata patre* or *prognata matre* as opposed to *prognatus patre*. If the collocation *prognata patre* was as rarely heard as the evidence suggests, then a feminine version of the collocation would be unexpected, so unexpected that Ilia may have come across as arrogating a masculine right to affirm one's paternity by means of the illocutionary phrase. Even if the impression that *prognata pater* is a transformation of *prognatus patre* can only be fleeting, the residue of that impression would have been only one feint in the direction of relativizing the binary opposition of male and female. Even the comparatively common feminine form *germana soror* reflects a choice and reminds the audience that Ilia and her sister inhabit a feminine world.

Prognatus patre has secondary ritual connotations, since the collocations *Iove patre prognatus* in the unknown tragedian and *ab Dite patre prognatos* in a theological context in Caesar indicate that the phrase was appropriate for describing the relationship between a god and his mortal offspring. *Iove patre prognatus* also plays on the ambiguity of the title *pater* when it is applied to divine parentage, an ambiguity that plays itself out in two ways in Ilia's dream. Her father is *Aeneas pater*, and the father of her unborn twins is the *homo pulcer*, who is apparently the venerable *Mars pater*. The private familial setting of the passage and its mythical context may therefore have prompted the audience to misconstrue *prognata pater* as *prognata patre*, a traditional collocation that evokes and is evoked by the dialogue between ritual and kinship system reference.

Ritual System Reference in Ilia's Dream

The term *pater* can refer to a god who is not one's parent. Gellius explicitly recognizes that *pater* is often added to divine names such as *Neptunuspater, Saturnuspater, Ianuspater,* and *Marspater,* not to mention *Jupiter* (NA 5.12.5). Moreover, the existence of a compound *Marspiter,* also cited by Gellius, suggests that the epithet was so closely associated with Mars that it could be the second element in a compound form just as *pater* in *Jupiter,* a grammatical connection that implies a very close relationship between the god and the epithet *pater.* If Mars was commonly known as *Marspiter,* as the form *-piter* suggests, then the implied presence of Mars alone may have lent some ambiguity to the repetition of *pater* in Ilia's dream to an audience who understood that the handsome stranger was in fact *Marspiter* the father of Romulus and Remus. If the close association between Mars and his title of *pater* was not enough to generate such an ambiguity, then the use of *pater* as a common title of male gods in the context of a recently apotheosized father's address to his mortal daughter invited some reflection on the ambiguity of *pater* as a signifier of both a familial relationship and godhood.

Nor is context the only factor that brings out the latent ambiguity of *pater* in the dream. Ilia addresses her father with her hands raised toward the sky, a posture that is often found in descriptions of prayer in Latin literature. The etymological figure *voce vocabam,* the expression that describes Ilia's speech to her father Aeneas, intensifies the ambiguity of the term *pater,* since it not only appears in literary descriptions of prayer but also has a cognate expression in Umbrian prayer. If the Umbrian collocation is, in fact, related to *voce vocabam,* then Ennius has yet again woven the language of ritual into his poetry in an unexpected manner to serve a literary purpose: a meditation on the implications of having a father who is immortal and the appropriate addressee of a prayer but who was once a mortal parent with a vested interest in the welfare of his child.

Tendebam Manus and Latin Ritual

At the end of her dream Ilia implores her father to appear to her as she raises her hands toward the sky. The act of raising the hands is explicitly recognized as an attitude of prayer in the *Servius Auctus* commentary on the *Aeneid.* The commentator asks *quis ad caelum manum tendens non aliud precatur,* "who raising his hands to the sky does not pray for something?" (*ad Aen.* 1.93). Although the authorship of the *Servius Auctus* commentary is unknown and the date of the commentary is late,[13] the assertion is confirmed implicitly in much earlier literary sources. Because the expression *ad caelum manum tendens* in *Servius Auctus* closely matches *manus ad caeli caerula templa / tendebam,* Ilia's imploring address to her father Aeneas may be couched in a traditional ritual collocation.

The action of raising the hands appears to occur in a ritual context in a fragment of Naevius, and the image of hands raised in prayer therefore predates Ennius in the Latin epic tradition:

> Isque susum ad caelum sustulit suas
> Amulius divis<que> gratulabatur (*Bell. Poen.* fr. 26)
>
> And he raised his (hands) up to the sky and Amulius thanks the gods.

Some editors, such as Jürgen Blänsdorf emend *isque* to *manus,*[14] but according to George Dunkel an ellipse of *manus,* or perhaps *palmas,* indicates "how current the posture (and its verbal expression was)."[15] Because the act of raising the hands is a common attitude of prayer in some cultures, including Hittite and Mesopotamian,[16] the act itself may be quasi-universal, even though the posture is common in the Homeric epics. Whether or not Naevius borrowed the phrase from Homer, its presence in a Saturnian poem had already begun the process of naturalizing the phrase in Latin, thereby rendering the image of the hands raised to the sky in prayer as much a reference to literary Latin ritual as to Homer.

Manus tendere expressed a posture of prayer in the poetry of the Augustan era and beyond. Vergil deploys a number of variations of the expression *manus tendere,* including a particularly close parallel in the *Aeneid* when Aeneas prays after the Penates have appeared to him and ordered him to leave Crete:[17]

> . . . Tendo supinas / ad caelum cum voce manus . . . (*A.* 3.176–77)
>
> I raise upturned hands to the sky with a call.

Ovid also makes use of variants of the same expression in the context of prayer. For example, in *Fasti* 5.57 Augustus vows to build a temple to Mars Ultor while holding up his hands (*ille manus tendens*). Because these expressions had a history in Latin as well as in Greek, they constitute a reference to Ennius and Naevius as much as to Homer, who could have been seen as the originator of the phrase. Augustan readers at least perceived *manus . . . tendebam* as a ritual collocation, perhaps on the basis of their experience with authors like Ennius.

If the collocation of *tendere* and *manus* was a literary conceit, it was not confined to poetry. In Book 35 of his *Histories,* Livy describes the angry reaction of Titus Quinctius Flamininus to a remark made by Eurylochus, the chief magistrate of the Magnesian league in Thessaly:

> Quinctius quidem adeo exarsit ira ut manus ad caelum tendens deos testes ingrati ac perfidi Magnetum invocaret (LIV. 35.31.13)
>
> Indeed, Quinctius was so consumed with anger that, raising his hands to heaven, he implored the gods to witness the ungrateful and treacherous spirit of the Magnetes.[18]

In Livy's account the ritual connotations of the action of the Roman envoy were not lost on the crowd, who witnessed his invocation and subsequently became terrified. There are three more examples of *manus tendere* in a ritual context in Livy (40.4.12, 26.9.8, and 25.37.9), and the prepositional phrase *ad caelum* modifies *manus tendere* in all four, as in Livy 26.9.8:

> Manus ad caelum ac deos tendentes
>
> Raising hands to the sky and gods.

Not only does Livy collocate *manus* and *tendere,* he also mirrors the use of *caelum* as the direction of raised hands in Ennius and elsewhere in Latin poetry. This correspondence therefore increases the number of elements of the expression and, in turn, the likelihood that the expression would stand out enough to recall collocations of *tendere, manus,* and *caelum* in other contexts.

The fact that the Thessalians were able to interpret Flamininus' gesture is a reminder that the raised hands as an attitude of prayer, and even a metonymy for prayer, may also be found in the Homeric poems. Dunkel lists no fewer than eight examples of the collocation χεῖρας ἀνασχεῖν in the Homeric poems, which accompany an act of prayer or stand for prayer metonymically.[19] Priam says to Hecuba, for example, that ἐσθλὸν γὰρ Διὶ χεῖρας ἀνασχέμεν, αἴ κ' ἐλεήσῃ, "for it is good to raise one's hands to Zeus, to see if he would feel pity" (*Il.* 24.301), an obvious case of the raising of the hands as a metonymy for prayer. The metonymy is made plain in another instance of the collocation when Odysseus prays to Zeus for a sign that his homecoming was the will of the gods, the phrase Διὶ δ' εὔξατο χεῖρας ἀνασχών, "he prayed to Zeus raising up his hands" (*Od.* 20.97). Even if *manus tendere* is a traditional ritual collocation, the expression itself is a hybrid of Homeric poetry and Roman ritual.

A near quotation of *ad caeli caerula templa / tendebam* elsewhere in the *Annals* also implies that the phrase was meaningful for the larger narrative of book 1. An unknown god, perhaps Jupiter or Mars, states that Romulus, the unborn child of Ilia, will become divine:

Unus erit quem tu tolles in caerula caeli
templa (*Ann.* 54–55)

One there will be one whom thou shalt raise to the blue precincts of the sky.[20]

Caerula caeli templa is an almost exact match for *ad caeli caerula templa. Tollo* is often substituted for *tendo* in descriptions of raising the arms in prayer in Roman literature,[21] including the Naevian parallel (*Bell. Poen.* fr. 26, discussed above). Moreover, after his quotation of the *devotio* (discussed in chapter 4) Macrobius describes different postures of prayer to be taken during the ceremony, among them: *cum Iovem dicit, manus ad caelum tollit,* "when (the officiant) says Jupiter, he raises his hands to the sky (3.9.10)." If the collocation is traditional, then the substitution may have been permitted in Roman ritual as well as in Latin literature. Both *quem tu tolles in caerula caeli templa* and *manus ad caeli caerula templa tendebam* may therefore have been variants of a traditional expression for the hands raised in prayer.

The substitution of *tollere* for *tendere* and the absence of *manus* also open the door for yet another interface between ritual and kinship system reference. *Tollere* is the technical term for picking up a child as a sign of formal recognition of paternity. It appears as early as Terence (*An.* 219, *Hau.* 627). Although it is not used in the exact sense of a father formally acknowledging a child, there is a close parallel to the Ennian fragment in the *Amphitruo* that suggests the form could simultaneously evoke comedy and solemnity. Jupiter enjoins Alcumena to raise the child who will be born of their liaison:

Quod erit natum tollito (*Am.* 501)

May you raise/rear the child whatever it will be

Both the Ennian and Plautine phrases collocate forms of *tollere, esse,* and *quis.* Moreover, the "future imperative" *tollito* gives the phrase an archaic feel that may indicate that it was a formal expression of the act of asserting the legitimacy of a child. The verb *tollere* not only describes the eventual apotheosis of Romulus, but it also implies that Mars must formally recognize his offspring, an act that can be signified with *tollere.* The word choice and the content of the short fragment therefore gives the impression that the Ennian version of the birth of

Romulus owes something to the standard comic plot that ends with the formal recognition of a child born of rape and the restoration of the social order.

The mixture of kinship and ritual system reference implied by *tolles in caerula caeli / templa* parallels the same ambiguity in the dream of Ilia. Although kinship is the primary mode of system reference in the latter passage, the ritual collocations in the passage remind the audience that Aeneas and Ilia are not a typical Roman family. There is a similar ambiguity in the phrase *tolles in caerula caeli / templa,* since *tollere* can be used instead of *tendere* for the act of raising the hands to sky (*caelum*) in prayer and to signify the act of recognizing one's offspring. Moreover, if the fragment describes the apotheosis of Romulus, it implies that Mars recognizes Romulus as his legitimate son (a recognition of kinship) and that mortals will pray to Romulus (a ritual act). The dialogue between ritual and kinship in book 1 of the *Annals* is not therefore confined to the dream of Ilia.

If a god is the speaker of the phrase *quem tu tolles in caerula caeli templa,* then a sort of tension between hierarchical difference and sameness characterizes the phrase in context. *Manus ad caelum tollere,* a ritual posture, is transformed into an apotheosis by changing the object *manus* to *unum quem.* There is a temptation to see the near quotation as a self-reflexive commentary on the requirements for godhood. In other words, godhood requires ritual, and by raising the hands in prayer an individual could achieve the apotheosis of a dead ancestor through illocutionary force. Given the Pythagorean precepts that color the prologue of the *Annals,* as well as the Empedoclean touches in book 7,[22] the wording of the expression, no matter who spoke it in the *Annals,* may imply that Ennius views the distinction between god and man as permeable.

A similar tension is at work in the dream of Ilia, where the raising of hands in prayer is transferred to an ambiguous context, thereby highlighting the unusual relationship of human daughter and divine father. Ilia's use of the phrase is further complicated by her own eventual status as the immortal consort of the river Anio. A mortal woman (Ilia) who will become immortal strikes an attitude of prayer while addressing a divinity who was once a man (Aeneas). This paradox raises a number of epistemological problems that are multiplied when another god couches the apotheosis of the same woman's son in a manner that recalls the same ritual posture.

Voce Vocabam and Umbrian *Suboco Subocau*

Although there are complications, Ennius ends the second-to-last line of Ilia's narrative with *voce vocabam,* a phrase that may also be a traditional collocation:

> Tendebam lacrumans et blanda voce vocabam (*Ann.* 49)

At least some of the collocations of *vox* and *vocare* in later literature are literary allusions, however, that cannot speak to whether the collocation was traditional in the age of Ennius or a literary invention.[23] Moreover, there are collocations of *vox* and *vocare* that do not occur in an obviously ritual context in other, later authors, even though several uses of this *figura etymologica* in an overt ritual context in Vergil suggest that the phrase had ritual connotations in Augustan poetry. The Italic proclivity toward etymological figures may be an indication that the Umbrian and Latin phrases are parallel developments owing to basic tendencies in Italic prayer. In either case, it is clear that the expression *could* be read as a ritual collocation. Whether the expression *was* a traditional Latin or common Italic ritual collocation is another matter entirely.

Because Vergil collocates *vox* and *vocare* in some ritual contexts in the *Aeneid,* it appears that Vergil read *voce vocabam* as a ritual collocation. For example, Aeneas tells Deiphobus that he invoked his shade three times after he set up a cenotaph for him:

> . . . magna manis ter voce vocavi. (*A.* 6.506)
>
> I invoked your shade three times with a great voice.

Anna uses the same expression in a similar context, an address to her sister Dido, who has just committed suicide:

> his etiam struxi manibus patriosque vocavi
> voce deos, sic te ut posita, crudelis, abessem? (*A.* 4.680–81)
>
> Did I strew (this pyre) for these shades and invoke our paternal gods so that, when you were placed upon (the pyre), I might be out of the way cruel one?

The appearance of these particular collocations of *vox* and *vocare* in these contexts implies that *voce vocare* was a formulaic description of a ritual posture within the *Aeneid.*

These ritual collocations may also be literary allusions to Ennius. The placement of *voce vocavi* at the end of the line in *Aeneid* 6.505 matches the position of *voce vocabam* in *Annals* 49. What is more, Aeneas is addressing someone who is absent because of death, just as Ilia addresses the absent Aeneas in the *Annals*. There is some irony in Aeneas using the same expression that was addressed to him in a similar context, an irony that suggests that *voce vocavi* is a deliberate allusion to the *Annals*. Anna's repetition of the terms *soror* (Aen. 6.677 and 682) and *germana* (*Aen.* 6.675 and 6.686) recalls not only Ilia's speech but also the general situation of calling upon a dead relative.

There are other instances of *voce vocare* in the *Aeneid*, however, that do not occur in an obvious ritual context or that appear to be allusions to the *Annals*. The challenge of Mezentius in book 10 of the *Aeneid* is one of several instances of *voce vocare* that lacks obvious ritual connotations:

> atque hic Aenean magna ter voce vocavit (*A.* 10.873)
>
> . . . and he called Aeneas with a great voice three times.

When Aeneas challenges Turnus while pursuing him in book 12, for example, he uses the phrase *voce vocat* (*A.* 12.483). Turnus also describes the Latin king Murranus as *me voce vocantem*, "calling out to me with his voice" (*A.* 12.638). Because the nightmare of Dido in book 4 of the *Aeneid* appears to be modeled on the dream of Ilia, Nita Krevans has also suggested that the phrase *voces et verba vocantis* in *Aeneid* 4.460 is an allusion to *voce vocabam* in Ennius.[24] These collocations of *voce* and *vocare* are consistent with the use of the expression to signify absence in the *Aeneid*, but they do not appear to have any ritual connotations.

There are, however, subtle connections to the dream of Ilia in these Vergilian examples of *voce vocare* in the *Aeneid* that may also allow for extremely subtle ritual connotations to come into play. The challenge of Mezentius restores Aeneas to the role of the addressee of the expression *voce vocavit*, a hint of an allusion to the dream of Ilia. Moreover, Aeneas responds to the challenge with a prayer to Apollo (*precatur* [*A.* 10.874]) that could be read "so may the father make him a god, so may lofty Apollo" (*sic pater ille deum faciat, sic altus Apollo* [*A.* 10.875]), even though the context dictates that *pater . . . deum* should be understood as "father of the gods." Thus both the ritual connotations of *voce vocavi* and the syntactic ambiguity of *ille deum faciat* are suggestive of apotheosis, perhaps as a nod to the pointed ambiguity of *voce vocabam* in Ilia's address to Aeneas in the *Annals*. The image of Murranus who calls upon Turnus is that of an absent loved one, as Aeneas is to Ilia in the *Annals*, a parallel that may be reinforced by the placement of the expression *me voce vocantem* at line end, where both *me voce videtur* and *voce vocabam* are found in Ennius. Even when Aeneas calls out to the absent Turnus, the situation is not dissimilar to Ilia's in the *Annals* when she seeks her absent father Aeneas.

The only use of the phrase in Livy (7.15.2) is a possible indication that it was traditional in ritual and military contexts. Although the reasons are not as transparent as for *donum dare,* the use of the phrase in a military context in Livy may indicate that the phrase vacillated between ritual and *militiae.* This range of contexts can be seen in Caesar's allusion to the *senatus consultum ultimum* in the *Bellum Civile,* provided that it is couched in traditional terms:

> Qua voce et quo senatus consulto populus Romanus ad arma sit vocatus (*Civ.* 1.7.5)
>
> . . . by which summoning and by which decree of the Senate the Roman people were called to arms

Given its use in Caesar, the phrase may also have been a solemn invocation of soldiers to report for duty, a context that may have overlapped with rituals like lustration and perhaps is a reason why Vergil sometimes uses *voce vocare* in a description of battle and sometimes in a description of a ritual.

There are no instances of *voce vocare* in Latin ritual that are not also literary, but there are multiple examples of a cognate expression in Umbrian in an overtly ritual and nonliterary context. In the Iguvine Tables the phrase *subocau suboco,* "I invoke an invoking," an obvious parallel to *voce vocabam,* occurs nine times in the sixth of the seven tablets in three different prayers to Jupiter Grabovius, Fisovius Sancus, and Tefer Iovius, respectively. The opening of the prayer to Jupiter Grabovius follows the same general pattern as the other two prayers:

> teio. subocau. suboco / dei. grabovi. ocriper. fisiu. totaper. iiouina. erer. nomneper. erar. nomneper. fos. sei. pacer. sei. ocre. fisei / tote. iiouine. erer. nomne. erar. nomne. arsie. tio. subocau. suboco. dei. grabove. arsier. frite. tio. subocau / suboco. dei. grabove. (Rix Um 1 VIa 22–25)
>
> I invoke an invoking to you Jupiter Grabovius for the Fisian Mount for the Iguvine People, in the name of this and in the name of that. Be favorable. Be propitious to the Fisian Mount and to the Iguvine people in the name of this and in the name of that. In the consecration I invoke an invoking to you Jupiter Grabovius. Trusting the consecration, I invoke an invoking to you Jupiter Grabovius.

Not only is the root of Umbrian *subocau* and *suboco* cognate with the root of Latin *voce* and *vocabam,* the verbs *subocau* and *vocabam* also have the thematic vowel *-a-*, extending the parallel from the level of root to that of stem.[25] Although *suboco* is in the accusative case and *voce* is in the ablative, the Umbrian formula is a very close parallel to *voce vocabam,* even though the Latin expression lacks the preverb *sub-*.

Because of the well-known tendency of Italic ritual texts toward *figurae etymologicae*—a tendency that has manifested itself more than once in the previous discussion—it is possible that both the Umbrian and Latin expressions are the result of iconicity. In other words, the solemn connotations are produced by the general syntactic figure rather than the specific collocation of *voce* and *vocare* (*voce vocabam* differs from *donum dare* because there is an abundance of evidence for the latter expression in the epigraphic record). Even if both expressions are the result of a tendency of common Italic ritual language, they still may indicate that Ennius is playing with the ambiguities inherent in speaking to a parent who has become immortal on the level of diction.

I emphasize again that ritual is not a phenomenon that exists independently of other forms of language such as poetry. Once a reader perceives an expression as a traditional ritual collocation, then for all practical purposes it is such a collocation. Although the traditional status of *voce vocabam* must remain an open question, the traditional qualities of the expression are evident, qualities that seem to have convinced other poets that the expression belonged to the realm of ritual. Tibullus, for example, uses the expression *voce vocare* without recalling the *Annals* in an overtly ritual context:

> vos celebrem cantate deum pecorique vocate
> voce: palam pecori, clam sibi quisque vocet. (2.1.83–84)

> Sing of the god honored by festivity, invoke (him) with an invoking for the flock: openly for the flock, secretly for himself each will each invoke him.

The resemblance of *cantate deum* to *divum empta cante* in the *Carmen Saliare* as quoted by Varro (*L.* 7.27) may be fortuitous, but the possibility remains that the Tibullan couplet is composed of genuinely archaic elements of Latin prayer.

Voce vocabam is also something of a hybrid of Latin and Greek. Both the infinitive phrase εἰπεῖν ἔπος and finite forms, such as εἴπῃσθα ἔπος occur multiple times in the *Iliad.* When she reproaches Zeus for his clandestine planning in the beginning of the *Iliad,* for example, Hera complains that Zeus never undertakes to say a word, εἰπεῖν ἔπος, about what he is thinking (*Il.* 1.543). In book 7, the Trojan herald Idaios relates that he was ordered to "speak a speech" (εἰπεῖν ἔπος [*Il.* 7.394]). In the heated dispute over what to do when the plague of Apollo strikes the Achaeans, Agamemnon reacts to Calchas' suggestion that he give up the daughter of Chryses with an invective against the priest:

> ἐσθλὸν δ᾽ οὔτε τί πω εἶπας ἔπος οὔτ᾽ ἐτέλεσσας (*Il.* 1.108)
>
> You have never spoken a good word at all nor accomplished anything good.

Another example comes from the fight between Achilles and Aeneas. The latter disparages talk in favor of action (an ironic statement, given that the following line is, in fact, the fifty-first line of a fifty-nine-line speech!), reflecting that there are many kinds of words:

> ὁπποῖόν κ᾽ εἴπῃσθα ἔπος, τοῖόν κ᾽ ἐπακούσαις (*Il.* 20.250)
>
> Whatever sort of word you would say, you could hear the same.

The Homeric parallels open the possibility that Ennius was able to exploit this ambiguity in order to further his poetic project of hybridization. These parallels do not, however, occur in a ritual context and do not explain why Vergil and other poets use the phrase in such a context.

As has been the case with almost every fragment I have analyzed, Ilia's dream is a hybrid of Greek poetry and Roman culture on every level of poetic composition. Although *pater* is a site of negotiation between kinship and ritual system reference in Latin in a manner that it cannot be in Greek, Zeus is still the πατὴρ ἀνδρῶν τε θεῶν τε, "father of gods and men," a title that enables some slippage in Greek. If *vires vitaque* is a common Italic ritual collocation, as the Oscan evidence suggests, then it is possible that such a phrase existed in the Greek of the Italian peninsula, since Greek was one of the cultures that participated in the central Italian *koinê*. *Manus . . . tendebam* and *voce vocabam* are more obvious hybrids of Greek poetry and Roman ritual, at least as Ennius' successors understood it. Even on the level of narrative, Greek and Roman elements have been synthesized. Nita Krevans has observed that the dream sequence is well attested in Greek tragedy and epic.[26] If Fabius Pictor was one of the sources for the story of Ilia, as is likely, then Ennius is using a Greek source text, perhaps more than one, since Plutarch (*Rom.* 3.1) claims that Diocles of Peparathus was the first to tell the story of Ilia. In addition to these Greek versions of Ilia, there are indirect parallels that may indicate the influence of Homer. Catherine Connors has suggested that Nausicaa may have been a partial inspiration for Ilia.[27] The hybrid nature of the fragment is evident.

The Language of Curses in the Dream of Ilia

Toward the beginning of her story, Ilia tells her sister that her very life force left her body, a statement that may be colored by a traditional ritual collocation:

Vires vitaque corpus meum nunc deserit omne (*Ann.* 37)

Now strength and life too leave all my body. (trans. Warmington)

As Calvert Watkins has observed,[28] *vires vitaque* is semantically and (partially) etymologically parallel to the Oscan doubling figure **biass biítam,** one of five pairings that comprise a *defixio* from Cumae:[29]

aginiss.	**urinss. úlleis**	his actions utterances
fakinss.	**fangvam**	deeds tongue
biass.	**biítam**	strength life
aftiím.	{a} **anamúm.**	ability(?) soul
aitatúm	**amirikum. (tíf[ei])**	lifespan livelihood to you. (Rix Cm13)

If the Oscan and Latin collocations are in fact reflexes of a common Italic collocation, as Watkins suggests, then the ritual context of the Oscan collocation implies that the Latin expression may have also been used in such texts. Ilia's dream therefore begins with a decidedly ominous tone.

There are examples of collocations in Latin curse tablets that have either *vita* or *vires* as constituents, although not together in the same collocation. *Vitam valitudinem,* a phrase that is characterized by the same semantics and the same initial sounds as *vires vitaque,* appears on a curse tablet from Roman Britain.[30] There are also examples of *vires* as the first member of an alliterative doubling figure in the Johns Hopkins *Tabellae Defixionum*. Several tablets ask Persephone to remove the *vires* and *virtutes* of the victim, who happens to be Plotius in the following example:[31]

Eripias salutem corp[us] colorem vires virtutes Ploti

May you snatch away the body, color, strength and courage of Plotius.

Vires virtutes also preserves the alliteration of *vires vitaque*. Because all of the Johns Hopkins *Tabellae* appear to be verbatim repetitions of the same curse with the names changed, it is almost certain all the tablets in the Johns Hopkins collection also used the same doubling figure found in three of the set of six.

The use of *corpus* in these tablets may be significant for identifying the extent of ritual system reference in the first line of Ilia's description of her dream and determining how dark the connotations of *vires vitaque* may be. *Corpus* is not only used in the Johns Hopkins *Tabellae,* it forms a "magic square" of two alliterative doubling figures, a structural principle that underlies the Oscan curse tablet quoted above:

corp[us] colorem
vires virtutes.

The arrangement establishes a relationship between *corpus* and *vires* as the first members in consecutive pairings that are bound by alliteration in the *defixio.* The sequence *vires vitaque corpus* is a near quotation of *corpus . . . vires virtutes.* Moreover, as the line unfolded it may have raised the expectation of the audience that the next word would form an alliterative doubling figure with *corpus* and that *vires, vitaque, corpus* would all be objects of a curse. Given that there is no evidence for such an arrangement outside of the Johns Hopkins *Tabellae,* it is more likely that the presence of three consecutive signifiers that appropriate the language of curses gave the opening of the dream a dark undertone.

According to at least one Roman writer, *vis* and *vita* may be both elements of a traditional collocation and derivations of the same root. Varro's claim that the *vita* is given to children by the *vis* of Venus may be an implicit etymology:

Poetae . . . coniunctione ignis et humoris, quam habent vim significant esse Ve<ne>ris. A qua vi natis dicta vita et illud a Lucilio:
Vis est vita, vides, nos facere omnia cogit (*L.* 5.63)

The poets . . . through the conjunction of fire and moisture are indicating that the *vis,* "force," which they have is that of Venus. Those born of *vis* have what is called *vita,* "life," and that was meant by Lucilius:
Life is force you see: to do everything force doth compel us.[32]

Varro's quotation of Lucilius, who implicitly derives *vis* from *vita,* pushes back the etymology to the late second century:

Vis est vita vides? Vis nos facere omnia cogit

Life is force you see: to do everything force doth compel us.

The insistent alliteration in Lucilius is also in play in Varro's discussion. If the folk etymology of *vita* and the *vis Veneris* is traditional, then it may have a direct bearing on the dream. Because Ilia is the granddaughter of Venus, her *vita* is literally derived from Venus, just as *vita* is etymologically derived from *vim Veneris* by Varro. An allusion to the *vis* of Venus in the *vita* could, in fact, foreshadow the intervention of Venus on behalf of her granddaughter that seems to have been part of the later narrative of book 1.

If *vires vitaque* is at once a traditional collocation and a *figura etymologica*, it suggests an etymology of *vir* as well as *vita*. In spite of the late dates of Lactantius and Cassiodorus, who derive *vir* from *vis*,[33] the roots of *vir* and *viris* (the oblique form of *vis*) are so nearly identical that a folk etymology must have suggested itself independently to speakers of Latin in the second century BCE. Some forms of *vir* and *vis* are indistinguishable when written, even though the roots differ in their vowel lengths and belong to different declensions. Moreover, the collocation of *virtutes vires* in the Johns Hopkins *Defixiones* suggests that *vires* and *virtutes* were associated in the language of curses, an association that implies a putative etymological relationship between *vis* and *vir*.

Ennius too may imply the same perceived relationship between *vir* and *vis* elsewhere in the *Annals:*

> Viri varia validis viribus luctant (*Ann.* 298)
>
> The soldiers struggled with sturdy strength. (trans. Warmington)

He ends another line with a similar expression when he describes some of Rome's faithful Italian allies, perhaps from a catalogue modeled after the census of 225:[34]

> Marsa manus, Paeligna cohors, Vestina virum vis (*Ann.* 229)
>
> Marsian troop, Paelignian company, Vestinian warrior force . . . (trans. Warmington)

In both phrases the alliterative pattern draws attention to the collocations of *vis* and *vir*. It is possible that *viri* and *viribus* and *virum vis* have simply been deployed near each other for the sake of alliteration, but the jingling combinations of *vis* and *vir* in these fragments imply that a folk-etymological relationship between *vis* and *vir* existed well before Lactantius and Cassiodorus.

A plurality of possible word choices that were perceived as derivations from a single root would explain why the Johns Hopkins *Tabellae Defixionum* pairs *vires* with *virtutes* whereas Ennius pairs *vires* with *vita*. The collocation *vires virtutes* in the Johns Hopkins *Defixiones* and *vires vitaque* may have been seen as variants of a single collocation of two different forms of *vis*. The underlying form of *vires vitaque* would therefore be the same for *viri . . . viribus* and *virum vis* in the other fragments of the *Annals*, an equation that may indicate that these collocations had ritual connotations. Even without such a folk-etymological connection, however, *vires vitaque* in Ennius could be perceived as a transformation of a pairing such as *virtutes vires* or *valitudinem vita.*

The introduction of a traditional (or at least appropriate) collocation specific to the language of cursing so early in a passage primarily characterized by kinship system reference does not strike as discordant a note as it may seem at first. Because curse tablets are very much private rituals that belong to the domestic and not the public sphere, the collocation *vires vitaque* is the type of ritual system reference that would be the least intrusive in the intimate space occupied by Ilia and her sister. Nor is it the only ritual collocation in the passage. It is only the first of several collocations with potential ritual connotations that are in dialogue with the traditional collocations of kinship that color the passage. The placement of the collocation so early in the narrative may therefore prepare the audience for the negotiation between kinship and ritual system reference that gives the dream a deeper and more complex meaning.

If *vires vitaque* has been appropriated from the language of curses, it performs narrative as well as cultural work. The ominous tone of such a collocation would serve as a reminder to the audience of what it already knew: despite its similarities to the generic plot of Roman comedy, Ilia's story will not have a comic ending. Although she will give birth after a rape, Ilia will not marry Mars but will be executed for violating her vows of chastity, which locate Ilia in a ritual system as a Vestal virgin, a position determined by her gender. In a manner similar to Decius Mus, who sacrifices himself (or tries to sacrifice himself, at any rate) by pronouncing the *devotio,* Ilia's inadvertent use of the language of curses may have implied to the audience of the *Annals* that she too has devoted herself to the gods of the underworld.

If the phrase *vires vitaque* is actually a collocation of two forms of the same root that yields *vir* (at least as the Romans etymologized it), then the expression may propel forward the dialogue between genders that began with the uncommon feminine expression *Eurydica prognata,* not to mention the similarity of the sequence *prognata pater* to the traditional collocation *prognatus patre. Vires vitaque* may emphasize that the dream is an encounter between a woman and a male divinity that leads to a pregnancy, or the beginning of *vita.* Because the word *vir* may be seen in the word *vir-es,* the loss of *vires* is the loss not only of *vis,* "strength," but also of the *vir,* or rather the *homo,* who abducted and seduced Ilia. In other words, *vires vitaque* could imply a connection between Ilia's loss of strength (*vir-es vitaque . . . deserit*) and the disappearance of the *homo pulcer* (i.e., *vir pulcer*) who abducts and leaves her (*deserit*).

Fathers and Sons: *Pater* and *Genitor* in Book 1 of the *Annals*

The ambiguity of the signifier *pater* enables an overlap between ritual and kinship system reference in the dream of Ilia and also in other fragments of book 1. In addition to enabling slippage between kinship and ritual, the word *pater* begins to erode incremental differences within the hierarchy of divinities. Although Aeneas may be classified as a *lar* in an inscription from Tor Tignosa (*CIL* I^2 2843),[35] he was called *Iovem indigetem* on the bank of the river Numicum near Lavinium, according to Livy (1.2.6), and *indigens*, a title presumably related to *Iovem indigetem*, in an inscription from Pompeii (*CIL* X 808). It is therefore possible that Aeneas could be confused with Jupiter linguistically, particularly *pater Aeneas*. Romulus is called *pater* and *genitor* after his own apotheosis (*Ann.* 108), a pairing that in turn recalls Ilia's address to Venus as *genetrix patris* (*Ann.* 58). If the parallel is salient, then Romulus is addressed in the manner of an Olympian. Because that Olympian is his grandmother, there is also some slippage between male and female. The instability of the signifier *pater* (and apparently its synonyms) appears to be endemic for the whole of book 1. This consistent semantic pressure on *pater* goes much further than the natural slippage that must have existed in the Latin language, a sign of a conscious manipulation for the purpose of making a point concerning the mythic subject matter of book 1 and apotheosis in general.

The language of the lamentation of the Roman people at the loss of Romulus almost wholly elides him with Jupiter:

> O Romule, Romule die,
> Qualem te patriae custodem di genuerunt
> O pater, o genitor, o sanguen dis oriundum! (*Ann.* 106–8)

> O Romulus, godly Romulus, what a guardian of your country did the gods beget you! O father, O begetter, O blood sprung from the gods! (trans. Warmington)

The intervening clause governed by *qualem* calls attention to the fact that the plural form of *dius* would be virtually indistinguishable from *di*, the plural of *deus*. I have already noted multiple instances in the *Annals* where a form of *deus* or *divus* occurs in proximity to *pater* in such a way as to etymologize *Iu-p(p)iter*. Moreover, the ablative form *dis* occurs in the phrase *o sanguen dis oriundum* and yields a third derivation of the root that underlies *deus, divus, dius* and the first element of *Iu-p(p)iter* in three lines, perhaps in order to buttress the etymological connection between *die* and *di.* Because the vocative *die* in combination with the title *pater* is a gloss of the name Jupiter, Romulus is another Jupiter on the level of language, just as his grandfather is when he is called *Iovem indigetem.*

There is no evidence for a traditional collocation *die pater genitor* in the languages of the central Italian *koinê,* but there is a single Greek parallel from Euripides' *Ion:*

Φοῖβος μοι γενέτωρ πατήρ (*Ion* 136)

Phoebus my begetter my father.[36]

Because allusions to Euripides are relatively rare in the *Annals* and Ennius does not apply the title to Apollo but to Romulus, the parallel phrase in the *Ion* is not likely to be the source of *o pater o genitor.* The lack of such a formulation *Ζεὺς πατὴρ γενέτωρ indicates that the collocation was not traditional in Greek. It is demonstrably absent in the most famous Greek texts, including the Homeric poems. If the collocation was more common in Greek than the evidence suggests, then it is also possible that it was borrowed during the central Italian *koinê* period into Latin, but the date of the borrowing would still mean the collocation was familiar to Ennius and his audience. In other words, in the unlikely event that it was borrowed from Greek, it almost certainly happened long enough before Ennius that it was a native collocation to the Romans of the second century BCE.

There is, however, an uncanny resemblance to Vedic Sanskrit collocations that mean "Father and begetter Sky," in the *Rig Veda* (*RV* 4.1.10d, 1.164.33a) that correspond exactly to *o die . . . o pater genitor* in the etymological sense. For example, the phrase *dyáuṣ pitā́ janitā́,* "Sky father begetter" (*RV* 4.1.10d), in a hymn to Agni, the Vedic fire god, is composed of the Sanskrit cognates of *die, pater,* and *genitor* in the same order as in Ennius. The similar expressions in Greek and Latin may therefore indicate that an equivalent phrase existed in Proto-Indo-European that was inherited into Latin as *die . . . pater . . . genitor,* into Vedic as *dyáuṣ pitā́ janitā́* and (partially) into Greek as γενέτωρ πατήρ.[37] Although a genetic relationship between two ritual collocations in two cultures separated by so much distance may at first seem far-fetched, the common origin of the name of *Iuppiter* and his Vedic counterpart is not in doubt. It is always preferable to rely primarily on evidence for a traditional collocation from within the Latin, or at least the common Italic tradition.[38] The parallel between the Latin and Sanskrit expressions, however, is so exact that the possibility that the Latin and Vedic collocations are genetically related cannot be dismissed.[39]

Whether or not the phrase *die . . . pater . . . genitor* is a traditional Roman ritual collocation, Ennius connects *die, pater,* and *genitor* by means of syntax and of etymological glosses for all three lexemes in the intervening relative clause:

O Romule, Romule **die,**
Qualem te PATRiae custodem **di** generunt
O PATER, o genitor, o sanguen **dis** oriundum!

The relative clause contains derivations of *genitor, die,* and *pater.* The etymologizing of all three constituents of the collocation therefore suggests that Ennius wanted to draw attention to the collocation. If he is drawing attention to *die, pater,* and *genitor,* the existence of a traditional ritual collocation would explain why.

The etymological play on *die . . . pater . . . genitor* probes the semantic overlap between kinship and ritual system reference. The act of breaking down the fossilized compound of *Iu-pater* (archaic vocative **(D)ieu pater > Iu pater*) into its constituent parts generates a tension between the holistic meaning of Jupiter and the individual elements of the collocation, a tension that in turn reminds the audience that there is a *pater* in *Iuppiter.* Given how much play there seems to be on the ambiguity of *pater* in the dream of Ilia, the audience is primed to see the slippage between divine epithet and kinship terminology in the address of Romulus. Moreover, the implicit division of the name *Iuppiter* into different roots highlights the irony of naming the childless Romulus as a *pater,* which is sharpened when the collocation *o die . . . o pater* is extended to *o die . . . o pater o genitor.* Although *genitor* may be used metaphorically, the common semantic ground of *pater* and *genitor* is reproduction, a state of affairs emphasized by the presence of *genuerunt* as a gloss of *genitor.* The probing of the difference and similarity of ritual and kinship system reference therefore seems not to be confined to the dream of Ilia but rather may be symptomatic of an overall thematic concern of book 1.

If the fragment precedes the deification of Romulus, as Skutsch suggests,[40] then the etymologizing of the name *Iu-p(p)iter* also has a deconstructive force similar to Ilia's use of the language of prayer to address her *pater,* Aeneas, in her dream. As I have already suggested, there is a hint in the parallels between Ilia raising her arms while entreating her father to appear and the image of Romulus being raised into the heavens that it is the act of raising one's hands in prayer that makes one immortal, not an actual innate quality. For the second time the deification of Romulus is as much the effect of a speech act that is performed by the citizens of Rome as it is an act of Jupiter. If Romulus can become a god who is addressed by what amounts to an etymological gloss on the name *Iu-p(p)iter,* there may be a hint at a euhemeristic point of view toward the gods that sees them as made by men but also made of language. Such skepticism may seem to be out of place in the *Annals,* but it seems less so when one recalls that Ennius also wrote a prose text based on the writing of Euhemerus, the author after whom euhemerism is named.

Grandmothers, Fathers, and (Grand) Daughters: *Pater* and *Genetrix* in Book 1 of the *Annals*

The interplay between ritual and kinship system reference may be seen in yet another fragment characterized by key verbal parallels with Ilia's dream. Ilia calls upon her grandmother Venus before she is thrown into the river Anio:

> Te saneneta† precor Venus, te genetrix patris nostri,
> Ut me de caelo visas, cognata, parumper. (*Ann.* 58–59)[41]

> Thee, hallowed Venus, thee now mother of my father, I pray look down on me from heaven a little while, my kinswoman. (trans. Warmington)

The keyword *pater,* this time in the genitive, resumes the repetition of *pater* in the dream sequence. *Cognata* is also a near match for *prognata,* and its proximity to *patris* generates a weak echo of *prognata pater,* and perhaps the underlying collocation *patre prognatus.* Ilia asks Venus to look down from the sky (*de caelo*), while she earlier raised her hands to the sky (*ad caeli caerula templa*) when she addressed her father in the dream. Although the verbal echoes of both the dream and the invocation of Venus are not striking in themselves, the number of repetitions spoken by the same speaker in two different passages suggests at the very least that Ilia is using the language of kinship to emphasize her connections with her father and her grandmother. Moreover, Ilia deploys at least one ritual collocation (*de caelo*) and thereby mixes the phraseology of ritual and kinship in her invocation of Venus.

The invocation of Venus also connects the dream of llia to the lamentation for Romulus both by means of verbal repetition and through the expression *genetrix patris,* a collocation of the root *gen-* and *pater* that parallels *prognata pater* in the dream (*Ann.* 36) and *o pater o genitor* in the lament (*Ann.* 108). When Ilia calls Venus *genetrix* and *cognata,* two forms of the same root *gen-*, it also faintly echoes the use of *genuerunt* as a gloss of *genitor* in *Annals* 109–10 and the implicit etymological comment upon *pro-gnata* through the use of *gnata* in the speech of Aeneas to Ilia. The repeated collocation of *pater* and the root *gen-* is another means of exploring the thematic knot of kinship, gender, and divinity.

Insofar as it retains the word *pater* while referring to a goddess, the feminine form of *genetrix patris* not only tests the boundaries of male and female in book 1, but it may also be a traditional means of contemplating the power of the gods to transcend mortal categories. A hexametrical couplet written by Quintus Valerius Soranus[42] quoted by Varro in his lost *De Cultu Deorum,* and in turn preserved by Augustine in the *De Civitate Dei,* may indicate that ambiguity of gender is an area touched upon even in the unmediated language of ritual:

Iuppiter omnipotens, regum rerumque deumque
Progenitor genetrixque, deum deus, unus et omnes (*C.D.* 7.9)

Jupiter all-powerful, begetter and mother of kings and things and gods, god of gods, one and all.

The placement of compound forms of *genetrix* (*pro-genitor*) and *pater* (*Iu-p(p)iter*) at the beginning of two consecutive lines may indicate that Soranus is alluding to a collocation of *pater* and *genitor. Progenitor* is most likely collocated with *genetrix* to emphasize that the Stoic Jupiter of Soranus is both male and female, a circumstance emphasized by the objective genitive *deumque,* which immediately precedes *progenitor* and follows *genetrix.*[43] If Soranus is alluding to Ennius, then at least one reader apprehended a ritual connection between the various collocations of *pater* and *gen-* and gender in the *Annals.* If the ambiguity of gender in Soranus is dependent on neither tradition nor Ennius, then the parallelism at least suggests that the language of ritual could be a means of thinking about gender.

A parallel expression to *progenitor genetrixque deum* in another fragment of the *Annals* (which I discussed in chapter 2) suggests that collocations of the root of *deus,* including *o die* and *genere,* are traditional in their own right:

O genitor noster, Saturnie, maxime divom (*Ann.* 444)

O son of Saturn, O our begetter, greatest of the gods. (trans. Warmington)

What is more, there are collocations of the cognates of the roots of *deus* and *genere* in Oscan ritual. The Oscan Agnone Tablet yields a theonym **deívaí genetaí** in two places (Rix Sa 1 A 15 and B 18). Although there are no instantiations of **deívaí genetaí** outside of the Agnone Tablet, the repetition of the expression implies that the collocation was traditional in Oscan. The name of the Roman goddess *Genita Mana* also suggests that the title **genetaí** is traditional. The archaic adjective *mana,* "good," likewise indicates that the name *Genita* is quite old.[44] Because *Genita, genitor,* and **genetaí** are cognate, their genetic relationship implies an ancient connection between the Latin and Oscan roots that may be grounded in the language of common Italic ritual. Collocations of forms based upon the roots of *deus* and *genere* may therefore have been "good to think with" for many generations before Ennius utilized the same collocation in a narrative that explored the interface between gender and divinity.

If some connection between *genetrix patris* and *Genita Mana* or **deívaí genetaí** is tenable, then these collocations could invite consideration of the relative position of male and female in the larger context of book 1. In other words, *genetrix patris,* among other ritual collocations in book 1, is not a deconstruction of the traditional gender roles but rather a traditional deconstruction of gender roles. The comic trope of the *uxor dotata* is a good example of an inversion of the usual relationship of the *paterfamilias* to the female members of his household. As Celia Schultz has convincingly demonstrated, gender was not necessarily a factor in determining who could participate in a given cult, a thesis that again emphasizes that the relative position of men and women could be fluid in the Roman Republic.[45] Such fluidity would have been tolerated only within certain limits, though, and there is no evidence for a sustained exploration of the intersection of gender and kinship in the *Annals* after Ilia has achieved her own apotheosis.

To return the focus to *genetrix patris,* the insistent association of *pater* and the root *gen-* is indicative of the overlap between kinship and ritual system reference throughout book 1. Venus is the *genetrix patris,* an expression that both identifies her as the mother of Aeneas and the grandmother of Ilia and recalls the cult title Venus *genetrix.* Whereas *prognata pater* consists of the same two roots as *prognatus patre,* an expression usually applied to mortals, there are also some examples of *prognatus patre* that refer to the sons of gods in a mythic, if not a ritual, context. The slippage between kinship and ritual system reference, however, begins to lose its momentum when Romulus, who fails to produce an heir, becomes *pater* and *genitor.* The use of collocations of *pater* and *genere* serve as a thematic thread that the audience may follow in order to arrive at the orderly and stable social structure of the future Roman state, but the path is neither short nor direct, as the three generations of the *Aeneidae* seek to find their proper place in mortal, and then in immortal, society.

The insistent use of the root *gen-* may explain the presence of the enigmatic *di genitales* in another fragment of the *Annals:*

> Romulus in caelo cum dis genitalibus aevom
> Degit. (*Ann.* 110–11)

Romulus lives from age to age in heaven with the gods that gave him birth. (trans. Warmington)

Henry Jocelyn suggests that the *di genitales* have a Pythagorean color and that they are connected with Pythagorean ideas of the divinity of "the visible bodies of the upper sky," who have some association "with the generation of living beings."[46] Jocelyn also suggests that Ennius added this Pythagorean coloring to a "Graecising story in which Romulus was taken after his earthly career to Olympus by his divine father Mars."[47] If Jocelyn is correct, then the fragment may be an attempt to rationalize the apotheosis of Romulus in philosophical terms and perhaps is another indication of some skepticism toward apotheosis in general on the part of Ennius. Even if the lament for Romulus also belongs to book 2, as Priscian says (*G.L.* 2 p. 250),[48] the phrase *dis genitalibus* may be a means of looking back to the three apotheoses in book 1 of three gen-erations that were born to mortals.

The language of ritual is not only a vehicle for themes in book 1, it is a means of affirming a deep connection between family and ritual. Although a connection between ritual and family in a poem composed in second-century Rome may not in itself be especially surprising, the overlap of the traditional expressions of familial relationships and divine titles in a narrative that details three apotheoses demonstrates a remarkable understanding of the use of language to create the boundaries between gods and men and men and women. In other words, there is an implicit recognition on the part of Ennius that kinship, gender, and divinity are all discourses.

The recognition of the discursive nature of categories such as mortal man or goddess, however, also implies a protodeconstructive undermining of such categories that would not be out of the realm of possibility for the man who translated Euhemerus and allegorized the gods in his *Epicharmus*.[49] It is hard to believe that the same writer would easily accept that three generations of mortals not only descended directly from a goddess but also that such mortals became immortal themselves.

I have suggested that some of the fragments of book 1 are characterized by a negotiation between the foreign and the familiar—the invocation of the Muses at the beginning of the *Annals*, a Greek *topos* that may also allude to the Italic *tripudium*, for example. The primary dialogue in the story of Aeneas, Ilia, and Romulus, however, is between the past and the present. In other words, most of the fragments of book 1, including the *augurium Romuli*, are primarily concerned with mediating the present of the second century BCE with the distant past. In spite of the fragmentary state of book 1, Ennius' mediation of past and present through language can be studied in some detail. Ennius not only shaped his narrative of the foundation of Rome as a family history; he was also able to partially elide the gap between the mythical family of Aeneas and the generic Roman family of the second century BCE, even as he implicitly recognized that kinship is a discourse by maintaining an insistent semantic pressure on kinship terms like *pater* and *genitor.*

By using kinship system reference, Ennius is able to familiarize a story that was used by Greek cities to situate Rome in the Greek world. This process of familiarization is analogous to the familiarization of the genre of Greek New Comedy in the plays of Roman comic playwrights like Plautus. If the myth of Aeneas was used primarily as a means to engage with Greek cities and was not a central myth of Roman identity in the Republic, as Andrew Erskine has argued, then book 1 of the *Annals* may represent an unsuccessful, or only partially successful, attempt at familiarizing the unfamiliar.[50] Whatever the status of the Aeneas myth in the second century BCE, it eventually took hold of the Roman imagination.

The combination of ritual and kinship system reference in the frame of a traditional story also allows Ennius to incorporate all three types of gods identified by Varro (quoted in Augustine [*C.D.* 6.5]).[51] The anthropomorphic gods of book 1 of the *Annals* interact with mortals, just as in Homer. These then are "the gods of the poets." Because the Roman people invoke Romulus with divine epithets, Romulus/Quirinus is one of the "gods of the state," who can be reached by means of ritual acts and prayers. Although "the gods of the philosophers" are not explicitly present, book 1 begins in the realm of philosophy, a fact that already engenders suspicion that the poet might not accept his traditional material at face value. The flux between divinity and humanity that continued over three generations surely challenged the credulity of some members of the audience.

Ennius was no mere encomiast or client poet who unreflectively transmitted the traditions of the founding of the city of Rome. The *Annals* is a sophisticated composition that allows for multiple points of view on the level of character and on the level of the most traditional ritual collocation. It is a poem that is surprisingly modern, contrary to comments by poets such as Ovid that Ennius was *rudis arte,* "unpolished" (*Tr.* 2.424), and that nothing was *hirsutius,* "more hairy" (*Tr.* 2.259), than the *Annals.* As I have shown, book 1 of the *Annals* is also current in its treatment of gender as a discourse. However archaic Ennius may have seemed to his Augustan successors, his discursive exploration of the ideological categories of the middle Republic suggests that the postmodern acknowledgment of the arbitrary nature of such categories is actually very ancient.

The Annals *of Quintus Ennius and the Modern Tradition*

The public high school that I attended had a Latin motto: *dum clavum teneam,* "until I may hold the helm." (My Latin teacher, Charles Speck, taught me that it was a temporal clause that expressed intent.) The motto is not only appropriate for an educational institution but also an allusion to the *Annals.* When I was reading all the fragments of the *Annals,* I came across the fragment that I assume was the ultimate source of *dum clavum teneam* (whether or not the clause expresses intent here is an open question):

> Dum clavom rectum teneam navemque gubernem
>
> So long as I hold the tiller straight and steer the ship . . .

Even in the experience of a high school student with little Latin and no Greek, the *Annals* of Quintus Ennius was present.

The fragment is also typical of the other fragments that have been discussed and interpreted in my study. The immediate source of *dum clavum teneam* is likely to be Quintilian (here it does not express intent), who does not even credit Ennius directly for inventing the expression, but rather says that the expression is known (*illud notum*) (2.17.24). As Skutsch observes, the content of the expression is proverbial, but the form of the expression "given by the poet seem[s] to have gained currency in Rome."[1] The distinction between Ennius and later authors and between traditional expression and poetry is collapsed in a manner that obscures the boundary separating the poet, the later authors who quote him, poetry, and tradition. In sum, the three-word motto conceals centuries of dialogue that can be partially recovered only by careful research.

Throughout the course of my argument I have emphasized that there is also a dialogue between cultures that helps shape even the diction of the *Annals.* Although the contributions of the member cultures of the central Italian *koinê* are not always obvious, I have identified several instances where a previous dialogue between the Romans and the other members of the *koinê* may be as important as the present dialogue between the Romans and the Greeks. Moreover, I have tried to show that what appears to be a dialogue between Greeks and Romans may in fact have once been between the foreign and the familiar.

Because the multicultural dialogue that is the *Annals* is polyphonic and not monophonic, it can be very difficult to hear the individual voices of this polyphony. Many of the voices of the central Italian *koinê* have been obscured by the passage of time. Even if much of the evidence is lost, the influence of the central Italian *koinê* on Roman culture is likely present, even when the *Annals* seems to be speaking in a purely Roman voice in harmony, or disharmony, with the voice of Greek culture. Although this combination was apparently taken as a single apologetic voice by the time of Cicero, I have tried to show just how deeply embedded these other voices are in the poem.

In my attempts at recovering these elements of a dialogue that had actually ended before Ennius was born, I also hope to give the reader a glimpse of a time when origins were not the only way one could classify a cultural element, a means of classification that I suggest had yet to be privileged over the experience of various aspects of Roman culture as foreign and familiar in the lifetime of Ennius. Origins have always been a convenient way to categorize various phenomena, but categories can also be defined by the cultural work they perform. Although the modern genre of comedy is not unaffected by its origins in classical Athens, few of the millions who watch situation comedies on television would classify them as a Greek, and therefore foreign, phenomenon.

Unlike modern comedy, however, many of the cultural elements in the *Annals* were adopted far more recently from other cultures, and the Romans may have possessed an awareness that they were once foreign, an awareness that would have enriched the dialogue of the foreign and familiar in the *Annals.* A similar process appears to be at work in the adoption of the novel and other forms of European literature by postcolonial cultures. Although the author of a "postcolonial" novel or poem may be a native speaker of English, she will likely be aware that English is of a recent, foreign origin in many of these cultures. The Romans were similarly very aware that epic poetry, comedy, and meter were Greek contributions to their culture, even though these phenomena were adopted at least a generation before the composition of the *Annals.* Nor does this awareness need to be limited to appropriations of Greek culture. The Romans may also have known that even the venerable cult of Jupiter Stator originated in an earlier encounter with Oscan culture.

We have learned the value of genetic diversity and the value of cultural diversity, but we often do not consider how many cultures of the past contributed to our own culture or how our own culture benefited from its own encounters with the foreign. Some of those cultures left traces of their contributions to Roman culture in the *Annals,* as I hope I have demonstrated, and some aspects of these ancient cultures have indirectly become part of modern culture. In sum, although we cannot read the *Annals* in its entirety, or even understand the fragments in the way its audience did, the *Annals* of Quintus Ennius can still tell us much about our own cultural and poetic traditions.

ABBREVIATIONS

All ancient sources are referred to by the abbreviations found in LSJ, *OLD,* and Rix (defined below) whenever possible.

Audollent	Audollent, Auguste, ed. *Defixionum Tabellae: Quotquot Innotuerunt tam in Graecis Orientis quam in Totius Occidentis Partibus praeter Atticas.* Paris: Albert Fontemoing, 1894.
LSJ	Liddell, Henry, Robert Scott, Henry Jones, and Roderick MacKenzie, eds. *A Greek-English Lexicon, Ninth Edition with a Revised Supplement.* New York: Oxford University Press, 1994.
OLD	Glare, Peter, ed. *Oxford Latin Dictionary.* New York: Oxford University Press, 1982.
Rix	Rix, Helmut. *Sabellische Texte: die Texte des Oskischen, Umbrischen und Südpikenischen.* Heidelberg: Winter, 2002.
Untermann	Untermann, Jürgen. *Wörterbuch des Oskisch-Umbrischen.* Heidelberg: Winter, 2000.

Chapter 1 · *Ennius and the Italic Tradition*

1. Twain, *Following the Equator,* 241. This book itself is a "classic" by Twain's definition.

2. All translations are my own unless otherwise indicated.

3. Albrecht, *Silius Italicus,* 164, suggests that the influence of Ennius on Silius is more general ("im Allgemeinen") than specific ("im Einzelnen"). Although such "general influences" could be filtered through secondary sources, I am not unconvinced that some of the verbal parallels adduced by Woodruff, *Reminisces of Ennius,* 365–93, are the result of direct acquaintance with the *Annals.*

4. Casali, "The Poet at War," 575–91, elaborates on parallels between the passage in Silius and Vergil suggesting that it is a nod to several passages from the *Aeneid.* The suggestion of Spaltenstein, *Commentaire des "Punica,"* Vol. 2, 179, that the episode was at least inspired by Ennius, however, cannot be verified, since the claim that Ennius was a descendant of Messapus, the one verifiable connection between this passage and the *Annals,* could have been filtered through a commentary on the *Aeneid.*

5. Skutsch, *The "Annals" of Quintus Ennius,* 29.

6. Goldberg, *Constructing Literature in the Roman Republic,* 24–28, cautions that, although the centrality of epic "seems natural, even self-evident," there is no reason to assume that the *Annals* would have survived without the work of scholars such as Q. Vargunteius in the second half of the second century.

7. Zetzel, "Influence of Cicero on Ennius," 2, observes, "Without Cicero's interest . . . we would have a great deal less to say about a great deal less of Ennius."

8. The two editions are Skutsch, *Annals* (in English) and a text and translation into Italian: Flores, *Annali,* Vol. I, and Flores, *Annali,* Vol. III. The text is accompanied by three volumes of commentary: Flores et al., *Annali,* Vol. II, Flores et al., *Annali,* Vol. IV, and Jackson and Tomasco, Vol. V. Both of these texts and commentaries owe much to previous editions, especially Vahlen, *Ennianae Poesis Reliquiae.* The first volume on Ennius is a special issue of *Arethusa* edited by Rossi and Breed (Vol. 39, no. 3, Fall 2006). The second is a supplementary volume of the *Proceedings*

of the Cambridge Philological Society edited by William Fitzgerald and Emily Gowers and published in 2007.

9. Kleve, "Ennius in Herculaneum," 5–16, identifies the papyrus—formerly thought to be from a comedy—as a hexameter poem, cross-references the fragments with fragments of book 6 of the *Annals*, and on that basis suggests that the roll once contained book 6, including the two previously unassigned fragments.

10. Zetzel, "Influence of Cicero on Ennius," 1–16. Elliott, "The Voices of Ennius' *Annals*," 40–46, constructs an extremely useful typology of motivations for preservation that may skew modern interpretations.

11. Zetzel, "Influence of Cicero on Ennius," 6.

12. I am not the first to suggest that Alexandrian or Callimachean poetry influenced the *Annals*. Jocelyn, "Poems of Quintus Ennius," 1015–17, Brink, "Ennius and the Hellenistic Worship of Homer," 547–67, Gratwick, "Ennius' *Annales*," 66–75, and Albrecht, *Roman Epic*, 63–73, have all made similar claims about different aspects of the *Annals*.

13. Halliday et al., *Lexicology and Corpus Linguistics*, 168.

14. Ibid., 93. I exclude the translations of phrases in the *OLD* as "dictionary senses" because those translations are, in fact, irreducible meanings of collocations.

15. Parry, *The Making of Homeric Verse*, 272.

16. Wolfgang Teubert, "Units of Meaning," 171.

17. Although others (e.g., Pallottino, *Genti e culture*, 44) have noted the existence of an Italian material cultural *koinê*, Campanile, "L'uso storico della linguistica italica," 36–45, is the first, to my knowledge, to discuss the cultural *koinê* in central Italy as a linguistic phenomenon that is separate from the Mediterranean cultural *koinê* and that postdates Proto-Italic.

18. Clackson and Horrocks, *Blackwell History of the Latin Language*, 41–48, identifies these common characteristics. including the common use of a personal *praenomen* and a family name or *nomen* not to mention that forms of the name "Titus" are found in Etruscan, Umbrian, Oscan, and Latin; the name "Aulus" in Etruscan, Oscan, and Latin and "Numerius" in Etruscan, Oscan, Umbrian, and Latin. The different linguistic communities of the *koinê* also appear to have worshipped similar gods, including some borrowed from the Greeks such as Apollo and Heracles. Schultz, *Women's Religious Activity in the Roman Republic*, 11, notes the existence of "similar (but not necessarily identical) priesthoods" and a type of votive deposit common to west-central Italy during the fifth and fourth centuries.

19. Eska and Mercado, "More on the Metrical Structure in the Inscription of Vergiate," 204–11.

20. The most recent attempt is Linderski, *Roman Questions II: Selected Papers*, 3–18.

21. Edmunds, *Intertextuality and the Reading of Roman Poetry*, 143, uses the word "system . . . to refer to verbal categories, literary and nonliterary, larger than single texts."

22. Macrobius 6.1.19 explicitly locates the fragment in book 7. Skutsch, *Annals*, 412–13, assigns it to Hannibal.

23. The text of the *Annals* throughout is Skutsch, *Annals*. All translations of Ennius are from Warmington, *Remains of Old Latin*, Vol. I, with adjustments to differences between his text and Skutsch.

24. The translation is from Lord, *Cicero*, Vol.10, 31.

25. Wallace-Hadrill, *Rome's Cultural Revolution*, 5–6, observes a process of "triangulation" of identities and a lack of anxiety over losing one's local identity by "Hellenizing." Although the nature of the *Annals* compels Ennius to "Romanize" and "Hellenize," his "local" identity does not seem to have much of an impact.

26. Ibid., 13.

27. Campanile, "Zur oskischen Inschrift Ve. 187," 47–48, offers alternative explanations to the possibility that the title is an appropriation of the Greek *Zeus Tropaios*.

28. E.g., Stephens, *Seeing Double*, 9, cites the following fragment of Callimachus: εἰδυῖαι φαλιὸν ταῦρον ἰηλεμίσαι (*SH* fr. 254.16), "knowing how to mourn the bull with the white marking," as a reference to the Egyptian Apis bull. Although the reference does not depend on a cross-linguistic pun as far as I am aware, Stephens does note that the Apis in this context "begins to lose otherness and to be incorporated into the allusive matrix of what has become an extended Greco-Egyptian mythological family."

29. Long, *Twelve Gods*, 56 prints the reconstructed text of Wendel, *Scholia in Apollonium Rhodium*, 172–73.

30. Long, *Twelve Gods*, 3–136, collects the written and visual evidence for the twelve gods.

31. Skutsch, *Annals*, 424, connects the names in the Ennian fragment to Livy's report that the number of gods for the *lectisternium* was raised to twelve (22.10.9). He also notes the exact correspondence of names between Ennius and Livy. On the basis of these parallels, he concludes that "there can be little doubt that the poet's catalogue of the same twelve gods was connected with this event."

32. Long, *Twelve Gods*, 4–5.

33. As Wiseman, *Unwritten Rome*, 84–139, has demonstrated, the cult of Liber was well established in ancient Italy and Rome before the Bacchanalian conspiracy.

34. Feeney, *Gods in Epic*, 124.

35. Varro mentions *Iana Luna*, perhaps a variant on the name Diana (*R.* 1.37.3) or perhaps the feminine of Janus. *Ianus* could be similarly derived from an older form *Dianus*, a masculine form of Diana, even though there are alternate ways to etymologize Janus. The fact that Nigidius *apud* Macrobius equates Janus with Apollo on the basis of *Iana* for Diana (Macrobius 1.9.8) suggests that there was an association of Janus with Diana in the mind of at least one Latin speaker.

36. Texts written in the native Umbrian alphabet are written in bold. Texts written in the Latin alphabet are conventionally written in italics.

37. Untermann s.v. Fενζηι understands the name as a borrowing from Latin.

38. Although the number of inscriptions that name Ceres is not large, she is named twice in the Agnone Tablet (Rix Sa 1) and three times in a curse tablet from Campania (Rix Cp 37), in addition to a plethora of adjectives derived from her

name. Untermann s.v. **çerfe** also derives the Umbrian divinity **çerfe** (a vocative) from the same root as Ceres.

39. Untermann s.v. **appelluneís.**

40. There are other *cistae* from Praeneste (e.g., *CIL* I² 563, 564, and 565) that name a long series of personalities depicted on them, but the others usually are mixed with names from Homeric poetry such as Achilles and Ajax.

41. Rix, "Teonomi," 209, suggests that the name Menerva is a derivation of the Proto-Indo-European root **men-*, "to think."

42. Ibid., 210, argues the Etruscan name is characterized by a Proto-Indo-European suffix. Wallace, *Zikh Rasna,* 132, suggests that the Etruscans borrowed the name from Umbrian speakers because the -*θ*- in *Neθuns* appears to reflect the simplification of the cluster -*pt*- to -*t*- in the Sabellic languages.

43. Rix, "Etrusco *un, une, unu* '*te, tibi, vos,*'" 674–76, compares a number of Etruscan phrases that appear to enjoin that the celebrant make a sacrificial offering to similar phrases in Latin and Umbrian. Weiss, *Language and Ritual,* 366 n. 24, considers the interpretation of Umbrian **spanti** as "platter" (based on Etruscan platters with the inscriptions such as **mi spanti nuzinaia**, "I am the platter of *Nuzinai*") to be "one of the most positive advances of the past thirty years of Umbrology." The Etruscan word *cletram* is also apparently a borrowing from Umbrian.

44. Rix, "Teonomi," 209–10.

45. Long, *Twelve Gods,* 4.

46. Festus cites "Alfius" as his source. It is unlikely that this Alfius is the same as the third-century CE author of *Libri Rerum Excellentium,* a poetic collection of episodes from Roman history.

47. The translation is from Long, *Twelve Gods,* 104.

48. Skutsch, *Annals,* 424, and Long, *Twelve Gods,* 236–37, observe that the previous *lectisternia* in Livy honored six gods. Both suggest that the *lectisternium* of 217 BCE was a radical change.

49. Skutsch, *Annals,* 29–30, suggests that Apuleius "probably knew the *Annals.*" Although the assumption is reasonable, given the popularity of Ennius in the Antonine age, the fact that Apuleius only quotes these two lines should give pause.

50. Feeney, "Interpreting Sacrificial Ritual," 1–21.

51. Rüpke, "*Acta aut agenda,*" 23–44, emphasizes that text and ritual are "interrelated systems, not alternatives."

52. Skutsch, *Annals,* 186. Hickson, *Roman Prayer Language,* 24, cautiously takes up Skutsch's suggestion.

53. The translation is from Foster, *Livy: Books I and II,* 251.

54. Skutsch, *Annals,* 186. Although the passage in Livy does have a vaguely dactylic shape, there are two tribrachs in the first eight words: -*ne pater* and -*te precor.*

55. Ibid., 250, lists a plethora of parallels besides Cicero. I quote him *exempli gratia.*

56. Fortson, *Language and Rhythm in Plautus,* 109–11, discusses a similar parallel in the *Persa* (228–336) and notes similar stylistic figures that are "characteristic of Plautus' frequent satirical treatment of solemn ritual language."

57. Poultney, *The Bronze Tables of Iguvium,* 232, notes the similarity and suggests that they are both "datives signifying the objects of divine favor."

58. Hickson, *Roman Prayer Language,* 75–76.

59. Skutsch, *Annals,* 749.

60. Jocelyn, "Poems of Quintus Ennius," 991 n. 43, and Adams, *Bilingualism,* 117 n. 23, both wonder whether Messapic was recognized as a language separate from Oscan by anyone outside of the area where it was spoken. If not, Gellius may have simply used *Osce* for *Messape,* an incomprehensible name to him.

61. Wallace-Hadrill, *Rome's Cultural Revolution,* 4.

62. Although she suggests epic, tragedy, and satire as the three "literary identities," Gowers, "The *Cor* of Ennius," 28–30, is noncommittal as to what three cultures the three hearts may represent.

63. Habinek, *Politics of Latin Literature,* 67, sees Ennius' claim of having three hearts as symptomatic of a struggle over the ultimate cultural identity of Roman Italy in the second century.

64. Untermann, "Beobachtungen an römischen Gentilnamen," 175–78, concludes the name Ennius is "*gut italisch.*" The name is widespread throughout Italy and neighboring territories, as Untermann's appendix clearly demonstrates, with concentrations in Campania and Apulia, as well as Liguria. In his treatment of the poet's name, ibid., 180–81, raises a number of possible origins for the name Quintus Ennius.

65. According to Cicero (*Brutus* 72) Accius reported that Livius was captured at Tarentum. Although Cicero does not dispute the place of origin of Livius, he does not accept the date of the capture given by Accius. Weiss, preface to Livingston, *Linguistic Commentary on Livius Andronicus,* xvii n. 11, observes that the name Ἀνδρόνικος is attested at Tarentum but wonders if Livius might not have been captured at Tarentum without being a native.

66. Sear, *Roman Theatres,* 145, mentions a hollow shape in the ground at the site of Rudiae that some have argued to be an Odeon and others an amphitheater.

67. Skutsch, *Annals,* 677.

68. Harvey, "Religion and Memory at Pisaurum," 132.

69. There is a tradition reported by Servius (*ad Aen.* 7.691) that Ennius claimed descent from Messapus, the eponymous colonizer of Messapian territory in Italy, a report that may suggest that Ennius' third heart and language was Messapic, not Oscan. Skutsch, *Annals,* 749, suggests that Ennius' Messapic descent is through his mother.

Chapter 2 · The Annals *and the Greek Tradition*

1. Skutsch, *Annals,* 147–53, discusses the sources, including Porphyrio, the scholiast to Persius 6.11, who explicitly states that Ennius claimed that Homer's soul had passed into his body.

2. The substitutions are not actually random. Fortson, *Language and Rhythm in Plautus,* argues that the "licenses" of Plautine prosody reflect the linguistic properties of the Latin language.

3. Skutsch, *Annals,* 66.

4. Ibid.

5. Watkins, "Greece and Italy outside Rome," 39.

6. Most accept this line as the opening of the *Annals.* Varro, who quotes it (*L.* 7.5), does not specify, however, that this is the first line of the epic. On the basis of Hesiod's *Catalogue of Women* and Solon 1, two poems that have a second line that begins with the word Μοῦσαι, however, Skutsch, *Annals,* 143, argues that it is not. I myself side with the majority opinion that it is the first line of the *Annals.*

7. Bettini, *Studi e note su Ennio.*

8. Lowrie, *Writing, Performance, and Authority in Augustan Rome,* 25–32, suggests that the fragment "embraces writing over against religious posturing," unlike Callimachus, who "follows Homer in referring to his own poetry as song" and makes claims to divine inspiration. She also suggests, however, that Ennius has not completely done away with the vocabulary of song, as in his use of *melos* (*Ann.* 293).

9. The passage was famous in antiquity and quoted in part or in full by several sources, among them Cicero (*Brut.* 71 and 75, *Div.* 1.114, and *Orat.* 171), Varro (*L.* 7.36), and Quintilian (*Inst.* 9.4.115). Wiseman, *Unwritten Rome,* 41–44, provides a valuable discussion of the various contexts in which quotations of *Annals* 207 are found. Although there are other parts of the passage that are taken to be fragments of the *Annals* and possibly the polemic of Ennius (Suerbaum, *Untersuchungen zur Selbstdarstellung älterer römischer Dichter,* 249–95, discusses this passage and other possible fragments of Ennius' polemic extensively), I will concentrate solely on this fragment because it is the only one that directly addresses Naevius, at least if Cicero can be trusted.

10. Although it was obviously different from dactylic hexameter, the nature of the Saturnian meter remains elusive. Freeman, "Saturnian Verse and Early Latin Poetics," 61–90, gives an overview of conflicting points of view, even though he adds little himself to the subject. Cole, "The Saturnian Verse," 3–73, is the classic exposition of the quantitative-syllabic argument. Parsons, "A New Approach to the Saturnian Verse and Its Relation to Latin Prosody," *TAPhA* 129 (1999): 117–37, argues that the Saturnian is based on the grouping of syllables.

11. I omit possible references to Ennius in the *Pro Archia* on the grounds that the possible quotations are not direct. Suerbaum, *Untersuchungen zur Selbstdarstellung älterer römischer Dichter,* 263–65, treats these references.

12. The text is from Courtney, *Fragmentary Latin Poets,* 10.

13. I have adjusted the translation of Warmington, *Remains of Old Latin,* Vol. I, 2, to reflect the discrepancy between *Italos* in Warmington's text and *latos* in Skutsch's.

14. The translation is from Hendrickson, *Brutus,* 71. Douglas, *Marci Tulli Ciceronis Brutus,* 65, glosses *reliquisset* as "left (virtually) untouched."

15. Skutsch, *Annals,* 370, accepts that these lines are an explanation (presumably his dismissal of the *faunei vatesque*) as to why Ennius did not give *a full account* of the war (emphasis mine) was in the text of the *Annals.*

16. The word *poeta* also occurs in two prologues (*Men.* 7 and *Cas.* 18). I exclude them from this list because the authorship of the prologues is not secure.

17. The identification is based on Paulus ex Festo's statement that Naevius was called a *poeta barbarus* in Plautus (PAUL. *Fest.* p. 36M). The entry could, however, be an educated guess made by ancient authors about the identity of the *poeta barbarus* rather than a known fact.

18. The translation is from de Melo, *Plautus,* Vol. III, 163.

19. As Gruen, *Studies in Greek Culture and Roman Policy,* 97, who is skeptical of the verse's authenticity, notes, "it is itself in dispute as to intent, significance and authenticity."

20. LSJ s.v. ποιητής lists no usage under the meaning "composer of a poem, author" earlier than the fifth century.

21. Wiseman, *Unwritten Rome,* 39–51.

22. Although Varro, who quotes the line, does not name his source (*L.* 7.25), it is a reasonable assumption that it is a fragment of the *Annals.* Both Skutsch and Flores include the line in their texts.

23. My discussion of code switching is based on Adams, *Bilingualism,* 18–29.

24. In addition to noting the tag, ibid., 131, suggests that the vocalism of *victurei* is a non-Latin feature in light of Oscan **víkturraí.**

25. Although Eumenius, the earliest explicit source for the connection with Fulvius, dates to the very late third century CE, I am convinced by the reference from Plutarch and the circumstantial evidence that Fulvius did bring the statues to Rome and build the temple. Sciarrino, "Introduction of Epic in Rome," 452, e.g., suggests that "the relationship between Ennius' poetic project and Fulvius' religious complex is . . . pervasive."

26. Skutsch, *Annals,* 145.

27. Hardie, "Juno, Hercules, and the Muses at Rome," 551–92.

28. Habinek, "Wisdom of Ennius," 476, sees *perhibere* as a signifier of either "interconvertability" or "substitution," depending on the specifics.

29. Gordon, *Letter Names of the Latin Alphabet,* 14–15.

30. The text of Lucilius is that of Marx, *C. Lucilii Carminum Reliquiae.* The translation is from Warmington, *Remains of Old Latin,* Vol. III, 123.

31. Hinds, *Allusion and Intertext,* 2. The term was coined by Ross, *Backgrounds to Augustan Poetry,* 78.

32. Hunter, *Shadow of Callimachus,* 27.

33. Skutsch, *Annals,* adds <*Iris*> as the beginning of the next line in his text. He also differs from Warmington, *Remains of Old Latin,* Vol. I, 142–43, who prints the line thus *arcus subscipiunt mortalibus quae perhibentur,* "they look up at the bows (?) which are said by mortals . . ." Warmington bases his emendation upon the reading *perhibentur* in the majority of manuscripts, whereas Skutsch (followed by Flores, *Annali,* Vol. III, 30) bases his on a reading of *perhibetur* in two manuscripts. I have adjusted Warmington's translation in order to fit Skutsch's text.

34. Watkins, "Language of Gods and Language of Men," 456–57, cites six instances of the language of gods in Homer (*Il.* 14.290–91, 2.813–14, 20.74, and 1.403, and *Od.* 10.305 and 12.61).

35. Flores, "Commentario al libro I," in Flores et al., *Annali,* Vol. II, 25.

36. Although a correspondence between Latin *sec/sequ-* and Umbrian **suk/siku-** is unexpected, many of the scholars cited by Untermann s.v. **sukatu** and **prusikurent** believe that the two roots are cognate.

37. Sheets, "The Dialect Gloss," 68.

38. *OLD* s.v. *pulso* 4.

39. Bettini, *Studi e note su Ennio,* 107–8, remarks that the phrase *pede pulsare* is "molto frequente" in Roman poetry and suggests that the phrase is traditional rather than a poetic creation.

40. So noted by Bettini, *Studi e note su Ennio,* 107–8.

41. The translation is from Rudd, *Horace,* 93.

42. Nisbet and Rudd, *Commentary on Horace,* 220, identify the festival as the *Faunalia* that took place on December 5th.

43. The translation is from Rudd, *Horace,* 189.

44. Bettini, *Studi e note su Ennio,* 107, suggests that the phrase recalls un genere di danza (*tripudium*) and defines the dance as a general category of dance performed by striking the ground with the feet, no matter who does the performing.

45. *OLD* s.v. *puls.*

46. The translation is from de Melo, *Plautus,* 425–27.

47. Skutsch, "New Words from Plautus," 166, suggests that *pultare* is actually derived from *puls* rather than *pulsare* and that *panem* implies *puls.*

48. Although Skutsch, *Annals,* 147, maintains that this correspondence is "probably accidental," the matching alliteration may be another indication that *Annals* 1 was, in fact, the first line of the poem.

49. Feeney, *Gods in Epic,* 124.

50. Lejuene, "Inscriptions de Rossano di Vaglio," 675.

51. The plural form ρεγο(μ) is roughly equivalent to Fανάκες, "lords, masters," an epithet of the Dioscuri found in Sparta. As Aldo Prosdocimi, "Sui grecismi dell'osco," in *Scritti in onore di Giuliano Bonfante* (Brescia: Paideia, 1976), 832, implies, the presence of a Spartan epithet in Tarentum, a Spartan colony, is not improbable.

52. *OLD* s.v. *regina* 2.

53. Feeney, *Gods in Epic,* 128.

54. Ibid., 121.

55. Kleve, "Ennius in Herculaneum," 8–9.

56. I have adjusted the translation of Warmington, *Remains of Old Latin,* Vol. I, 207, to reconcile the differences between his and Skutsch's text of the fragment.

57. Whatever the original reading was, it is not in the manuscript reading, because the transmitted *at* is not metrical. Skutsch, *Annals,* 629, notes that it would be plausible for *at* to be a corruption of the abbreviation *qb* and that there are no syntactic objections that might otherwise arise from the mixture of the imperfect and

present subjunctives *saperet* and *sint*. Skutsch's intuition that *a-* conceals an original *q-* appears to be confirmed by Kleve, "Ennius in Herculaneum," 8–9.

58. Flores, *Annali,* Vol. I, 66 n. 109, observes that a letter *-i-* remains from the otherwise missing line preceding *Ann.* 469, a letter that could be the *-i-* in *ingentis,* even though it is not possible to know with complete certainty. Suerbaum, "Die Pyrrhos-Krieg in Ennius' *Annales* VI," 42, also joins the two fragments without citing Flores, whom Giorgio Jackson, "Commentario al Libro VI," in Flores et al., *Annali,* Vol. II, 103, credits with being first to join the fragments; it appears that both scholars independently arrived at the same conclusion.

59. The epitaph is preserved by Gellius (GEL. 1.24.2) with other epitaphs supposedly written by Plautus and Ennius. Luck, "Naevius and Virgil," 275, credits "some scholars" with the idea that the epigram is from Varro's *Imagines* and composed by Varro himself.

60. Although there is some debate over the original meaning of *naenia* or *nenia,* Cicero considers the *nenia* to be a funeral custom (*Leg.* 2.62), as Habinek, *World of Roman Song,* 234, observes. Paulus ex Festo (PAUL. *Fest.* p. 163M) also defines *nenia* (*sic*) as *carmen quod in funere laundandi gratia cantatur ad tibiam.* Whether *naenia* originally meant funerary song, as Habinek, *World of Roman Song,* 234, suggests, or "plaything," as Heller, "Nenia 'παίγνον,'" 215–68, suggests, *naenia* demonstrably meant "funeral dirge" to Cicero, a meaning that very likely predates Cicero.

61. Versnel, "'May He Not Be Able to Sacrifice,' 247, prints the entire text and a brief account of the curious history of the study of the tablet that was apparently originally thought to be an example of Gaulish.

62. Fox, *The Johns Hopkins "Tabellae Defixionum,"* 23.

63. Text and translation are from Tomlin, Frere, and Hassall, "Roman Britain in 1987," 485–87.

64. Adams, *Bilingualism,* 139, observes that the Oscan curses are earlier than their Latin counterparts and that Oscan influence on Latin curse tablets "would accord with the tendency in Latin literature for certain magical practices to be associated with Italic peoples such as the Sabelli, Paeligni and Marsi."

65. Gager, *Curse Tablets and Binding Spells,* 118, observes that early curses against legal rivals "name the opponents; they sometimes invoke local deities by their familiar names . . . and they mention physical and mental faculties, usually tongue and mind, to be bound or tied up so that the targets will be unable to pursue their case."

66. The fragment has been analyzed in great detail in the previous literature, especially with respect to its influence on Vergil, and little can be added concerning its similarity to Homer. Whereas Hinds, *Allusion and Intertext,* 11–13, and Dominik, "From Greece to Rome," 83–84, are both concerned with the influence of Ennius upon Vergil, Nadeau, "Ennius, *Annales* 175–179 (Skutsch)," 309–12, suggests that the fragment actually describes the building of the Roman fleet under Gaius Duilius, but Macrobius explicitly attributes the fragment to book 6 and his report appears to be confirmed by a partial match between the sequences]RAT[and]SP[in Pezzo 1 fr. 2. As Kleve "Ennius in Herculaneum," 7, notes, the two sequences match *frangitu*]*r*

at[que and *procera]s p[ervortunt* in *Annals* 177–78, a match that confirms that the fragment is from book 6. No evidence from the Herculaneum papyrus in any way suggests that book 6 dealt with the first Punic War. The fragment may refer to the building of Pyrrhus' fleet, however, if Nadeau is correct about the subject matter of the fragment.

67. Flores, *Annali,* Vol. I, 72.

68. Adams, *Bilingualism*, 181–82, observes several linguistic features that suggest a date of no earlier than the Flavian era for the prophecy, an argument that I find very persuasive, even though an earlier date would strengthen my own suggestion that Etruscan thought has influenced the Ennian fragment.

69. Edlund-Berry, "Ritual Space and Boundaries in Etruscan Religion," 118–19.

70. Torelli, "Un *templum augurale* d'età repubblicana a Bantia," 293–315, first identified a series of six *cippi* as markers of an augural temple. Some of these *cippi* appear to assign an augural point to a god, including Jupiter (*IOVI*), Flusa (*FLUS*), an Oscan form of Flora, and perhaps the sun (*SOLEI*), if it refers to it as a god. Upon the discovery of three more augural cippi from the same site, Torelli, "Contributi al supplemento del *CIL* IX," 39–48, revised his initial suggestion that two other *cippi* named gods and instead argued that both stones were abbreviations of augural terms.

Chapter 3 · Ritual and Myth in the Augurium Romuli *(*Annals *72–91)*

1. Here, I change the translation of Warmington, *Remains of Old Latin,* Vol. I, 31, ". . . [on a hill] . . . Remus devotes himself to watching" in order to match Skutsch's text.

2. I have inserted "by" to clarify what I think Warmington means when he translates "luckiest far."

3. Skutsch, *Annals,* 233–34, does not provide any examples of *pulcer* and *praepes* together outside Ennius but makes a convincing case for the individual elements as examples of augural terminology.

4. Linderski, *Roman Questions II: Selected Papers,* 17–18, notes that a stone used to mark the boundaries of augural *templa* from Bantia reads *R AVE* or *R(emore) AVE.* He also cites the definition of *remores aves* as "a sign to delay" in Paulus ex Festo (PAUL. *Fest.* p. 276M).

5. Mineur, *Callimachus,* 211.

6. O'Hara, *Inconsistency in Roman Epic,* 28, notes that Callimachus does not say that he accepts the Arcadian version instead of the Cretan but rather "all Cretans are liars."

7. Hunter, *Apollonius of Rhodes, Argonautica, Book III,* 21, gives this allusion to a variant tradition as one example of "the process of selecting between variants, either by referring to a rejected version in the course of telling the selected one or by combining previously competing versions."

8. Aicher, "Ennian Artistry," 222–24, suggests that the simile prefigures the Augustan tendency to compare the rustic past of Rome to its present grandeur.

9. Although Skutsch, *Annals,* 225–26, is tentative, he supposes that "Naevius . . . deriving the name of Aventine . . . may or may not have had the birds of Romulus in mind." Servius *A.* 657 says that *Aventinus mons urbis, quem constat ab avibus esse nominatum.* Servius may refer to Naevius' etymology, but the verb *constat* implies agreement among several authorities. It is possible, however, that other authors appropriated the etymology from Naevius, leading to a perceived state of agreement. On balance, Servius' failure to credit Naevius with the etymology inclines me to believe that the derivation of *Aventinus* from *avis* was a popular etymology employed by Naevius.

10. Skutsch, *Annals,* 223. Although *OLD* does not list *dare operam . . . auspiciis* as a formula, Linderski, *Roman Questions,* 526, calls it an example of "Roman divinatory terminology." Elsewhere, it only appears in prose writers such as Cicero and Livy (*Fam.* 10.12.3 and LIV. 38.26.1).

11. *OLD* s.v. *inferus* 2.

12. Flores, *Annali,* Vol. I, 46.

13. Skutsch, *Annals,* 224–25, objects that, in addition to the metrical problems, the use of *se devovet* outside of sacrifice to the nether gods is not found before Curtius (9.6.21).

14. Wiseman, *Remus,* 12, mentions an etymology of *Lemuria* as *Remuria* in Ovid's *Fasti* (5.445–49 and 478–79) that may also suggest such a variant.

15. Merula, *Quinti Enni Annalium LIBB XIIX,* ccx, has suggested that the *sol albus* is the moon, but as Skutsch, *Annals,* 231, points out, Ennius could have simply written *luna alba* in the same position in the line. Jocelyn, "*Urbs Augurio Augusto Condita,*" 70–72, suggests that the *sol albus* is the morning star, but Skutsch also objects to this interpretation, albeit less vehemently. Skutsch himself suggests that *sol* should be taken as sun and notes that *albus* is the usual Latin rendering of Greek λευκός, an adjective sometimes applied to the sun in Greek as early as Homer (*Il.* 14.185). Flores, *Annali,* Vol. I, 46–48, avoids the problem of the close proximity of the two suns by transposing line 92 (*interea sol albus recessit in infera noctis*) to the line immediately before the extended simile.

16. Powell and Rudd, "Explanatory Notes," 177, note other occurrences of two suns in Cicero (*Div.* 1.97), Livy (28.11.3, 41.21.13), and Pliny (*Nat.* 2.99).

17. Linderski, *Roman Questions II: Selected Papers,* 10.

18. Steuart, *"Annals" of Quintus Ennius,* 116.

19. Linderski, *Roman Questions II: Selected Papers,* 15, notes that the eagle observed by Marius flies toward the east after turning from the west and implies that the birds seen by Romulus also fly east. He also notes that Jupiter thunders on the left.

20. The text is that of Courtney, *Fragmentary Latin Poets,* 175.

21. Linderski, *Roman Questions II: Selected Papers,* 15.

22. Fantham, *Ovid, Fasti IV,* 244, observes that Ovid is alone in separating the day of the augural contest from that of the foundation.

23. Thomas, *Virgil and the Augustan Reception,* 25–54, gives a concise overview of the debate between the "pessimistic" and "optimistic" readers of Vergil. Important

landmarks in this debate are Clausen, "Interpretation of the *Aeneid,*" 139–47, an early formulation of the "pessimist" view of the *Aeneid,* and Johnson, *Darkness Visible,* who is the first that I am aware of to refer to the opposing sides of the debate as "pessimists" and "optimists." O'Hara, *Death and the Optimistic Prophecy,* is the most relevant to my study here.

24. Elliott, "The Voices of Ennius' *Annals,*" 49–54.

25. Zetzel, "Influence of Cicero on Ennius," 1–16.

26. MacBain, *Prodigies and Expiation,* 50–51, notes that *haruspices* are present in the record of ten of the thirteen lightning prodigies that are accompanied by a description of the response to the prodigies. On the basis of this evidence he observes that "it seems a reasonable presumption that it was their expertise in the handling of lightning bolts, perhaps more than any other aspect of the discipline, which principally attracted Roman interest to them" (i.e., Etrsucan *haruspices*). Ibid., 51 n. 123, also lists several sources confirming that the Romans, including Cicero (*Div.* 1.92), considered lightning omens to be a central concern of the Etruscan divination.

27. The text and translation are from Turfa, "The Etruscan Brontoscopic Calendar," 181 and 189.

28. Valmaggi, *I frammenti degli Annali,* 45, is apparently the first to suggest this context for *Annals* 145.

29. *De Legibus* 3.11 occurs in the part of the text without commentary.

30. Bréal, *Les tables eugebines,* 7, enigmatically quotes *Annals* 74–76 without further comment in a footnote to his discussion of the participle *anzeriates.* It is unclear, however, whether he is simply making a general semantic or a specific etymological connection.

31. The translation is from Poultney, *The Bronze Tables of Iguvium,* 230.

32. Untermann s.v. *curnaco.*

33. Untermann s.v. *desua.*

34. Poultney, *The Bronze Tables of Iguvium,* 228.

35. As Vine, "An Umbrian-Latin Correspondence," 126, observes, "The tendency of Umbrian ritual language toward marked effects based on rhyme, alliteration and rhythm is well documented."

36. Ibid., 111–27, collects the evidence for both the Umbrian and Latin collocations and concludes that they are "ritually cognate, reflecting a two-member phrase assignable to Common Italic ritual practice." Vine believes that the Umbrian *ficla* is "a purely Umbrian replacement" created for the purpose of assonance.

37. Sandoz, "Le nom d'une offrande à Iguvium," 345–46, suggests that *vestiçia* is cognate with Latin *depsticium.* He imagines that the discrepancy between the *v-* in Umbrian and *d-* in Latin to be the result of a borrowing from Sabine, a language that appears to change *d-* to *l-* under some circumstances, into Umbrian.

38. Benveniste, "Le valeurs économiques dans la vocabulaire indo-européen," 309, notes the striking similarity between the Latin and Umbrian phrase and suggests that the phrases are genetically related.

39. Linderski, *Roman Questions II: Selected Papers,* 9.

40. MacBain, *Prodigies and Expiation,* 59, cautions against reading the episode as evidence for conflict between the two groups. The senate, as MacBain observes, appears to have heeded the advice of the *decemviri* and the *haruspices.*

Chapter 4 · *Ritual,* Militia, *and History in Book 6 of the* Annals

1. Fantham, "'*Dic si quid potis de Sexto Annali,*' 551.
2. The lack of sources for the Pyrrhic War renders any attempt at reconstructing a more specific context difficult. Ibid., 550–51, provides a good, concise summary of what is known of the events of the war. The two major historical problems that affect the reconstruction of book 6 are the placement of the speech of Pyrrhus treated below and the historicity of the *devotio* of Decius Mus, also treated below.
3. Dench, *Romulus' Asylum,* 58. Fantham, "'*Dic si quid potis de Sexto Annali,*'" 551–52, also suggests that the Pyrrhic war was also important to the debate over whether Rome would have prevailed had Alexander ever made it to Italy.
4. Dench, *Romulus' Asylum,* 66, sees these traits as an aspect of Roman self-definition within a framework of Greek ethnography.
5. Kleve, "Ennius in Herculaneum," 6.
6. Whether Pyrrhus released his prisoners unconditionally or only granted them a temporary release on condition of a settlement as in Appian (Samn. 10) and in Plutarch (Pyrrh. 20), Skutsch, *Annals,* 348, observes that in other sources the release is unconditional, even if such a release occurred during negotiations for peace, as Lefkowitz, "Pyrrhus' Negotiations with the Romans," 162–63, argues.
7. Coffee, *The Commerce of War,* 7–30. In terms of reciprocal and commodity exchange, however, the speech is a straightforward "declaration of Roman values," as observed in ibid., 31.
8. Valmaggi, *I frammenti degli Annali,* 55–56, puts the speech in the mouth of Appius Caecus, but Skutsch, *Annals,* 358, objects that "Roman statesman can hardly be credited with learned allusions to Greek mythology, or with flattering references to the enemy's military prowess." The first objection is not valid if one allows anachronism, such as Ovid and later poets employ when treating past events. The second is also not valid if the fragment is read as an implicit criticism.
9. Habinek, "Wisdom of Ennius," 485.
10. Skutsch, *Annals,* 8 and 358, suggests *Troades* 1158–59 as a model for the fragment, a tragedy that Ennius translated at least in part in his *Andromacha.*
11. Elliott, "The Voices of Ennius' *Annals,*" 53–54, notes a "productive ambivalence" in the use of *Aeacidae* and other indications of Aeacid descent.
12. McDonnell, *Roman Manliness,* 92, suggests that the pairing is borrowing from Greek, since it is rare in early Latin literature and "the few passages where it does occur seem to be modeled on Greek works."
13. Gildenhard, "Virgil vs. Ennius, or: The Undoing of the Annalist," 83.
14. Ibid.

15. As Fantham, "'*Dic si quid potis de Sexto Annali*,'" 566, observes, a temple of Jupiter would be an odd place for what could be read as a reproach of the god.

16. Skutsch, *Annals*, 352, and Jackson, "Commentario al libro VI," in Flores et al., *Annali*, Vol. II, 139, note the parallel. Jackson remarks on the possible implications of its ritual context in passing. Skutsch does not.

17. Skutsch, *Annals*, 353, notes the cult title of the Penates but curiously does not suggest the obvious Greek parallel.

18. Euler, dōnum dō-, 13–16.

19. Vine, *Studies in Archaic Latin Inscriptions*, 198–205. I omit CIL I^2 2828 because it is extremely fragmentary.

20. Skutsch, *Annals*, 352 n. 6, identifies several commentators and readers, most notably Dante, who appear to have taken *dono* as a noun.

21. Euler, dōnum dō-, 15–16.

22. Ibid., 11–16, collects sixteen examples under the category of *Inschriften der italischen Sprachen*. Three of the sixteen appear to be Oscan and two Umbrian. Although the others appear to be in Latin, some contain Oscan words and phrases. Ibid., 36, also cites CIL I^2 364 in an appendix.

23. There are a number of dedications to Aesculapius (*CIL* I^2 26–28) among the early inscriptions as well as to Hercules (*CIL* I^2 61, 62, 2675a), but other divinities such as Fortuna, Jupiter, Diana, and Apollo are also represented.

24. In some of these inscriptions *merito(d)* immediately follows *donum dare* (e.g., *CIL* I^2 27, 31, 32, 384, and 386), and in one at least, *mereto* is inserted between *donum* and *dedit* (*CIL* I^2 976). In addition to these examples of *donum dare merito(d)*, the phrase *libens merito(d)* immediately follows *donum dare* sometimes (e.g., *CIL* I^2 28, 388).

25. The obscurity of the syntax has led to some disagreement as to how to understand the sentence. Although Skutsch, *Annals*, 352–53, understands the phrase as modifying *ducite*, Fantham, "'*Dic si quid potis de Sexto Annali*,'" 560, and Goldberg, *Epic in Republican Rome*, 101–2, suggest that the phrase modifies all three verbs.

26. Norden, *Ennius und Vergilius*, 162, argues that the speaker of the line is Aeneas when he meets the king of Alba Longa. Skutsch, *Annals*, 191, suggests that Latinus is the speaker instead of Aeneas.

27. Valmaggi, *I frammenti degli Annali*, 28.

28. The translation is from Foster, *Livy: Books I and II*, 83.

29. *OLD* s.v. *verbum* 9.

30. Although Watson, *International Law in Archaic Rome*, 7, claims that "there is . . . a general agreement among scholars that the *ius fetiale* . . . existed even before the city was founded," Wiedmann, "The Fetiales," 478–90, observes that much of the evidence for the archaic date of the Fetial rite only establishes what the Augustan age thought and that earlier evolutionary models that viewed the discussions of Augustan date as proof have been abandoned by modern scholarship. Because there seems to be little dispute that the Fetials were active in the middle Republic and because there is independent evidence that *foedus ferire* is a traditional colloca-

tion, the controversy has little bearing on my argument that the audience of the *Annals* would recognize the collocation and its connotative meaning.

31. I have taken the text from Richardson, *Hispaniae*, 199.

32. Riggsby, *Caesar in Gaul and Rome*, 196, defines the "category of 'general's inscriptions'" as "any inscriptional text that makes overt reference to a military action or its aftermath." He also identifies a "focus on plunder," ibid., 197, including territory, and a focus on the general to the exclusion of the armies that he led.

33. I omit the six from the list of thirty-one "general's inscriptions" in ibid., 217–21, that were taken from literary sources. I have also chosen to cite these inscriptions by *CIL* number rather than Riggsby's numbers. Some of the texts collected in Riggsby are emended, sometimes heavily, and I do not cite any emendation as evidence for any of my own subcategories of inscriptions.

34. *CIL* I^2 9, 613 and 2954. Although *CIL* I^2 2836 may be emended to *M Fo[lvios Q. f. cos]ol / [dede]d V[olsi]nio cap[to,* I err on the side of caution and exclude it.

35. *CIL* I^2 48 and 49.

36. *CIL* I^2 25, 608, 7, 615, 616, 622, 625, 626, 630, 631, and 741 and I^2 2836 and 2926. Out of these, a form of the verb *dare* has been supplemented for *CIL* I^2 630, as well as for *CIL* I^2 2836 (discussed above). Although these emendations shift the statistical shape of the evidence somewhat, I again err on the side of caution because these emended texts are not essential to my argument.

37. The epitaph is one of five composed for various members of the *Gens Cornelia Scipionis* found in their family tomb. The texts may be metrical. Van Sickle, "The *Elogia* of the Cornelii Scipiones," 42, identifies the four epitaphs not composed in elegiacs as Saturnians.

38. The *CIL* notes that the last two letters of *dedit,* among other letters, are no longer visible, but older authorities transcribe the inscription thus. The presence of *ded*[, as the inscription now reads, is sufficient for my point. *Dedit* is apparently written over the erasure of the verb *vovit.* The significance of this alteration is obscure, but it may indicate that *vovere,* and perhaps *votum solvit,* were acceptable variants of *dare.*

39. The translation is based on Riggsby, *Caesar in Gaul and Rome,* 220, but I have made some adjustments.

40. Ibid., 217, places this text first in his collection. The translation is also his.

41. Courtney, *Archaic Latin Prose,* 109, notes that Servilius was a pontifex. Note also Servilius' cognomen *vatia,* which may stem from *vates.*

42. Ibid.

43. Leigh, *Comedy and the Rise of Rome,* 37–45, does not discuss the formulaic nature of *vera virtute,* but the repeated attention drawn to the phrase suggests that he understands it as a traditional collocation.

44. If the opposition of *era Fors* and *virtute* is an appropriation of the opposition of ἀρετή, "excellence," and τύχη, "fortune," in Greek thought, as McDonnell, *Roman Manliness,* 84–95, has suggested, then the opposition of *virtute* and *Fors* in Ennius could be a mixture of Greek and Latin diction similar to *volentibus cum*

magnis Dis. Because I have not been able to find a single, fixed expression that collocates ἀρετή and τύχη in Greek, however, especially in poetry, and also because of the inexact match between Greek ἀρετή and Latin *virtus,* I have elected not to pursue the implications of the possible mixture of Greek and Latin diction here.

45. Gildenhard, "Virgil vs. Ennius, or: The Undoing of the Annalist," 83.

46. Jackson, "Commentario al Libro VI," in Flores et al., *Annali,* Vol. II, 166, conscientiously notes that the line is not explicitly assigned to the *Annals,* or even Ennius, by Cicero, who quotes it in the *De Re Publica* (3.6), although there have been no objections on that basis to its placement in the *Annals.*

47. Skutsch, *Annals,* 350, makes this observation on the pairing of *aurum* and *ferrum* in line 185 in the speech of Pyrrhus. He also notes a parallel in Plautus (*Truc.* 929) that may indicate that the collocation was proverbial before Ennius.

48. I present this text *exempli gratia.* The readings of the papyrus are those of Kleve, "Ennius in Herculaneum," 5–16. The supplements are an amalgam of those of Kleve, "Phoenix from the Ashes," 61–62, and Suerbaum, "Die Pyrrhos-Krieg in Ennius' *Annales* VI," 45–51

49. Gildenhard, "Virgil vs. Ennius, or: The Undoing of the Annalist," 83.

50. Although Aurelius Victor (*Vir. Ill.* 36) reports that a Decius suppressed a revolt at Volsinii in 265, Cornell, "Ennius, *Annals* VI: A Reply," 515, calls this author "unreliable."

51. Although it is suspicious that both the grandfather and father of Decius perform *devotiones* in Livy (8.9.6–8 and 10.28.15–18) but not the grandson, Cicero twice asserts that all three devoted themselves (*Fin.* 2.61 and *Tusc.* 1.89). Skutsch, "Book VI of Ennius' Annals," 514, suggests the third *devotio* is a fabrication by Ennius or "an obscure variant."

52. As Skutsch, *Annals,* 354, notes, the mouse (*mus*) is "believed to be connected with death and to foretell it and therefore the name of the character whether mentioned explicitly or not in the *Annals* would resonate with the cult of the underworld gods."

53. The translation is from Foster, *Livy: Books VIII–X,* 37.

54. Text and translation are from Kaster, *Macrobius: Saturnalia,* 68–71.

55. Rawson, "Scipio, Laelius, Furius and the Ancestral Religion," 172–74, reviews the evidence for and against the *devotio* at Carthage.

56. Bömer, *Ahnenkult und Ahnenglaube im alten Rom,* 127–30, adduces a number of uses of *mittere,* especially with the object *inferias,* in chthonic contexts in later literary sources and some later inscriptions such as *CIL* XI 1420.

57. Skutsch, *Studia Enniana,* 57–58.

58. The translation is from Shackleton-Bailey, *Cicero: Letters to Friends,* Vol. II, 107.

59. The only source of fragments cited by Ribbeck (Accius *praet.* 1–16) for the play is Nonius, who usually refers to the play as *Aeneadis vel Decio.*

60. The second line is especially opaque. It reads *ASTEDNOISIOPETOITESIAI PACARIVOIS.* Tichy, "Gr. οἴσειν und Lat. åti und die Mittlezeile der Duenos-Inschrift," 196–201, suggests that the second be read thus: *As*(*t*) *ted n' oisi opet, oit*

esiai paka rivois or *ast te ne uti optet utere ei, paca rivis.* I paraphrase her German translation thus: "and if she will not walk off with you, walk off with (this) instead of her, satisfy yourself in streams."

61. Although I cite the *CIL*, I follow the reading put forth in Vine, *Studies in Archaic Latin Inscriptions*, 85–95. I also omit the problematic form *HOI* that begins the inscription.

62. As Vine, "A Note on the *Duenos* Inscription," 295, notes, Festus is "generally accurate" when identifying archaic *-sn/sm-* clusters.

63. Ibid.

64. Although the precise phonological shape of the root $^*h_2$mei(*H*)- has not been determined to the satisfaction of all, as Vine "A Note on the *Duenos* Inscription," 296, notes, this imprecision is, in any case, not relevant to the Latin form *mitat*, because any of the roots proposed would be spelled *mitat.*

65. The text is a combination of ibid., 293, and the revised reading of ENMANOMEINOM, in ibid., 300.

66. Peirano, "Hellenized Romans and Barbarized Greeks," 52 n. 82, cites the fragment in connection with the bribing of the soldiers but hesitates to draw any conclusions about its relevance, because it is unclear where it was placed in the narrative.

67. Elliott, "The Voices of Ennius' *Annals*," 53–54, observes that "all recognizable references to Pyrrhus' person dwell on a heroized version of his descent."

68. Although I am sympathetic with Suerbaum, "Die Pyrrhos-Krieg in Ennius' *Annales* VI," 48, when he objects that Kleve, "Phoenix from the Ashes," 62, is overreading the fragments from the Herculaneum papyrus, I find Kleve's general suggestion that Pyrrhic War narrative in Ennius has tragic elements to be compelling.

Chapter 5 · *Ritual, Kinship, and Myth in Book 1 of the* Annals

1. The engagement was not always direct. Skutsch, *Annals*, 24, notes that in one instance the author of the *Origo* "merely repeats the much quoted line 207 [of the *Annals*]."

2. McCarthy, *Slaves, Masters, and the Art of Authority in Plautine Comedy*, 1–29.

3. Zetzel, "Influence of Cicero," 13.

4. There is some question as to whether Ennius explicitly describes the rape of Ilia or only suggests it by means of Ilia's dream. Skutsch, *Annals*, 194, suggests that Ilia recounts the dream after a description of Mars coming to her in her bedroom.

5. Although the text of the fragment is generally sound, there are some minor textual issues. The *etcita* in the manuscripts may conceal *excita* and not *et cita.* Skutsch, *Annals*, 195, concedes that the "possibility that E. wrote *excita* cannot be ruled out." Flores, *Annali*, Vol. I, 38, prints *excita*, appealing to *lectio difficilior* (2002: 42). The phrase *corde capessere* is considerably opaque. Vine, "*Corde Capessere* (Ennius *Ann.* 42 Sk.)," 123–26, has suggested that *colla capessere* underlies the manuscript reading, but he does not fully commit to the emendation, because the artistic effect of the repetition of *corde cupitus* five lines later would be lost. Skutsch, *Annals*,

199, offers the possibility that the name of the sister may have been corrupted into *corde.*

6. Keith, *Engendering Rome,* 42–46, understands Ilia as virgin territory in the literal and metaphorical sense, noting the emphasis on space in the dream and suggesting a connection between the topography of Ilia's dream and metaphors of female sexuality. Elliott, "The Voices of Ennius' *Annals,*" 46–49, reads the fragment as a particularly sophisticated tapestry of male and female, tragic and epic, poetic and historical, and Greek and Roman. My debt to her reading will be clear to anyone familiar with it.

7. Van Sickle, "The *Elogia* of the Cornelii Scipiones," 51.

8. Klingner, *Studien zur griechischen und römischen Literatur,* 415.

9. Fontaine, *Funny Words in Plautine Comedy,* 176–83, borrows the term from psycholinguistics. He provides the following "stock example": "The horse raced past the barn fell (i.e. the horse *that was* raced past the barn fell)."

10. Although ibid., 177, cites no occurrences of the phrase *manedum asta* in Plautus, he lists a number of very similar phrases such as *mane atque asta* (*Cas.* 737).

11. Ibid., 179, suggests that Sceparnio pronounced the *-t-* in *ventris* more like a glottal stop than a dental stop and that the speaker inserted an epenthetic short *-e-* between the glottal stop and *-r-*.

12. In addition to the variants mentioned in f.n. 6, the *corpus meum* is reversed in one manuscript and *-que* after *vires vitaque* (both *Ann.* 37) is omitted in another. *O gnata* (*Ann.* 44) is an emendation of *cognata.*

13. Fowler, "The Virgil Commentary of Servius," 73, discusses the relationship of the seventh- or eighth-century *Servius Auctus* commentary to that of the fourth-century commentary by Servius.

14. Nonius s.v. *gratulari,* the source of this fragment, reads *isque susum ad caelum sustulit suas.*

15. Dunkel, "Old Latin Orality," 329–30, sees the Naevian version as a formulaic variant, or an "allo-formula," of an expression for raised hands in prayer.

16. Dunkel, "Periphrastica Homerohittitovedica," 111–14, notes a number of expressions for hands raised in prayer in Hittite, Greek, and Vedic. The Akkadian expression *nãs qàttim* (literally raising of hands) is an idiomatic expression for "prayer."

17. Sullivan, "*Tendere Manus,*" 358–62, surveys the permutations of *tendere manus* in the *Aeneid,* as well as the semantic variations of the phrase. He concludes that these collocations "normally mark(s) a prayerful gesture" in the *Aeneid.*

18. The translation is from Sage, *Livy: Books XXXV–XXXVII,* 93.

19. Dunkel, "Periphrastica Homerohittitovedica," 111.

20. Although the line is not directly attributed to Ennius, Skutsch, *Annals,* 205, points out that hexameters quoted by Varro are invariably from Ennius, even if the poet is not named.

21. E.g., Livy 5.21.14 and 24.16.10 and Ovid *Fasti* 6.449 and *Metamorphoses* 9.703. Sullivan, "*Tendere Manus,*" 359, includes two collocations of *sustulit* and *manus* in *Aeneid* 2.153 and 9.16–17 among his list of examples of *manus tendere* in the *Aeneid.*

22. Skutsch, *Annals,* 394, notes the use of the four elements in *Annals* 220–21 parallels Empedocles. He also sees the *paluda virago* (*Ann.* 220) and *Discordia taetra* (*Ann.* 225) as closely related to the principle of Strife in Empedocles.

23. Wills, *Repetition in Latin Poetry,* 247, asserts that the collocations of *voce* and *vocare* are not "a prose syntagm," even though he himself cites Livy 7.15.2.

24. Krevans, "Ilia's Dream," 266–68.

25. If *suboco* is an *-o-* stem, then it matches *voce* only on the level of the root, but *suboco* may be a consonant stem. Untermann s.v. *suboco* favors neither possibility, but simply acknowledges it may be an *-o-* stem or a consonant stem.

26. Krevans, "Ilia's Dream," 259–61.

27. Connors, "Ennius, Ovid, and Representations of Ilia," 105.

28. Watkins, *How to Kill a Dragon,* 155–56. Although the etymological correspondence between *vires vitaque* and **biass biítam** is not exact, Oscan **biítam** and Latin *vita* are both reflexes of the Indo-European root **gʷit-*, and both **biass** and *vires* carry essentially the same semantic message, "strength and life." Moreover both expressions are bound by alliteration. *Vires* is not cognate with Oscan **biass,** however, because the Latin root of vires is a reflex of the Indo-European root **wiH-r-* (the same underlying root of Latin vir and other words for "man" in the daughter languages), whereas **biass** is a reflex of the root **gʷih$_2$-* (the underlying root of Greek βία, "physical force."

29. The translation is from Watkins, *How to Kill a Dragon,* 220, who translates **Aftiím,** following Pisani, *Le lingue dell' Italia antica oltre il Latino,* 95.

30. Tomlin et al., "Roman Britain in 1996," 456–57.

31. Fox, *The Johns Hopkins "Tabellae Defixionum,"* 19. The restoration of *corp[us]* is guaranteed by the reading *c.rpus* on another tablet since all the tablets appear to repeat the same curse formulation.

32. Text and translation are from Kent, *Varro: On the Latin Language,* 60–61.

33. Lactantius *Opif.* 12.16: *vir nuncupatus est, quod maior in eo vis est quam in femina,* "*Vir* is called (thus) because there is greater force in man than in woman." Cassiodorus *In psalm* 1.11.109: *vir . . . vocatur a viribus.* Isidore (10.274) also etymologizes *vir* from *vis: vir nuncapatus . . . quod vi agat feminam.*

34. The line is not securely attributed by a reliable ancient source to Ennius. Although "Sergius" explicitly names Ennius as the author (*Explan. In Don.* 4.65), his attribution is likely a guess, and some of his obvious guesses are wrong. Skutsch, *Annals,* 409, notes that "Sergius" assigns a confirmed fragment of the *Annals* to Plautus. Nevertheless, Skutsch argues, "It is difficult to see to what other poet the line could belong."

35. Weinstock, "Two Archaic Inscriptions from Latium," 116, suggests that taking *Lare Aineia* as a dative is the "most natural."

36. West, *Indo-European Poetry and Myth,* 87, cites ὁ γεννήσας πατήρ (*S. El.* 1412) as a parallel and alludes to "similar phrases" without elaborating.

37. Although Schmitt, *Dichtung und Dichtersprache in indogermanische Zeit,* 152–53, posits that the Vedic and Euripidean expressions are reflexes of a collocation

of Indo-European date, he believes that the collocation in Ennius is a borrowing from Greek.

38. There are good reasons for this assumption. Dunkel, "Old Latin Orality," 330, summarizes the problem well: "the typically Roman literary and cultural dependence reduces the trustworthiness of the comparison."

39. If the correspondence between the Latin and Vedic phrases is not indicative of the inheritance of a common Indo-European collocation, then a number of other parallels between phrases in Italic and Indo-Iranian languages would also have to be accidental. The close parallel between Umbrian *veiro pequo* and a phrase in Young Avestan noted by Wackernagel, *Kleine Schriften herausgegeban von der Akademie Wissenschaften zu Göttingen,* Vol. I, 280–83, could have arisen from a common Indo-European source. Dunkel, "Old Latin Orality," 329, suggests that *manus tendebam* is a reflection of one of a number of "PIE competing formulas" for the ritual posture. Matasovic, *A Theory of Textual Reconstruction in Indo-European Linguistics,* 114, notes that expressions such as *voce vocans* in *Aeneid* 6.247 are different enough in "syntax of the cases and the meaning" to be considered reflexes of an inherited Indo-European collocation into Latin rather than a borrowing of Greek expressions such as εἰπεῖν ἔπος,

40. Skutsch, *Annals,* 256.

41. Ibid., 209, proposes that *saneneta* is a corruption of *ted* and *Aeneia,* a cult title of Aphrodite *Aineias,* who had a temple in Ambracia, where Ennius could have seen it while accompanying Fulvius Nobilior. The existence of a shrine of Aeneas in the same region could have led Ennius to connect the epithet *Aineias* with Aeneas. The proximity of *cognata* may also be a gloss on Aenean Venus, i.e., Venus the mother of Aeneas and therefore related to Ilia.

42. Murphy, "Valerius Soranus and the Secret Name of Rome," 127–28, discusses what is known about the life and contributions of Valerius Soranus, a learned man credited with the invention of the table of contents and vilified by ancient sources for revealing the secret name of Rome.

43. The shifting of gender in Soranus may reflect the influence of Stoic pantheism on the fragment. Courtney, *Fragmentary Latin Poets,* 66–67, believes Stoic pantheism ultimately stems from Orphic thought.

44. Watmough, "The Suffix *-tor-*," 90–91, connects the Latin and Oscan names.

45. Schultz, *Women's Religious Activity in the Roman Republic,* 151, concludes that "religion is another area of daily life in which Roman women took an active role in both the private and the public spheres."

46. Jocelyn, "Romulus and the *Di Genitales,*" 55.

47. Ibid.

48. Ibid., 46–47, makes an especially good case for placing *Annals* 110–11 at the beginning of book 2. It seems to me that his observation that the line is several times referred to in Pompeian graffiti and that these graffiti tend to quote the first lines of books of Vergil and Lucretius is especially important.

49. Lowrie, *Writing, Performance, and Authority in Augustan Rome,* 28, cites a comment made by Cotta in the *De Natura Deorum* (1.119) indicating that Ennius

was a follower of Euhemerus as well as his translator. Courtney, *Fragmentary Latin Poets,* 30–39, edits and comments on the fragments of this poem, evidently a translation of a philosophical work attributed spuriously to the Sicilian comedian Epicharmus. Feeney, *Gods in Epic,* 121–22, suspects that Ennius is allegorizing Saturn in *Annals* 444 and raises the possibility that the story of Saturn in the *Annals* has Euhemeristic qualities.

50. The thesis of Erskine, *Troy between Greece and Rome,* has met with some criticism for being overstated. Cornell, "Cicero on the Origins of Rome," 48 n. 31, suggests that the fact that Augustan authors could use Republican sources for the Aeneas myth indicates a dependence upon the Republican authors rather than a post-Vergilian bias. Rose, "Reevaluating Troy's Links to Rome," 480, cites material evidence indicating that the Romans did view themselves as the descendants of the Trojans, including a coin struck during the Pyrrhic War with Roma wearing a Phrygian cap. Even if Erskine is correct, there is no reason not to claim that book 1 of the *Annals* is an attempt to familiarize an Aeneas myth that had not succeeded in embedding itself in the Roman consciousness.

51. The idea must be older than Varro, but how much older is hard to say. After a thorough review of the scholarship on the *tria genera theologiae,* Lieburg, "Die 'theologia tripertita' in Forschung und Bezeugung," 107, concludes that the idea cannot be attributed to a single Greek thinker or school of thought but must be a "universale Denkform."

Conclusion · *The* Annals *of Quintus Ennius and the Modern Tradition*

1. Skutsch, *Annals,* 661.

BIBLIOGRAPHY

Adams, J. N. *Bilingualism and the Latin Language.* New York: Cambridge University Press, 2003.

Aicher, P. J. "Ennian Artistry: *Annals* 175–179 and 78–83 (Sk.)," *CJ* 85, no. 3 (1990): 218–24.

Albrecht, Michael von. *Silius Italicus: Frieheit und Gebundenheit römischer Epik.* Amsterdam: P. Schippers, 1964.

———. *Roman Epic: An Interpretative Introduction.* Leiden: E. J. Brill, 1999.

Benveniste, Émile. "Le valeurs économiques dans la vocabulaire indo-européen." In *Indo-European and Indo-Europeans: Papers Presented at the Third Indo-European Conference at the University of Pennsylvania,* edited by George Cardona, Henry Hoenigswald, and Alfred Senn, 307–20. Philadelphia: University of Pennsylvania Press, 1970.

Bettini, Maurizio. *Studi e note su Ennio.* Pisa: Giardini, 1979.

Blänsdorf, Jürgen. *Fragmenta Poetarum Latinorum Epicorum et Lyricorum Prater Enni Annales et Ciceronis Germanicique Aratea.* New York: De Gruyter, 2011.

Bömer, Franz. *Ahnenkult und Ahnenglaube im alten Rom.* Leipzig: Teubner, 1943.

Bréal, Michel. *Les tables eugebines.* Paris: A. Franck, 1875.

Brink, C. O. "Ennius and the Hellenistic Worship of Homer." *AJP* 93, no. 4 (1972): 547–67.

Campanile, Enrico. "L'uso storico della linguistica italica: l'osco nel quadro della koiné mediterannea e della koiné italiana." In *Oskisch-Umbrisch Texte und Grammatik: Arbeittagung der Indogermanichen Gesellschaft und der Società Italiana di Glottologia vom 25. Bis 28. September 1991 in Freiburg,* edited by Helmut Rix, 26–35. Wiesbaden: Reichert, 1993.

———. "Zur oskischen Inschrift Ve. 187." In *Sprachen und Schriften des antiken Mittelmeerraums: Festschrift für Jürgen Untermann zum* 65. *Geburtstag,* edited by Frank Heidermanns, Helmut Rix, and Elmar Seebold, 47–52. Innsbruck: Institut für Sprachwissenschaft der Universität Innsbruck, 1993.

Casali, Sergio. "The Poet at War: Ennius on the Field in Silius' *Punica.*" *Arethusa* 39, no. 3 (2006): 569–93.

Clackson, James, and Geoffrey Horrocks. *The Blackwell History of the Latin Language.* Walden: Blackwell Publishing, 2007.
Clausen, Wendell. "An Interpretation of the *Aeneid.*" *HSCP* 68 (1964): 139–47.
Coffee, Neil. *The Commerce of War: Exchange and Social Order in Latin Epic.* Chicago: University of Chicago Press, 2009.
Cole, Thomas. "The Saturnian Verse." *YCS* 21 (1969): 3–73.
Connors, Catherine. "Ennius, Ovid, and Representations of Ilia." *Materiali e discussioni per l'analisi dei testi classici* 32 (1994): 99–112.
Cornell, T. J. "Ennius, *Annals* VI: A Reply." *CQ* 37 n.s., no. 2 (1987): 512–14.
———. "Cicero on the Origins of Rome." *Bulletin of the Institute of Classical Studies* 45 (2001): 41–56.
Courtney, Edward. *Archaic Latin Prose.* Atlanta: Scholar's Press, 1999.
———. *The Fragmentary Latin Poets.* New York: Oxford University Press, 2003.
Dench, Emma. *Romulus' Asylum: Roman Identities from the Age of Alexander to the Age of Hadrian.* New York: Oxford University Press, 2005.
Douglas, A. E. *Marci Tulli Ciceronis Brutus.* Oxford: Clarendon Press, 1966.
Dunkel, George. "Periphrastica Homerohittitovedica." In *Comparative-Historical Linguistics: Indo-European and Finno-Ugric Papers in Honor of Oswald Szemerényi III,* edited by Bela Brogyanyi and Reiner Lipp, 103–18. Philadelphia: Benjamins, 1993.
———. "Old Latin Orality Seen through Indo-European Lenses." In *ScriptOralia Romana: Die römische Literatur zwischen Mündlichkeit und Schriftlichkeit,* edited by Lore Benz, 321–40. Tübingen: Narr, 2001.
Edlund-Berry, Ingrid. "Ritual Space and Boundaries in Etruscan Religion." In *The Religion of the Etruscans,* edited by Nancy Thomason de Grummond and Erika Simon, 116–31. Austin: University of Texas Press, 2006.
Edmunds, Lowell. *Intertextuality and the Reading of Roman Poetry,* Baltimore: Johns Hopkins University Press, 2001.
Elliott, Jacqueline. "The Voices of Ennius' *Annals.*" In *Ennius Perennis: The "Annals" and Beyond,* edited by William Fitzgerald and Emily Gowers, 38–54. Cambridge: Cambridge Philological Society, 2007.
Erskine, Andrew. *Troy between Greece and Rome: Local Tradition and Imperial Power.* New York: Oxford University Press, 2001.
Eska, Joseph, and Angelo Mercado. "More on the Metrical Structure in the Inscription of Vergiate." *Historische Sprachforschung* 124 (2009): 202–12.
Euler, Wolfram. dōnum dō-: *Eine* figura etymologica *der Sprachen Altitaliens.* Innsbruck: Institut für Sprachwissenschaft der Universität Innsbruck, 1982.
Fantham, Elaine. *Ovid, Fasti IV.* New York: Cambridge University Press, 1998.
———. "'*Dic si quid potis de Sexto Annali*': The Literary Legacy of Ennius' Pyrrhic War." *Arethusa* 39, no. 3 (2006): 549–68.
Feeney, Denis. *The Gods in Epic.* New York: Oxford University Press, 1991.
———. "Interpreting Sacrificial Ritual in Roman Poetry: Disciplines and Their Models." In *Rituals in Ink: A Conference on Religion and Literary Production in Ancient Rome,* edited by Alessandro Barchiesi, Jörge Rüpke, and Susan Stephens, 1–21. Stuttgart: Franz Steiner, 2004.

Flores, Enrico. *Annali (Libri I–VIII): Introduzione, testo critico con apparato, traduzione di Enrico Flores,* Vol. I. Naples: Liguori, 2000.

———. "Commentario al libro I." In *Annali (Libri I–VIII): Commentari a cura di Enrico Flores, Paolo Esposito, Jackson, Giorgio, Domenico Tomasco,* Vol. II, by Enrico Flores, Paolo Esposito, Giorgio Jackson, and Domenico Tomasco, 23–63. Naples: Liguori, 2002.

———. *Annali (Libri IX–XVIII): Introduzione, testo critico con apparato, traduzione di Enrico Flores,* Vol. III. Naples: Liguori, 2003.

Flores, Enrico, Paolo Esposito, Giorgio Jackson, Mariantonietta Paladini, Margherita Salvatore, and Domenico Tomasco. *Annali (Libri IX–XVIII): Commentari a cura di Enrico Flores, Paolo Esposito, Giorgio Jackson, Mariantonietta Paladini, Margerita Salvatore, Domenico Tomasco,* Vol. IV. Naples: Liguori, 2006.

Flores, Enrico, Paolo Esposito, Giorgio Jackson, and Domenico Tomasco. *Annali (Libri I–VIII): Commentari a cura di Enrico Flores, Paolo Esposito, Giorgio Jackson, Domenico Tomasco,* Vol. II. Naples: Liguori, 2002.

Fontaine, Michael. *Funny Words in Plautine Comedy.* New York: Oxford University Press, 2010.

Fortson, Benjamin. *Language and Rhythm in Plautus: Synchronic and Diachronic Studies.* New York: De Gruyter, 2008.

Foster, Benjamin Oliver, ed. and trans. *Livy: Books I and II with an English Translation.* Cambridge: Harvard University Press, 1919.

———. *Livy. Books VIII–X with an English Translation.* Cambridge: Harvard University Press, 1926.

Fowler, Don. "The Virgil Commentary of Servius." In *The Cambridge Companion to Virgil,* edited by Charles Martindale, 73–78. New York: Cambridge University Press, 1997.

Fox, William Sherwood. *The Johns Hopkins "Tabellae Defixionum."* Baltimore: Johns Hopkins University Press, 1912.

Freeman, Philip. "Saturnian Verse and Early Latin Poetics." *Journal of Indo-European Studies* 26, nos. 1 and 2 (1998): 61–90.

Gager, John. *Curse Tablets and Binding Spells from the Ancient World.* New York: Oxford University Press, 1992.

Gildenhard, Ingo. "Virgil vs. Ennius, or: The Undoing of the Annalist." In *Ennius Perennis: The "Annals" and Beyond,* edited by William Fitzgerald and Emily Gowers, 73–102. Cambridge: Cambridge Philological Society, 2007.

Goldberg, Sander. *Epic in Republican Rome.* New York: Oxford University Press, 1995.

———. *Constructing Literature in the Roman Republic: Poetry and Its Reception.* New York: Cambridge University Press, 2005.

Gordon, Arthur. *Letter Names of the Latin Alphabet.* Berkeley: University of California Press, 1973.

Gowers, Emily. "The *Cor* of Ennius." In *Ennius Perennis: The "Annals" and Beyond,* edited by William Fitzgerald and Emily Gowers, 17–37. Cambridge: Cambridge Philological Society, 2007.

Gratwick, Adrian. "Ennius' *Annales.*" In *The Cambridge History of Classical Literature,* Vol. 2: *Latin Literature,* edited by E. J. Kenney and Wendell Clausen, 60–76. New York: Cambridge University Press, 1982.

Gruen, Erich S. *Studies in Greek Culture and Roman Policy.* Leiden: E. J. Brill, 1990.

Habinek, Thomas. *The Politics of Latin Literature: Writing, Identity and Empire in Ancient Rome.* Princeton: Princeton University Press, 1998.

———. *The World of Roman Song: From Ritualized Speech to Social Order.* Baltimore: Johns Hopkins University Press, 2005.

———. "The Wisdom of Ennius." *Arethusa* 39, no. 3 (2006): 471–88.

Halliday, M. A. K., Wolfgang Teubert, Colin Yallop, and Anna Cermakova. *Lexicology and Corpus Linguistics: An Introduction.* London: Continuum, 2004.

Hardie, Alex. "Juno, Hercules, and the Muses at Rome." *AJP* 128, no. 4 (2007): 551–92.

Harvey, Paul, Jr. "Religion and Memory at Pisaurum." *YCS* 33 (2006): 117–36.

Heller, John L. "Nenia 'παίγνον.'" *TAPhA* 70 (1943): 215–68.

Hickson, Frances. *Roman Prayer Language: Livy and the "Aeneid" of Vergil.* Stuttgart: B. G. Teubner, 1993.

Hinds, Stephen. *Allusion and Intertext: Dynamics of Appropriation in Roman Poetry.* New York: Cambridge University, 1998.

Hunter, Richard. *Apollonius of Rhodes, Argonautica, Book III.* New York: Cambridge University Press, 1989.

———. *The Shadow of Callimachus: Studies in the Reception of Hellenistic Poetry at Rome.* New York: Cambridge University Press, 2006.

Jackson, Giorgio. "Commentario al libro VI." In *Annali (Libri I–VIII): Commentari a cura di Enrico Flores, Paolo Esposito, Giorgio Jackson, Domenico Tomasco,* Vol. II, by Enrico Flores, Paolo Esposito, Giorgio Jackson, and Domenico Tomasco, 101–76. Naples: Liguori, 2002.

Jackson, Giorgio, and Domenico Tomasco. *Annali Frammenti di collocazione incerta: Commentari a cura Giorgio Jackson e Domenico Tomasco,* Vol. V. Naples: Liguori, 2009.

Jocelyn, Henry. "*Urbs Augurio Augusto Condita.*" *Proceedings of the Cambridge Philological Society* 17 (1971): 44–51.

———. "The Poems of Quintus Ennius." *Aufstieg und Niedergang der römischen Welt* 1, no. 2 (1972): 987–1026.

———. "Romulus and the *Di Genitales* (Ennius, *Annales* 110–11 Skutsch)." In *Studies in Latin Literature and Its Tradition in honour of C. O. Brink,* edited by J. Diggle, J. B. Hall, and H. D. Jocelyn, 39–65. Cambridge: The Cambridge Philological Society, 1989.

Johnson, W. R. *Darkness Visible: A Study of Vergil's "Aeneid."* Berkeley: University of California Press, 1976.

Kaster, Robert, trans. and ed. *Macrobius: Saturnalia,* Vol. II: Books 3–5. Cambridge: Harvard University Press, 2011.

Keith, Allison. *Engendering Rome: Women in Latin Epic.* New York: Cambridge University Press, 2000.

———. "Women in Ennius' *Annales.*" In *Ennius Perennis: The "Annals" and Beyond,* edited by William Fitzgerald and Emily Gowers, 55–72. Cambridge: Cambridge Philological Society, 2007.

Kent, Roland, ed. and trans. *Varro: On the Latin Language,* Vol. I: Books V–VII. Cambridge: Harvard University Press, 1938.

Kleve, Knut. "Ennius in Herculaneum." *Cronache Ercolanesi* 20 (1990): 5–16.

———. "Phoenix from the Ashes: Lucretius and Ennius in Herculaneum." In *The Norwegian Institute at Athens: The First Five Lectures,* edited by Oivind Anderson and Helène Whittaker, 57–64. Athens: Norwegian Institute at Athens, 1991.

Klingner, Friedrich. *Studien zur griechischen und römischen Literatur.* Zurich: Artemis Verlag, 1964.

Krevans, Nita. "Ilia's Dream: Ennius, Virgil and the Mythology of Seduction." *HSCP* 95 (1993): 257–71.

Lefkowitz, Mary. "Pyrrhus' Negotiations with the Romans, 280–279 B.C." *HSCP* 64 (1959): 147–77.

Leigh, Matthew. *Comedy and the Rise of Rome.* New York: Oxford University Press, 2004.

Lejuene, Míchel. "Inscriptions de Rossano di Vaglio." *Atti della Accademia nazionale dei Lincei: Rendiconti Classe di Scienze morali, storiche e filologiche* 26 (1971): 663–84.

Lieburg, Godo. "Die 'theologia tripertita' in Forschung und Bezeugung." *Aufstieg und Niedergang der römischen Welt* 1, no. 4 (1973): 63–115.

Linderski, Jerzy. *Roman Questions.* Stuttgart: Franz Steiner, 1996.

———. *Roman Questions II: Selected Papers.* Stuttgart: Franz Steiner, 2007.

Long, Charlotte. *The Twelve Gods of Greece and Rome.* Leiden: Brill, 1987.

Lord, Charles, ed. and trans. *Cicero: In Catilinam I–IV; Pro Murena; Pro Sulla; Pro Flacco,* Cambridge: Harvard University Press, 1937.

Lowrie, Michèle. *Writing, Performance, and Authority in Augustan Rome.* New York: Oxford University Press, 2009.

Luck, Georg. "Naevius and Virgil." *Illinois Classical Studies* 8, no. 2 (1983): 267–75.

MacBain, Bruce. *Prodigies and Expiation: A Study in Religion and Politics in Republican Rome.* Brussels: Collection Latomus, Vol. 177, 1982.

Manuwald, Gesine. *Roman Republican Theatre.* New York: Cambridge University Press, 2011.

Marx, Friedrich. *C. Lucilii Carminum Reliquiae: Recensuit, Ennaravit Fridericus Marx.* Amsterdam: Hakker, 1963.

Matasovic, Ranko. *A Theory of Textual Reconstruction in Indo-European Linguistics.* New York: Peter Lang, 1996.

McCarthy, Kathleen. *Slaves, Masters, and the Art of Authority in Plautine Comedy.* Princeton: Princeton University Press, 2004.

McDonnell, Myles. *Roman Manliness: Virtus and the Roman Republic.* New York: Cambridge University Press, 2006.

Melo, Wolfgang David Cirilo de, ed. and trans. *Plautus: Amphitryon; The Comedy of Asses; The Pot of Gold; The Two Bacchises; The Captives.* Cambridge: Harvard University Press, 2011.

Merula, Paullus. *Quinti Enni Annalium LIBB XIIX Fragmenta conlecta, composita, inlustrata ab Paullo Merula.* Leiden: Paetsius and Elzevir, 1595.

Mineur, W. H. *Callimachus: Hymn to Delos.* Leiden: Brill, 1984.

Murphy, Trevor. "Valerius Soranus and the Secret Name of Rome." In *Rituals in Ink: A Conference on Religion and Literary Production in Ancient Rome,* edited by Alessandro Barchiesi, Jörge Rüpke, and Susan Stephens, 127–40. Stuttgart: Franz Steiner, 2004.

Nadeau, Yvan. "Ennius, *Annales* 175–179 (Skutsch). A Footnote." *Latomus* 66 (2010): 309–12.

Nisbet, Gideon, and Niall Rudd. *A Commentary on Horace,* Odes, *Book III.* New York: Oxford University Press, 2004.

Nixon, Paul, ed. and trans. *Plautus,* Vol. III: *The Merchant, The Braggart Warrior, The Haunted House, The Persian, with an English Translation by Paul Nixon.* Cambridge: Harvard University Press, 1970.

Norden, Eduard. *Ennius und Vergilius: Kriegsbilder aus Roms grosser Zeit.* Leipzig: B. G. Teubner, 1915.

O'Hara, James. *Death and the Optimistic Prophecy in Vergil's "Aeneid."* Princeton: Princeton University Press, 1990.

———. *Inconsistency in Roman Epic: Studies in Catullus, Lucretius, Vergil, Ovid and Lucan.* New York: Cambridge University Press, 2007.

Pallattino, Massimo. *Genti e culture dell'Italia preromana.* Rome: Jouvence, 1981.

Parry, Milman. *The Making of Homeric Verse: The Collected Papers of Milman Parry.* Edited by Adam Parry. New York: Oxford University Press, 1971.

Parsons, Jed. "A New Approach to the Saturnian Verse and Its Relation to Latin Prosody." *TAPhA* 129 (1999): 117–37.

Peirano, Irene "Hellenized Romans and Barbarized Greeks: Reading the End of Dionysius of Halicarnassus, *Antiquitates Romanae.*" *JRS* 100 (2010): 32–53.

Pisani, Vittore. *Le lingue dell' Italia antica oltre il* Latino. Turin: Rosenberg and Sellier, 1964.

Poultney, James. *The Bronze Tables of Iguvium.* Baltimore: American Philological Association, 1959.

Powell, Jonathan, and Niall Rudd. "Explanatory Notes," to Cicero, *The Republic and the Laws,* translated by Niall Rudd. New York: Oxford University Press, 1998.

Prosdocimi, Aldo. "Sui grecismi dell'osco." In *Scritti in onore di Giuliano Bonfante.* Brescia: Paideia, 1976.

Rawson, Elizabeth. "Scipio, Laelius, Furius and the Ancestral Religion." *JRS* 63 (1973): 161–74.

Richardson, J. S. *Hispaniae: Spain and the Development of Roman Imperialism, 218–82 BC.* New York: Cambridge University Press, 1986.

Riggsby, Andrew. *Caesar in Gaul and Rome: War in Words.* Austin: University of Texas Press, 2006.

Rix, Helmut. "Etrusco *un, une, unu 'te, tibi, vos'* e le preghiere dei rituali paralleli nel Liber Linteus." *ArchClass* 43 (1991): 665–91.

———. "Teonomi Etruschi e teonomi italici." *Annali della fondazione per il museo <<Claudio Faina>>* 5 (1998): 207–29.

Rose, Charles. "Reevaluating Troy's Links to Rome: A Review of Andrew Erskine, *Troy between Greece and Rome* (Cambridge University Press, 2001)." *Journal of Roman Archaeology* 16 (2003): 479–81.

Ross, David. *Backgrounds to Augustan Poetry: Gallus Elegy and Rome.* New York: Cambridge University Press, 1975.

Rudd, Niall, ed. and trans. *Horace: Odes and Epodes* (Cambridge: Harvard University Press, 2004).

Rüpke, Jörge. "*Acta aut agenda:* Relations of Script and Performance." In *Rituals in Ink: A Conference on Religion and Literary Production in Ancient Rome,* edited by Alessandro Barchiesi, Jörge Rüpke, and Susan Stephens, 23–44. Stuttgart: Franz Steiner, 2004.

Sandoz, Claude. "Le nom d'une offrande à Iguvium: ombr. Vestiçia." *Bulletin de la Société de Linguistique de Paris* 74 (1979): 339–46.

Schmitt, Rüdiger. *Dichtung und Dichtersprache in indogermanische Zeit.* Wiesbaden: Harrasowitz, 1967.

Schultz, Celia. *Women's Religious Activity in the Roman Republic.* Chapel Hill: University of North Carolina Press, 2006.

Sciarrino, Enrica. "The Introduction of Epic in Rome: Cultural Thefts in Social Contexts." *Arethusa* 39, no. 3 (2006): 449–70.

Sear, Frank. *Roman Theatres: An Architectural Study.* New York: Oxford University Press, 2006.

Shackleton-Bailey, D. R., ed. and trans. *Cicero: Letters to Friends,* Vol. II. Cambridge: Harvard University Press, 2001.

Sheets, George. "The Dialect Gloss: Hellenistic Poetics and Livius Andronicus." *AJP* 102, no. 1 (1981): 58–78.

Skutsch, Otto. "New Words from Plautus." *CR* 51, no. 5 (1937): 166.

———. *Studia Enniana.* London: Athlone, 1968.

———. *The "Annals" of Quintus Ennius.* Oxford: Clarendon Press, 1985.

———. "Book VI of Ennius' Annals." *CQ* n.s., 37, no. 2 (1987): 514.

Spaltenstein, François. *Commentaire des "Punica" de Silius Italicus,* Vol. 2: *Livres 9 à 16. Publications de la Faculté de lettres / Université de Laussane 28.* Geneva: Droz, 1990.

Stephens, Susan. *Seeing Double: Intercultural Poetics in Ptolemaic Alexandria.* Berkeley: University of California Press, 2003.

Steuart, Ethel. *The "Annals" of Quintus Ennius.* Cambridge: Cambridge University Press, 1925.

Suerbaum, Werner. *Untersuchungen zur Selbstdarstellung älterer römischer Dichter.* Hildesheim: Olms, 1968.

———. "Die Pyrrhos-Krieg in Ennius' *Annales* VI im Lichte der ersten Ennius-Papyri aus Herculeneum." *Zeitschrift für Papyrologie und Epigraphik* 106 (1995): 31–52.

Sullivan, Francis. "*Tendere Manus:* Gestures in the *Aeneid.*" *CJ* 63, no. 8 (1968): 358–62.

Teubert, Wolfgang. "Units of Meaning, Parallel Corpora, and Their Implications for Language Teaching." In *Applied Corpus Linguistics: A Multidimensional Perspective,* edited by Ulla Connor and Thomas A. Upton, 171–89. New York: Rodopi, 2004.

Thomas, Richard. *Virgil and the Augustan Reception.* New York: Cambridge University Press, 2001.

Tichy, Eva. "Gr. οἴσειν und Lat. uti und die Mittlezeile der Duenos-Inschrift." *Glotta* 78 (2002): 179–202.

Tomlin, R. S. O., B. C. Burnham, L. J. F. Keppie, and A. S. Esmonde Cleary, "Roman Britain in 1996." *Britannia* 28 (1997): 395–472.

Tomlin, R. S. O., S. S. Frere, and M. W. C. Hassall, "Roman Britain in 1987." *Britannia* 19 (1988): 415–508.

Torelli, Mario. "Un *templum augurale* d'età repubblicana a Bantia." *Atti della Accademia nazionale dei Lincei: Rendiconti Classe di Scienze morali, storiche e filologiche* 21 (1966): 293–315.

———. "Contributi al supplemento del *CIL* IX." *Atti della Accademia nazionale dei Lincei: Rendiconti Classe di Scienze morali, storiche e filologiche* 24 (1969): 9–48.

Turfa, Jean. "The Etruscan Brontoscopic Calendar." In *The Religion of the Etruscans,* edited by Nancy Thomson de Grummond and Erika Simon, 173–90. Austin: University of Texas Press, 2006.

Twain, Mark. *Following the Equator: A Journey around the World.* Hartford: American Publishing Company, 1898.

Untermann, Jürgen. "Beobachtungen an römischen Gentilnamen in Oberitalien." *Beiträge zur Namenforschung* 7 (1956): 173–94.

Vahlen, Johannes. *Ennianae Poesis Reliquiae. Iteratis Curis.* Leipzig: B. G. Teubner, 1928.

Valmaggi, Luigi. *I frammenti degli Annali. Commento e note di L. Valmaggi.* Turin: Chiantore, 1900.

Van Sickle, Jon. "The *Elogia* of the Cornelii Scipiones." *AJP* 108, no. 1 (1987): 41–55.

Versnel, H. S. "'May He Not Be Able to Sacrifice . . .' concerning a Curious Formula in Greek and Latin Curses." *Zeitschrift für Papyrologie und Epigraphik* 58 (1985): 247–69.

Vine, Brent. "An Umbrian-Latin Correspondence." *HSCP* 90 (1986): 111–27.

———. "*Corde Capessere* (Ennius *Ann.* 42 Sk.)." *Glotta* 67 (1989): 123–26.

———. *Studies in Archaic Latin Inscriptions.* Innsbruck: Institut für Sprachwissenschaft der Universität Innsbruck, 1993.

———. "A Note on the *Duenos* Inscription." In *UCLA Indo-European Studies,* Vol. 1, edited by Vyacheslav V. Ivanov and Brent Vine, 293–305. Los Angeles: Program in Indo-European Studies, 1999.

Wackernagel, Jacob. *Kleine Schriften herausgegeban von der Akademie Wissenschaften zu Göttingen,* Vol. I. Göttingen: Vandenhoeck and Ruprecht, 1953.

Wallace, Rex. *Zikh Rasna: A Manual of the Etruscan Language and Inscriptions.* Ann Arbor: Beech Stave, 2008.

Wallace-Hadrill, Andrew. *Rome's Cultural Revolution.* New York: Cambridge University Press, 2008.

Warmington, E. H., ed. and trans. *Remains of Old Latin,* Vol. I: *Ennius and Caecilius.* Cambridge: Harvard University Press, 1967.

———. *Remains of Old Latin,* Vol. III: *Lucilius, The Twelve Tables.* Cambridge: Harvard University Press, 1967.

Watkins, Calvert. "Language of Gods and Language of Men: Remarks on Some Indo- European Metalinguistic Traditions." In *Calvert Watkins: Selected Writings,* Vol. II: *Culture and Poetics,* edited by Lisi Oliver, 456–72. Innsbruck: Institut für Sprachwissenschaft der Universität Innsbruck, 1994.

———. "Greece in Italy outside Rome." *HSCP* 97 (1995): 35–50.

———. *How to Kill a Dragon: Aspects of Indo-European Poetics.* New York: Oxford University Press, 1995.

Watmough, Margaret. "The Suffix *-tor-*: Agent Noun Formations in Latin and the Other Italic Languages." *Glotta* 73 (1996): 80–115.

Watson, Alan. *International Law in Archaic Rome: War and Religion.* Baltimore: Johns Hopkins University Press, 1993.

Weinstock, Stefan. "Two Archaic Inscriptions from Latium." *JRS* 50 (1960): 112–18.

Weiss, Michael. Preface to *A Linguistic Commentary on Livius Andronicus,* by Ivy Livingston, xi–xix. New York: Routledge, 2004.

———. *Language and Ritual in Sabellic Italy: The Ritual Complex of the Third and Fourth* Tabulae Iguvinae. Boston: Brill, 2009.

Wendel, Carl. *Scholia in Apollonium Rhodium vetera recensuit Carolus Wendel.* Berlin: Weidmann, 1935.

West, M. L. *Indo-European Poetry and Myth.* New York: Oxford University Press, 2007.

Wiedmann, Thomas. "The Fetiales: A Reconsideration." *CQ* 36 n.s., no. 2 (1986): 478–90.

Wills, Jeffrey. *Repetition in Latin Poetry: Figures of Allusion.* New York: Oxford University Press, 1996.

Wiseman, T. P. *Remus: A Roman Myth.* New York: Cambridge University Press, 1995.

———. *Unwritten Rome.* Exeter: University of Exeter Press, 2008.

Woodruff, Loura Bayne. *Reminisces of Ennius in Silius Italicus.* New York: MacMillan, 1910.

Zetzel, James. "The Influence of Cicero on Ennius." In *Ennius Perennis: The "Annals" and Beyond,* edited by William Fitzgerald and Emily Gowers, 1–16. Cambridge: Cambridge Philological Society, 2007.

INDEX